WATERGATE
The Fall of Richard M. Nixon

Stanley I. Kutler is Edward I. Fox Professor of American Institutions at the University of Wisconsin. He is the author of *The Wars of Watergate, Privilege and Creative Destruction: The Charles River Bridge Case, The American Inquisition, The Supreme Court and the Constitution,* and other books and articles.

WATERGATE

THE FALL OF RICHARD M. NIXON

Edited by

STANLEY I. KUTLER

Brandywine Press • **St. James, NY**

ISBN 1-881-089-30-4

1st Printing 1996

Telephone Orders: 1-800-345-1776

Printed in the United States of America

Table of Contents

Introduction

The Watergate scandal will inevitably color any considerations of Richard Nixon's presidency and his political career. Nixon was the first and so far the only President of the United States to resign from office. The Constitution provides for such action, but for over two hundred years, resignation of a President had never occurred and was almost unthinkable. Impeachment by the House of Representatives and removal of a President by the Senate appeared equally remote from the American mind. Andrew Johnson, the only President to be impeached, was spared conviction and removal by the Senate in a very controversial affair in 1868. Only death, it seemed, would intervene to shorten a presidential term.

Richard Nixon's presidency is closely bound to a public career that dated back nearly a quarter century before his election in 1968. From his first election to Congress in 1946 until his death in 1994, he was an ongoing presence in American politics, always to be reckoned with. Yet few political leaders in modern times have been so controversial and so polarizing.

During his congressional career, Nixon rode to fame by exploiting fear of communism, making him a paladin for whoever believed the nation in peril from enemies within. At the same time, his behavior was so provocative that he earned the undying enmity of perhaps an equally large group. But Nixon's fall from grace in 1973–1974 must be considered against the backdrop of his loss of support from a hard-core constituency that had loyally supported him for nearly thirty years as the best and brightest his party could offer.

As Dwight Eisenhower's Vice President, Nixon suffered by his contrast to a chief executive enormously popular and open to no moral reproach. In 1968, Nixon for the second time was the Republican standard-bearer (having lost to John F. Kennedy in

1960). The nation had to choose between Hubert H. Humphrey, representing the discredited administration of Lyndon B. Johnson, and Nixon, one of the most deeply divisive figures in American life. While Nixon promised to "bring us together," he was no more likely than Humphrey to reconcile the passionate political forces that divided the nation. He vaguely promised an end to the Vietnam War, but peace did not come for another four years. During his first term, he remained an object of distrust for many people, but in 1972 he had the good fortune to confront a fragmented Democratic Party and its nominee, Senator George McGovern, a man who seemed to embody the upheavals and dissent that so distressed the nation. Nixon won in a landslide, losing only Massachusetts and the District of Columbia.

Nixon's support proved wide but not deep. He had done little to aid his party, and the opposition retained control of Congress. Nixon remained a figure distrusted and scorned, particularly as the Vietnam War dragged on with mounting casualties and public despair. Meanwhile, in the White House, Nixon raged at enemies, both real and imagined. Later, John Mitchell, his Attorney General, campaign manager, and former law partner, spoke of the "White House Horrors" of the first term, by which he meant a variety of actions, illegal or unethical, taken to preserve power and punish Nixon's enemies. Eventually, in the impeachment charges against Nixon, these acts were referred to as "abuses of power." The break-in of Democratic National Committee headquarters at the Watergate office complex in June 1972 did not begin "Watergate." That event merely lifted the veil and exposed a variety of wrongdoing by Nixon and his men. Democratic dominance of the legislative body was certainly crucial to Nixon's woes, but his downfall cannot be blamed on partisan politics. In the end, a large number of Republicans, including most of the party's leaders, called for Nixon's resignation.

For two decades after he left office, Richard Nixon labored mightily in his campaign for history. He wrote books, appeared on television, and entertained journalists, all in an attempt to refurbish his reputation. This last campaign was as much to establish himself as elder statesman, a wise and authoritative voice on public matters ranging from foreign affairs to politics, as it was an attempt to eradicate the memory of Watergate from public consciousness. But Watergate will haunt Nixon's reputation throughout history.

This collection of documents is designed to take the reader through the events of Watergate in their actual succession, as far as possible. They open with the promise of Nixon's commitment to "law-and-order," and then trace some of the White House Horrors before the break-in. After the Watergate burglary, we follow the Administration's response and its instigation of a cover-up, which eventually led to the crime of obstruction of justice. The workings of the various investigatory agencies and individuals, including the United States Attorney, the Special Prosecutor, the Senate Select Committee on Watergate, and the House Impeachment Inquiry, are presented in chronological order. Nixon's responses to events also are included. The documents offer the reader a factual narrative of the key players, events, and moments in the nation's most memorable constitutional crisis since the disputed presidential election of 1876. And, it is hoped, they will provide some understanding of the political passion and turmoil that so engulfed the nation.

Watergate:
A Brief History

During the middle of Nixon's first term, some members of the White House staff had begun to use their power to pursue partisan vendettas. Nixon's assistants, most of them conservative young lawyers and former advertising men lacking political experience, ignored the traditional rules of Washington politics. By 1972 many of the President's men, claiming that the national interest required Nixon's reelection, justified crimes as necessary for national security.

CREEP

The Committee to Re-Elect the President (CREEP) organized the burglary in June of Democratic Party offices at the Watergate Building in Washington. A White House official, G. Gordon Liddy, and a man working for him, E. Howard Hunt, recruited a group of anti-Castro Cubans; and CREEP's director of security, James McCord, led this small band of seven people on two raids. The burglars planted microphones and took pictures of files of the Democratic National Committee. During a second raid, a night watchman discovered their entry and called police. Moments later the burglars were under arrest. Evidence at the scene quickly connected them to Liddy and to CREEP.

Some newspaper reporters continued to investigate the Watergate incident. Amid media speculation, Nixon ordered a staff inquiry and told the public that "what really hurts is if you try to cover up" a crime. A federal grand jury indicted McCord and his accomplices, along with Liddy and Hunt. All pleaded guilty, and thus no trial or legal reckoning could be made. But Judge John Sirica, who presided over the grand jury, doubted that these brief judicial proceedings had solved the Watergate case. Then in mid-March 1973 McCord wrote to Sirica, charging that the White House had pressured the defendants into silence with offers of executive clemency and hush money. Government officials had approved the Watergate burglary, McCord claimed, and conspired also to cover up their own involvement. McCord's letter prompted the Watergate grand jury and the Senate's special Watergate committee, chaired by Sam Ervin of North Carolina, to probe further these mysterious White House activities.

Nixon loyalists could not contain the scandal. One of them, John Dean, thought that the President might blame the whole affair on him, and began to bargain with federal prosecutors from the grand jury. At about the same time, the former deputy chairman of CREEP, Jeb Stuart Magruder, admitted that he had lied in his appearances before the grand jury. He confessed that the bugging of Democratic headquarters was not "a wild scheme concocted by Hunt" but a much-discussed plan, which Attorney General John Mitchell had approved directly.

Nixon tried to seal off the Oval Office from the spread of Watergate. Before a national television audience on April 30, 1973, he accepted the responsibility—but not the blame—for the actions of "overzealous subordinates." Absorbed in the business of running the country, he explained, he had failed to monitor their campaigning. He also announced the resignations of John Ehrlichman and H. R. Haldeman, "two of the finest public servants it has been my privilege to know." Dean also left the staff. Under pressure from Congress and even close friends, Nixon appointed a special prosecutor, Harvard law professor Archibald Cox, and promised him "complete independence" to investigate the Watergate affair. These acts provided only temporary surcease for the embattled President.

In the televised Senate Watergate hearings, Senator Sam Ervin with his shock of white hair and trembling jowls became a national symbol of honor and rectitude. The star witnesses, Magruder and Dean, told their stories. Magruder suggested presidential involvement in the cover-up, and Dean linked Nixon directly with illegal activities. Dean quoted the President as saying that it would be "no problem" to raise a $1 million hush fund and that payments should be made through E. Howard Hunt.

The White House Tapes

Then the committee staff stumbled upon a stunning discovery. A former White House aide, Alexander Butterfield, testified that recording equipment had taped most presidential conversations for the last two years. Presumably these reels could determine the extent of Nixon's role in the Watergate affair. The Senate committee, as well as Special Prosecutor Cox and the Watergate grand jury, requested segments of the tapes. The President argued that their disclosure would violate the confidentiality of the presidency and erode the separation of powers. A complicated legal battle ensued. Frustrated, Cox finally told a televised press conference that he would ask Judge Sirica to declare the President "in violation of a court ruling" for his delay in turning over a set of tapes. When Nixon fired Cox, the top two officials in the Justice Department quit in protest. This "Saturday Night Massacre" produced an outpouring of popular protest, appearing as it did that Nixon was trying to get Cox before Cox got Nixon.

Continuing revelations plagued Nixon. When the White House finally handed over a few tapes, prosecutors discovered the recordings contained sizable gaps, erasures that technical experts later judged intentional. The Watergate grand jury, now directed by a new special prosecutor, Texas attorney Leon Jaworski, indicted forty-one people for obstruction of justice and other crimes committed during the 1972 campaign. Convinced of Nixon's involvement, yet unwilling to confront constitutional issues, the jurors listed Nixon as an "unindicted coconspirator."

Pressed by public skepticism and a growing pile of subpoenas and court orders for more and more tapes, in late April 1974 Nixon released edited transcripts, not the actual recordings, of meetings concerning Watergate. Even Nixon's version—he had deleted a number of items that damaged his claims of innocence—showed a dubious morality. The new evidence implicated him in the cover-up and openly told of schemes for political revenge against "enemies."

The Final Days

Already at work on articles of impeachment was a judiciary committee of the House of Representatives, twenty-four Democrats and fourteen Republicans. Nixon made a last, double-edged counterattack. His lawyer fought to prevent release of further tapes. Nixon himself spoke to carefully selected audiences, often in the very conservative deep South, hoping for a show of public support. But his statement, "I am not a crook," shocked more than it soothed. And his lawyer-like argument that only criminal acts would justify impeachment sounded like a tacit admission of serious wrongdoing.

During late July and early August 1974, rapid events finally ended any doubts about the President's fate. The Judiciary Committee heard its Democratic and Republican counsels urge impeachment. On July 24 the Supreme Court ordered the White House to turn over sixty-four additional tapes. That same day the Judiciary Committee began its televised debate on impeachment.

In compliance with the Supreme Court order, Nixon released additional tapes on Monday, August 5. After seeing the new evidence, the President's chief of staff, Alexander Haig, began preparations for the accession of Vice President Gerald Ford to the presidency. Ford, previously Republican minority leader in the House, had been appointed by Nixon when Vice President Spiro Agnew resigned in a scandal unrelated to Watergate. The tape of a conversation on June 23, 1972—Nixon's first day back in Washington after the Watergate break-in—showed the President and Haldeman planning to cloak White House involvement in the crime. Here, after eighteen months of protestations of innocence, was the "smoking gun." Nixon's defenders on the Judiciary Committee switched their votes, and leading Republican senators visited the White House, telling the President that his removal was a certainty. On August 9, 1974, Nixon resigned.

The Cast of Characters

Agnew, Spiro T.—Nixon's Vice President, who resigned after pleading no contest on charges of income tax evasion

Baker, Senator Howard H. Jr.—Tennessee Republican, vice chairman of the Senate Watergate committee

Barker, Bernard—convicted Watergate burglar

Bernstein, Carl—*Washington Post* reporter

Buchanan, Patrick J.—special consultant to the President

Bull, Stephen—special assistant to President Nixon

Burger, Warren E.—Chief Justice of the United States

Bush, George—Republican national chairman

Butterfield, Alexander P.—presidential aide

Buzhardt, J. Fred Jr.—special counsel to President Nixon

Byrd, Senator Robert C.—West Virginia Democrat

Byrne, W. Matthew Jr.—presiding judge at Ellsberg-Russo trial

Campbell, Donald E.—U.S. attorney, a prosecutor at the Watergate break-in trial

Caulfield, John J.—employee of John Ehrlichman, investigator and undercover agent

Chapin, Dwight L.—presidential appointments secretary

Chotiner, Murray—political adviser to President Nixon until his death in January 1974

Clawson, Ken W.—director for communications, White House

Colson, Charles W.—special counsel to the President

Connally, John B.—Secretary of the Treasury; domestic and foreign affairs adviser to President Nixon

Cushman, General Robert E. Jr.—Marine Corps commandant; deputy director, C.I.A.

Dahlberg, Kenneth H.—treasurer, Finance Committee to Re-elect the President

Dash, Samuel—chief counsel and staff director, Senate Watergate committee

Dean, John W. 3d—counsel to President Nixon

De Diego, Felipe—indicted for taking part in break-in of Ellsberg's psychiatrist

DeLoach, Cartha D.—assistant director, F.B.I.

Doar, John M.—chief counsel, House Judiciary Committee

Eastland, Senator James O.—Mississippi Democrat

Ehrlichman, John D.—chief domestic affairs adviser to President Nixon

Ellsberg, Dr. Daniel J.—defendant in the Pentagon Papers case

Ervin, Senator Sam J. Jr.—North Carolina Democrat, chairman of the Senate Watergate committee

Fielding, Fred F.—assistant to John W. Dean 3d

Fielding, Dr. Lewis—Daniel Ellsberg's psychiatrist

Flug, James F.—chief counsel, Senate Subcommittee on Administrative Practice and Procedure

Ford, Vice President Gerald R.—successor to Spiro T. Agnew, Vice President, minority leader of the House of Representatives

Garment, Leonard—counsel to President Nixon

Gesell, Gerhard A.—judge, U.S. District Court, District of Columbia

Glanzer, Seymour—Assistant United States Attorney for the District of Columbia, a prosecutor at the Watergate trial

Goldwater, Senator Barry—Arizona Republican

Gonzalez, Virgilio R.—convicted Watergate burglar

Gray, L. Patrick 3d—acting director, F.B.I.

Gurney, Senator Edward J.—Florida Republican, member of the Senate Watergate committee

Haig, General Alexander M. Jr.—Haldeman's successor as White House chief of staff

Haldeman, H. R.—White House chief of staff

Harlow, Bryce—White House liaison chief

Helms, Richard M.—Director, C.I.A.

Higby, Lawrence M.—assistant to H. R. Haldeman

Hoover, J. Edgar—Director of the F.B.I. until his death in May 1972

Hruska, Senator Roman L.—Nebraska Republican

Humphrey, Senator Hubert H.—Minnesota Democrat and former Vice President

Hunt, E. Howard Jr.—former C.I.A. agent and White House consultant, convicted Watergate conspirator

Hunt, Dorothy—wife of E. Howard Hunt Jr., killed in plane crash Dec. 8, 1972

Huston, Tom Charles—White House aide who designed 1970 intelligence-gathering plan

Jaworski, Leon—Houston lawyer, Cox's successor as Watergate special prosecutor

Jenner, Albert E.—chief minority counsel, House Judiciary Committee

Kalmbach, Herbert W.—personal attorney to President Nixon

Kennedy, Senator Edward M.—Massachusetts Democrat

Kennedy, Senator Robert F. (Bobby)—New York Democrat and presidential contender at the time of his assassination in 1968; former U.S. Attorney General

Kissinger, Henry A.—presidential adviser on national security; Secretary of State

Klein, Herbert G.—White House communications director

Kleindienst, Richard G.—U.S. Attorney General

Krogh, Egil Jr.—chief assistant to John D. Ehrlichman; co-head "Plumbers"

Laird, Melvin H.—counselor to the President for domestic affairs; Secretary of Defense

LaRue, Frederick C.—White House aide, assistant to John N. Mitchell at the Committee for the Re-election of the President

Liddy, G. Gordon—former counsel of Committee for the Re-election of the President; convicted of conspiracy, burglary, and wiretapping in the Watergate case

MacGregor, Clark—director of the Committee for the Re-election of the President (succeeded Mitchell)

Magruder, Jeb Stuart—deputy director, Committee for the Re-election of the President

Mansfield, Senator Mike—Montana Democrat

Mardian, Robert—deputy manager, Committee for the Re-election of the President; Assistant Attorney General

Martinez, Eugenio R.—convicted Watergate burglar

McCord, James W. Jr.—convicted participant in the Watergate break-in

McGovern, Senator George—South Dakota Democrat and 1972 Democratic presidential nominee

Mitchell, John N.—former U.S. Attorney General; former director, Committee for the Re-election of the President

Mitchell, Martha—wife of John N. Mitchell

Montoya, Senator Joseph M.—New Mexico Democrat, member of the Senate Watergate committee

Moore, Richard A.—special counsel to the President

Muskie, Senator Edmund S.—Maine Democrat and 1972 presidential contender

Nixon, Donald—President Nixon's nephew, son of F. Donald Nixon

Nixon, Richard—37th President of the United States

O'Brien, Lawrence F.—Democratic national chairman at the time of the Watergate break-in

O'Brien, Paul L.—attorney for Committee for the Re-election of the President

Odle, Robert C. Jr.—director of administration, Committee for the Re-election of the President

Pappas, Thomas A.—Massachusetts millionaire, long-time Nixon supporter

Parkinson, Kenneth W.—attorney for Committee for the Re-election of the President

Patman, Representative Wright—Texas Democrat, chairman of the House Banking and Currency Committee

Petersen, Henry E.—assistant attorney general, headed the Justice Department's Watergate inquiry

Porter, Herbert L. (Bart)—scheduling director, Committee for the Re-election of the President; convicted for lying to the F.B.I. about his knowledge of Segretti

Rather, Dan—White House correspondent for C.B.S.

Reisner, Robert—assistant to Jeb Stuart Magruder at the Committee for the Re-election of the President

Rhodes, Representative John J.—Arizona Republican, succeeded Gerald Ford as minority leader of the House

Richardson, Elliot L.—Attorney General

Richey, Charles R.—U.S. District Court Judge, Washington, D.C.

Rodino, Representative Peter W. Jr.—New Jersey Democrat; Chairman of the House Judiciary Committee

Rogers, William P.—Secretary of State

Ruckelshaus, William D.—deputy attorney general

Russo, Anthony J. Jr.—co-defendant with Ellsberg in the Pentagon Papers trial

St. Clair, James D.—special counsel to the President

Saxbe, William B.—successor to Elliot L. Richardson as U.S. Attorney General; former Republican senator of Ohio

Schlesinger, James R.—former Director, C.I.A.; Secretary of Defense

Scott, Senator Hugh R.—Pennsylvania Republican and minority leader of the Senate

Segretti, Donald H.—former Treasury Department attorney who directed a campaign of political espionage and sabotage against the Democrats; convicted for these activities

Shaffer, Charles N.—attorney for John W. Dean 3d

Silbert, Earl J.—principal assistant U.S. attorney, original chief prosecutor at the Watergate break-in trial

Sirica, John J.—chief judge of the U.S. District Court, Washington, D.C.

Sloan, Hugh W. Jr.—treasurer, Finance Committee to Re-elect the President

Stans, Maurice H.—Secretary of Commerce; chairman, Finance Committee to Re-elect the President

Stennis, Senator John C.—Mississippi Democrat

Strachan, Gordon C.—assistant to H. R. Haldeman

Sturgis, Frank A.—convicted Watergate burglar

Timmons, William E.—director of congressional relations for the White House

Titus, Harold H. Jr.—U.S. attorney, District of Columbia

Ulasewicz, Anthony T. (Tony)—former detective, New York City Police Department; aide to John J. Caulfield

Wallace, George C.—Democratic governor of Alabama and 1972 presidential contender until an assassination attempt on his life

Walters, Johnnie—I.R.S. commissioner

Walters, Lieutenant General Vernon A.—deputy director, C.I.A.

Warren, Earl—Chief Justice of the United States

Weicker, Senator Lowell P. Jr.—Connecticut Republican and member of the Watergate committee

Wilson, John J.—attorney for John D. Ehrlichman and H. R. Haldeman

Woods, Rose Mary—executive assistant and personal secretary to the President

Woodward, Bob—*Washington Post* reporter

Wright, Charles Alan—special White House legal consultant on Watergate

Young, David R. Jr.—White House aide; co-head of "Plumbers" unit

Ziegler, Ronald L.—White House press secretary

I

Richard Nixon: At Work and in His Own Words

"[L]et us begin by committing ourselves to the truth, to see it like it is, to find the truth, to speak the truth and to live the truth. That's what we will do."

Richard Nixon, 1968

Acceptance Speech: 1968

On August 8, 1968, Richard Nixon was nominated for the presidency by the Republican Party for the second time. Nixon would always regard his acceptance speech as one of his best. It had powerful allusions to the American Dream, evoking a young boy growing up in the hinterlands, who found himself on the verge of the nation's highest office. The shattering of Nixon's presidency exactly six years later, and the subsequent conviction of his Attorney General, imparts a special irony to his remarks about "law and order."

And tonight it's time for some honest talk about the problem of order in the United States. Let us always respect, as I do, our courts and those who serve on them, but let us also recognize that some of our courts in their decisions have gone too far in weakening the peace forces as against the criminal forces in this country.

Let those who have the responsibility to enforce our laws, and our judges who have the responsibility to interpret them, be dedicated to the great principles of civil rights. But let them also recognize that the first civil right of every American is to be free from domestic violence. And that right must be guaranteed in this country.

And if we are to restore order and respect for law in this country, there's one place we're going to begin: We're going to have a new Attorney General of the United States of America.

I pledge to you that our new Attorney General will be directed by the President of the United States to launch a war against organized crime in this country. . . .

Because, my friends, let this message come through clear from what I say tonight. Time is running out for the merchants of crime and corruption in American society. The wave of crime is not going to be the wave of the future in the United States of America. . . .

New York Times, August 9, 1968.

The Personality of the President

Alexander Butterfield, best remembered as the man who revealed the existence of the White House taping system, was a presidential aide, constantly at the President's elbow, ushering in visitors and preparing "talking papers" for Nixon's meetings. With the exception of Chief of Staff H. R. Haldeman, no one else observed Nixon so closely. Butterfield's remarks to the House Impeachment Committee in July 1974 are extraordinary for their insights about Nixon's work habits, his attitudes, and his intolerance of any diversity of views around him.

[F]rom my observations, from my having seen thousands and thousands of memoranda over this period of time—I may be using those figures loosely—hundreds and hundreds of memoranda over this period of time, from working directly with the President and Haldeman, I know him [Nixon] to be a detail man. But I think any successful person is a detail man to a degree. . . .

The President often, of course, was concerned whether or not the curtains were closed or open, the arrangement of state gifts, whether they should be on that side of the room or this side of the room, displayed on a weekly basis or on a monthly or daily basis.

Social functions were always reviewed with him, the scenario, after they came to me from Mrs. Nixon. Each was always interested in the table arrangements. He debated whether we should have a U-shaped table or round table.

He was deeply involved in the entertainment business, whom we should get, for what kind of group, small band, big band, black band, white band, jazz band, whatever. He was very interested in meals and how they were served and the time of the waiters and was usually put out if a state dinner was not taken care of in less than an hour or an hour's time.

He debated receiving lines and whether or not he should have a receiving line prior to the entertainment for those relatively junior people in the administration who were invited to the entertainment portion of the dinners only and not to the main dinner. He wanted to see the plan, see the scenarios, he wanted to view the musical selections himself. He was very interested in whether or not salad should be served and decided that at small dinners of eight or less, the salad course should not be served.

He was interested in who introduced him to guests and he wanted it done quite properly. I did it for a while and I don't think I was altogether satisfactory. Sometimes a military aide did it. Then one time Mr. Macomber from the State Department did a superb job and he was hired on to introduce the President to guests henceforth. That lasted a month or two. Emil Mosbacher, the Protocol Ambassador, did it for a while.

He wanted a professional producer to come and actually produce the entertainment, especially the entertainment which was for television, et cetera.

Guests lists were of great interest to him. He did review all the guest lists very carefully and no one would put someone on a guest list or take some one person off a guest list as a rule without going to the President. He was interested in knowing how many Republicans or Democrats were on the list, he would review it for that. Too many or too little—it always got his personal view—how many from the South, East, West, North regions of America, how many blacks, how many ethnics, how many labor members might be invited to this—he would review all of these lists personally and approve them personally.

He was very conscientious of criticism of the worship services, yet he wanted to continue having the worship services. There was criticism, especially, that he was using them for political purposes, so he purposely invited a number of Democrats, people who might be considered enemies—I do use that word loosely. It may be inappropriate, but I mean precisely that, because he felt there was some benefit from worship services. There were no pictures taken.

He debated having worship services on a monthly basis or bimonthly or whatever or not at all and he wanted to know who sat where among the VIP's in the first couple of rows, and he wanted to see a chart, a setup of the worship services. . . .

Ceremonies—he was interested, of course, in whether or not they should be public on the south grounds or whether we should have only administrative personnel; the details of the drive up the walkway, whether the military would be to the right or left, which uniforms would be worn by the White House police, whether or not the Secret Service would salute during the Star-Spangled Banner and sing, where the photographer would be, and such things as that. In fact, all Presidential activities quite naturally had his interest.

He was interested in the press followup. He wanted to see a copy of the press coverage. He wanted to note who was going to be on hand to record this; which recorder do you have? He suggested after a while that we nominate a number of anecdotists, color reporters as we call them, to go to these events at which some human interest item might occur, little vignettes of human interest. He wanted those recorded for the President's file, for history. . . .

Yes, there was a lot of leisure time for the President, but he chose not to take it in the form of indulging, by way of indulging in recreation. It was my observation that he had no hobbies. The Presidency was his hobby. He bowled occasionally—very seldom—once every three weeks at best on an average. He meditated, he thought, he pondered. He worked on his yellow pad. He thought things over. He thought over his schedule.

He seemed to me to be preoccupied with the Presidency. I say that in a complimentary way. He seemed to me to be preoccupied with his place in history, with his Presidency as history would see it. Perhaps this is normal, I think all of us care a little bit. . . . I would guess that the concept is normal, but that the preoccupation probably is not. . . .

Testimony of Witnesses, *Hearings*, Committee on the Judiciary, July 2, 1974, 31–33, 65–66.

The Man on Top

Whatever explanations are offered for Watergate—the connection to Vietnam, the role of overzealous aides, the efforts of an opposition Congress—the personality of the President is central. One aide has described him as "The Man on Top." In comparison to several of his successors, Richard Nixon has been characterized as a "hands-on" President. He liked so to regard himself and, as eventually demonstrated, he actively participated in the events that occurred immediately following the Watergate break-in and those of the succeeding fourteen months.

The Nixon Archives contain an extraordinary number of memoranda to various aides that reflect the President's thinking and desires. We see a President deeply conscious of public relations, preoccupied with enemies, real and imagined; mulling even from the time of his first inauguration over his prospects for reelection, fixating on trivial matters, constantly compelled to compare himself with his predecessors, John F. Kennedy and

Lyndon B. Johnson. The Nixon Papers contain surprisingly little of the President's interest or involvement in policy. Most clearly, his memoranda reflect his abiding interest in his own image and his dealings with opponents.

JUNE 16, 1969
TO: H. R. Haldeman
FROM: The President

I have an uneasy feeling that many of the items that I send out for action are disregarded when any staff member just reaches a conclusion that it is unreasonable or unattainable. I respect this kind of judgment. On the other hand, I want to know when that kind of decision is made. In the future, I want you to keep a check list of everything I order and I want you to indicate what action has been taken (and I want no long memoranda indicating why it can't be taken) and particularly I want to know when the action that I have ordered has *not* been taken.

Nixon Papers, Nixon Archives, National Archives.

JUNE 16, 1969
TO: Bob Haldeman
      John Ehrlichman
FROM: The President

I have noted an increasing number of instances in the news reports of columnists indicating that "White House staffers privately" were raising questions about some of my activities. One of these instances was the Chamber of Commerce speech on student revolt. The other on the Air Force Academy speech. I want the whole staff in the strongest possible terms to be informed that unless they can say something positive about my operations and that of the White House staff they should say nothing. I also would like to get your report on who has been responsible for this kind of statement.

Ibid.

OCTOBER 10, 1969
TO: Mr. Haldeman
FROM: The President

In talking with Ehrlichman, I was concerned about the fact that we apparently have not been getting across the theme which I have been emphasizing to you for four or five months—the long hours, hard-working image which we deserve and on which we have a really good case to sell.

I recall that you told me that this theme had been covered and that an adequate job had been done. Ehrlichman feels that there is an urgent need for a more effective job to be done on this score. I do not want to get into the nuts and bolts, but there are so many things that could be covered—no lunches or breakfasts, working in the office after dinner, calls and appointments which do not appear on the official schedule, etc., etc. Obviously, this has been an area where we have dropped the ball in a grossly inept way. I would like to see a game plan as to how this can be corrected, both as to the past where Ehrlichman has an idea or two that might be useful, and particularly as to the future. Here again, this shows why the Ziegler operation is deficient; he just can't get across what we do day by day, because he cannot sell . . . he can only report. Somebody constantly has to be telling the press until it runs out of their ears that the President is working hard, even though he may be at Camp David, Florida or in California. Johnson was away from the White House almost more than any other President and yet his staff got across the fact that he was the hardest working President in our history. I have probably spent less time away than any President in recent history—very little golf and no vacations without work, yet this story has not been told except, I understand from Ehrlichman, by Thimmesch who, of course, is not read by too many people.

I am really quite disappointed that, since I have mentioned this on at least a dozen occasions over the past four months, we apparently have not followed up. I hope you will get me an action plan that will reverse the situation, since on this issue I know we have a good case to sell.

Ibid.

DECEMBER 1, 1969
TO: Mr. Haldeman
FROM: The President

I would like for you to discuss the conclusions I will be presenting in this memorandum [with] Klein, Ziegler and whoever else may be advising Administration or Cabinet people with regard to their relations with the press. It is important that you use this only as a Talking Paper because I do not want any distribution of my thoughts among the staff.

I have noted that within the staff and among some Cabinet people there has been criticism of Martha Mitchell for her appearance on TV, and also criticism of CBS and Maria McLaughlin, who was the interviewer. Both of these criticisms completely miss the mark. Neither Martha Mitchell nor the interviewer is to blame. The responsibility rests with those who advise Cabinet people and their staffs and families with regard to the press.

It is essential that some fundamental principles be borne in mind.

1. Before talking to any member of the press, remember that a great majority of the press are opposed to the Administration and, therefore,

will subconsciously or consciously be after a story which will be harmful to the Administration.

2. Clearly apart from whether individual members of the press may be "friends" or not, it is vital to remember that virtually all members of the press, including those we may think are friends, owe their first loyalty to the story. As a matter of fact, we really wouldn't want to have it any other way.

3. This means, in other words, that it is vital always to be on guard regardless of what protestations the member of the press will make with regard to his or her friendship when he or she is after a story. As a matter of fact, that is the time to be most suspicious . . . when they come in and say "I want to do something that will be helpful" or "This story is going to be written anyway, and I wanted to be sure you got your side into the story" or "You can count on my not using anything that is harmful." These are the oldest dodges in Washington, but people, particularly new people, and even some of the old timers, have to be reminded of them or they will fall into the traps.

4. Another rule that I want followed for all of my family, including Pat, Tricia, Julie and David and myself, and that I would advise for everybody else, is *never tape more than the interviewer is going to use*. Mrs. Mitchell answered 83 questions. Of course, I know that in many cases the interviewer will say that they will submit the part they are to use as they did when they interviewed Tricia and Julie for that President's Daughters series. This, however, is a bad deal. In any event, first we should not be in the position of having to "censor" a script and, second, when these interviewers go on too long, the person being interviewed inevitably will not be at his best toward the end and slips are bound to occur. It is vitally important that Ziegler, Klein and Connie Stuart carry out my instructions on this with regard to the RN family, and I would strongly urge that Klein give this advice to Cabinet people. If they are not bright enough to understand it, then that's just too bad. Just keep this one fundamental rule in mind: Over-taping is *always* in the interest of the interviewer; it is very seldom in the interest of the person being interviewed. Therefore, never over-tape regardless of how good a "friend" is doing the job.

Haldeman Papers, Nixon Archives, National Archives.

SUNDAY, MAY 9, 1971
TO: H. R. Haldeman
FROM: The President
RE: White House Correspondents' Dinner

Before you get reports from some of the naive members of our staff who were present, let me give you a hard-nosed appraisal of the White House Correspondents' Dinner, the mistakes our staff made in scheduling me at the dinner, and some lessons for the future.

You will recall that I noted that the reporters receiving the awards were way out left-wingers. Obviously, anybody could have done a little checking to find out why they were being honored at this dinner. Every one of the recipients was receiving an award for a vicious attack on the Administration—[Supreme Court nominee] Carswell, wire tapping, Army surveillance, etc. I had to sit there for 20 minutes while the drunken audience laughed in derision as the award citations were read.

I'm not a bit thin-skinned, but I do have the responsibility and everybody on my staff has the responsibility to protect the office of the Presidency from such insulting incidents. I'm sure that Ziegler, Klein, and possibly Scali and Price approved this charade because it would demonstrate that the President was a "good sport." I do not have to demonstrate that. I have done so many times over the past 24 years. As one of the few friendly reporters told me after the dinner, he had been attending Gridirons, White House Correspondents' and other dinners for 24 years and that this was by far the worst, but that he had never seen one in which the audience was friendly or the program, as far as the press participation was concerned, was not directly or indirectly aimed at embarrassing me. . . .

What I want everybody to realize is that as we approach the election we are in a fight to the death for the big prize. Ninety-five percent of the members of the Washington press corps are unalterably opposed to us because of their intellectual and philosophical background. Some of them will smirk and pander to us for the purpose of getting a story but we must remember that they are just waiting for the chance to stick the knife in deep and to twist it. I just feel that Ziegler and his people and even more, of course, a newcomer like Scali, haven't the slightest idea of what we are up against. Like Ray Price, Len Garment and Herb Klein, they always bemuse themselves by thinking that "Well, if we just keep trying we may win some of them or at least soften them." Forget it. They will neither be won nor softened by giving them the opportunity to insult the President and more important the opportunity to insult his office as they did so at the White House Correspondents' dinner. . . .

Ibid.

II
The
White House
Horrors

Plumbers and Enemies

 John Mitchell, Nixon's former Attorney General and his 1972 campaign manager, in testimony before the Senate Select Committee in July 1973, memorably characterized as the "White House Horrors" a number of the Administration's first-term activities. The 1972 Watergate break-in parted the veil to reveal a larger pattern of wrongdoing and abuse of power in the Nixon Administration. Mitchell bluntly maintained that the purpose of the eventual cover-up of the Administration's role in the break-in had been to conceal the "horrors" for fear they would be revealed and endanger Nixon's reelection bid. Watergate, he said, "did not have the great significance that the White House horror stories . . . had." Mitchell's stories included forging cables to implicate Kennedy Administration officials in the assassination of South Vietnamese President Ngo Dinh Diem; a planned firebombing of the liberal think-tank, the Brookings Institution; "a lot of miscellaneous matters" relating to Senator Edward Kennedy and the drowning at Chappaquiddick; and "alleged extracurricular activities in the bugging area." Mitchell's most significant reference was to the burglary of the offices of the psychiatrist of Daniel Ellsberg, the man known to have leaked the Pentagon Papers to *The New York Times* and *The Washington Post*. The perpetrators were the "plumbers," a group of White House operatives authorized by John Ehrlichman in 1971, probably with Nixon's full knowledge. The incident linked the Vietnam War to Watergate. Mitchell's former aide, White House Counsel John W. Dean, concurred and told the Senate in June 1973 that "the Watergate matter was an inevitable outgrowth of a climate of excessive concern over the political impact of demonstrators, excessive concern over leaks, an insatiable appetite for political intelligence, all coupled with a do-it-yourself White House staff, regardless of the law."

The Plumbers

MEMORANDUM

THE WHITE HOUSE
WASHINGTON

CONFIDENTIAL   September 29, 1971
MEMORANDUM FOR: H. R. Haldeman
FROM: Fred Malek
SUBJECT: Leaks

The purpose of this memo is to brief you on my plan for dealing with the problem of leaks.

BACKGROUND

Since the President's forceful direction on this problem, there have been a minimum of major improper disclosures requiring your attention. However, the number of minor, hard to track down, infractions has continued. In fact, a CIA study predicts that at the present rate, we will have 4 times the number of improper disclosures of national security information this year as we had in 1970. This study is attached at Tab A, and John Ehrlichman tells me it is the basis for his recent comments to you on this subject.

PLAN OF ATTACK

Responsibility for dealing with this problem has been centralized with me. However, it will be necessary to have separate approaches for national security leaks and domestic leaks.

National Security. As you know, Bud Krogh and David Young, under Ehrlichman's direction, are already conducting a comprehensive investigation of national security leaks. They plan to continue this, and any efforts on my part to actually investigate will be redundant. Rather, my role will be to keep informed of their efforts, to crack down hard on any violators who are uncovered, and to report to you on any cases needing your intervention. Their problem to date is identifying the violators, but I feel they are on the right track.

Domestic. This covers all leaks not involving national security, some of which could involve State or DOD. There are, of course, a large number of minor infractions in this area, and I do not believe we at the White House should try to locate the origins except in the most obvious cases. Rather, I plan to remain continually alert to leaks, forcefully call them to the attention of Department Heads, insist on actions, and follow through to ensure actions are taken. Where multiple sources are involved, we would coordinate the follow through from here. When a violator is identified, I would ensure a hard crackdown. . . .

Hearings, June 26, 1973, SSC, Book 3:1114–15.

EYES ONLY
July 22, 1971
TO: John Ehrlichman
FROM: Charles Colson
RE: Further on Pentagon Papers

As we discussed earlier this week I met today with Bud Krogh and reviewed with him what he has done to date and what his immediate plans are.

We both agreed that the major task at hand is to pull together all of the information that is available in Justice, Defense, CIA, State and outside. We must determine whether we have a case that can be made public with respect to Ellsberg and any conspiracy with his colleagues.

At the moment I think Bud has a good investigative mechanism (although he thinks he will need the full time services of Jack Caulfield, a matter I would like to discuss with you). Leddy [sic] is an excellent man. Hunt can be very useful. . . .

Whether we can make the case publicly is one question; a second question is where the political punch line is even if we can make the case. To paint Ellsberg black is probably a good thing; to link him into a conspiracy which suggests treasonous conduct is also a good thing, but the real political payoff will come only if we can establish that there is what the *National Review* has called a "counter government" which is deliberately trying to undermine U.S. foreign policy and the U.S. position in the world and that it is the President who stands against this "counter government," who conquers them and who rescues the nation from the subversion of these unsavory characters. We must be certain we can direct this effort in a way that gives us the political positions we need and ties our political opposition into the enemy camp.

There is a second objective, however, as to which I think the political payoff is even more significant. Congressional hearings will begin this fall in both the Senate and the House on the revelations of the Kennedy/Johnson papers. It is in this forum that we can clearly nail our prospective Democratic opponents, thoroughly discredit the Kennedy power elite which masterminded our foreign policy during the Kennedy Administration and which LBJ unfortunately inherited. There is considerable research which must be done into the events and personalities of the entire era. We need to know the vulnerable points like the Diem coup, build our case from what is in the public record and what we can dig out ourselves and see that it is adequately fed to the people on the Hill who will be on our side during the hearings. Bud had not focused on the second objective. In my opinion, it is politically more promising to us, although I am clearly in favor of doing both.

As to the first effort (i.e., Ellsburg) [sic] Bud and Dave Young are working in tandem. I question, however, whether Dave should be involved at this stage in the second effort.

I have assigned Howard Hunt the job of going through the Pentagon Papers, picking out those areas where we might be able to expose the Harrimans, the Warnkes, the Cliffords, the Vances, the McGeorge Bundys and McNamaras, etc. He will begin an independent investigation of the facts surrounding each of these key targets as he has done with the coup episode. Each of the prospective Democratic opponents next year can be vulnerable if we can tie them or their advisers into gross misjudgments committed during this period.

There is some considerable internal delicacy to this second phase. My thought is that Howard should do a complete evaluation both substantively and politically over the next few weeks. When that is completed we will have to make a decision as to the points that we can and want to make and the modus operandi.

It seems to me that at this point you and I need to spend a few minutes to be sure that we are tracking correctly on this and to cover one or two administrative points that have been raised.

Colson Papers, Nixon Archives, National Archives.

JULY 28, 1971
MEMORANDUM FOR: Charles Colson
FROM: Howard Hunt
SUBJECT: Neutralization of Ellsberg

I am proposing a skeletal operations plan aimed at building a file on Ellsberg that will contain all available overt, covert and derogatory information. This basic tool is essential in determining how to destroy his public image and credibility.

Items:
Obtain all overt press material on Ellsberg and continue its collection;
Request CIA to perform a covert psychological assessment/evaluation on Ellsberg;
Interview Ellsberg's first wife;
Interview Ellsberg's Saigon contact: the restaurant owner, Nicolal, and his mistress whom Ellsberg coveted;
Request CIA, FBI, and CIC for their full holdings on Ellsberg;
Examine Ellsberg personnel files at ISA (Pentagon) and the Rand Corporation, including clearance materials;

Obtain Ellsberg's files from his psychiatric analyst;

Inventory Ellsberg's ISA and Rand colleagues; determine where they are, and whether any might be approachable.

I realize that, as a practical matter, not all the foregoing items can be accomplished; even so, they represent desiderata.

Statement of Information Impeachment Inquiry,
Committee on the Judiciary, H.R., 93 Cong., 2 Sess., 208.

Break-In at Ellsberg's Psychiatrist: A Burglar's Tale

Q. Had you been told when you entered what you were going in to do in the doctor's office?

A. No. It was told by Barker at that time, when we get inside the doctor's office.

Q. Now, you saw some cameras in this suitcase that was put in there earlier; is that correct?

A. Right.

Q. Had anybody told you that you were going to photograph any papers in the doctor's office.

A. Some paper, but we didn't know what kind of paper.

Q. Were you told before you went in that you were going to take anything from the doctor's office?

A. No, not before. . . .

Q. Showing you Exhibit Number 19, a photograph, with Suite Number "212" and "Lewis J. Fielding" showing, does this look like the hallway door that you went in through?

A. Right.

Q. Do you remember how you got in through that door? How it was forced?

A. With the—I—I can't say in English. I don't know the name.

Q. A pry bar (indicating)?

A. Right. Correct.

Q. Were you wearing any gloves to avoid leaving fingerprints?

A. We did.

Q. Then I take it you got in Dr. Fielding's office?

A. Right.

Q. Did anybody tell you after you got inside what you were there to do?

A. Well, at that time, Barker told us, "We are here because we are doing a great job for the country. And we have to find some paper of a great traitor to the United States, which is an s.o.b., and he's—and which will help enemies of this country."

So we asked who was the guy, and he said, "Daniel Ellsberg."

Q. You asked who the guy was, and he said Daniel Ellsberg?
A. Right.
Q. Did you know who Daniel Ellsberg was at that time?
A. Of course.
Q. By the way, did you think you were working for the United States Government at this time?
A. Yes. No question about it.
Q. Now, after he told you you were after papers on Daniel Ellsberg, what did you do inside the office?
A. We tried to find papers, and we—I mean, I did not find any.
Q. Did you break anything open inside the office—
A. We did. . . .
Q. And did you look through the files in the cabinets?
A. That's correct.
Q. What were you looking for, you, yourself?
A. I was looking for any paper with the name of Daniel Ellsberg on it.
Q. Did you see any name of Daniel Ellsberg on anything?
A. I did not. . . .

Felipe DeDiego Testimony, June, 6, 1973,
Grand Jury, People v. Ehrlichman, 191–99.

Using the IRS

EYES ONLY
JULY 14, 1970
TO: Mr. [Tom Charles] Huston
FROM: L. Higby [Former assistant to H.R. Haldeman]

Bob asked that I pass the following along to you:
It is reported that a growing number of New Left Congressional Staffers are associating themselves more and more closely with the activist, peace-loving groups on the Hill. These staffers are becoming a more effective group through the intellectual guidance of the new weekly seminars conducted by Brookings and by the Institute for Foreign Policy Studies. The seminar structure includes the rank-and-file "Government in Exile" and serves members of the Departments of State and Defense. Other instructors like Noam Chomsky and Richard Barnet are occasional visitors to Hanoi.
With regard to the above you should go after Brookings and the Institute for Policy Studies. You should have the Internal Revenue make some discreet inquiries *if* it is political. . . .

Haldeman Papers, Nixon Archives, National Archives.

JULY 16, 1970
TO: H. R. Haldeman
FROM: Tom Charles Huston

I have the following observations on the problems posed by Brookings, Institute for Foreign Policy Studies; etc.

1. Making sensitive political inquiries at the IRS is about as safe a procedure as trusting a whore. With the bark on, the truth is we don't have any reliable political friends at IRS whom we can trust and, as I suggested nearly a year ago, we won't be in control of the Government and in a position of effective leverage until such time as we have complete and total control of the top three slots at IRS. . . . I think the risks of leakage from making inquiries about major tax exempt foundations is greater than any benefits which might accrue. Over a year ago, I requested, at the direction of the President, that IRS conduct an examination of several radical tax exempt organizations which were clearly operating in violation of existing IRS regulations. To date, nothing has come of this request. . . . This is too typical of the type of non-cooperation we get in those quarters. . . .

3. Pat Buchanan has been researching the activities of Ford, Brookings, and other tax-exempt organizations for some time in anticipation of preparing a series of broadsides for the Veep to launch. These attacks would be on higher and less vulnerable ground than an attack based merely on their anti-Administration foreign policy briefings, and would thus be more effective. In short, the material is available to blast the hell out of these outfits and to scrare the living hell out of them. . . . I suggest that Pat be asked to crank these speeches out and that the Veep unload at the earliest possible time.

4. There is also the low road which should not be passed by. We can gather a great deal of material about the pro-Hanoi and anit-American activities of some of these outfits which would arouse the wrath of the Unenlightened folks west of the Appalachians. I think John Lehman and I could pull this material together and put together a hefty package which could be turned over to some people on the Hill and some friendly columnists to soften up the enemy in anticipation of the Veep's more gentlemanly attacks. . . .

5. If we reach the point that we really want to start playing the game tough, you might wish to consider my suggestion of some months ago that we consider going into Brookings after the classified material which they have stashed over there. There are a number of ways we could handle this. There are risks in all of them, of course; but there are also risks in allowing the government-in-exile to grow increasingly arrogant and powerful as each day goes by.

Haldeman Papers, Nixon Archives, National Archives.

EYES ONLY
DECEMBER 9, 1970
TO: H. R. Haldeman
FROM: John Dean
RE: IRS

In response to your memorandum of December 2, 1970, regarding my activities on reorganization and infusing new personnel at IRS, I want to advise you that after conversations with persons knowledgeable in this area both within government (Tax Division—Justice) and outside government, I have concluded that a major reorganization is neither necessary nor wise. There is a serious problem in politicizing IRS or taking action that would give the appearance of politicizing IRS. A reorganization which infused a large number of politically appointed people into IRS would undoubtedly have such an effect or give such an appearance. This is not to say that we cannot vastly improve upon the existing situation, where we have a 60,000 man agency vital to the government, with *one* political appointee.

Accordingly, I have been working with Fred Malek, who has devised the overall game plan for IRS. More specifically, I have given Jamie McLane my thoughts and had him attend a meeting in my office with Assistant Attorney General Johnnie Walters (Tax Division) to discuss how IRS might be organizationally improved.

I concur fully in Malek's game plan and I anticipate further discussion with Malek and McLane this week regarding what *can* be done to improve the organization of IRS.

Haldeman Papers, Nixon Archives, National Archives.

The Enemies List

Colson Memo to Dean
(June 12, 1972)

I have received a well-informed tip that there are income tax discrepancies involving the returns of Harold J. Gibbons, a vice president of the teamsters union in St. Louis. This has come to me on very, very good authority.

Gibbons, you should know, is an all out enemy, a McGovernite, ardently anti-Nixon. He is one of the three labor leaders who were recently invited to Hanoi.

Please see if this one can be started on at once and if there is an informer's fee, let me know. There is a good cause at which it can be donated.

Colson Memo to Dean
(Nov. 17, 1972)

I have received from an informer some interesting information on Jack Anderson, including a report that Jack Anderson was found in a room with wiretap equipment and a private investigator in connection with the Dodd investigation. Anderson, according to my source, had the wiretape equipment supplied to him by a Washington, D.C., man.

According to the same source, Anderson and Drew Pearson were paid $100,000 in 1958 by Batista to write favorable articles about the former Cuban dictator. In 1961 Anderson wrote several very favorable articles on Fidel Castro. Fredo de la Campo, Batista's Under Secretary of State, sent Anderson a telegram saying "I hope you were paid well, as well for the Castro articles as you were for the Batista articles." My source has a copy of the telegram.

You know my personal feelings about Jack Anderson. After his incredibly sloppy and malicious reporting on Eagleton, his credibility has diminished. It now appears as if we have the opportunity to destroy it. Do you agree that we should pursue this activity?

Dean Memo on 'Enemies'

Memorandum from Dean to Lawrence Higby, former assistant to Haldeman, dated Aug. 16, 1971 and entitled "Dealing with our political enemies."

This memorandum addresses the matter of how we can maximize the fact of our incumbency in dealing with persons known to be active in their opposition to our Administration. Stated a bit more bluntly— how we can use the available federal machinery to screw our political enemies.

After reviewing this matter with a number of persons possessed of expertise in the field, I have concluded that we do not need an elaborate mechanism or game plan, rather we need a good project coordinator and full support for the project. In brief, the system would work as follows:

—Key members of the staff (e.g., Colson, Dent, Flanigan, Buchanan) could be requested to inform us as to who they feel we should be giving a hard time.

—The project coordinator should then determine what sorts of dealings these individuals have with the Federal Government and how we can best screw them (e.g., grant availability, federal contracts, litigation prosecution, etc.).

—The project coordinator then should have access to and the full support of the top officials of the agency or departments in proceeding to deal with the individual.

I have learned that there have been many efforts in the past to take such actions, but they have ultimately failed—in most cases—because of lack of support at the top. Of all those I have discussed this matter with, Lyn Nofizger [President's California manager] appears the most knowledgeable and most interested. If Lyn had support he would enjoy undertaking this activity as the project coordinator. You are aware of some of Lyn's successes in the field, but he feels that he can employ limited efforts because there is a lack of support.

As a next step, I would recommend that we develop a small list of names—not more than ten—as our targets for concentration. Request that Lyn "do a job" on them and if he finds he is getting cut off by a department agency, that he inform us and we evaluate what is necessary to proceed. I feel it is important that we keep our targets limited for several reasons: (1) a low visibility of the project is imperative; (2) it will be easier to accomplish something real if we don't over expand our efforts; and (3) we can learn more about how to operate such an activity if we start small and build.

Hearings, Senate Select Committee,
93 Congress, 1 Sess., Book 4: 1686–98.

Nixon and "Dirty Tricks"

Richard Nixon, priding himself on his ability in campaigning, claimed that he had personally managed his previous campaigns. He publicly proclaimed that he would not be so personally involved in 1972. Yet despite protests to the contrary, the 1972 campaign found him immersed in minutiae and detail—and what he called "dirty tricks."

Finally I wrote that I was going to take the advice of nearly all those around me and firmly and flatly keep out of my re-election campaign until as late as possible in 1972.

In fact my determination to keep politics out of the White House was short-lived. I should have known that the attempt would be futile. . . . So I ended up keeping the pressure on the people around me to get organized, to get tough, and to get information about what the other side was doing. Sometimes I ordered a tail on a front-running Democrat; sometimes I urged that department and agency files be checked for any indications of suspicious or illegal activities involving prominent Democrats. I told my staff that we should come up with the kind of imaginative dirty tricks that our Democratic opponents used against us and others so effectively in previous campaigns.

John Mitchell was going to be my campaign manager, but he would have his hands full organizing and running the Committee to Re-elect the President. Increasingly I turned to Chuck Colson to act as my political point-man. Colson had joined the administration in late 1969 in the role of White House liaison with special interest groups. He worked on policy matters with energy and devotion. He spent hours with labor groups, veterans' organizations, ethnic minorities, and religious groups. He was positive, persuasive, smart, and aggressively partisan. His instinct for the political jugular and his ability to get things done made him a lightning rod for my own frustrations at the timidity of most Republicans in responding to attacks from the Democrats and the media. When I complained to Colson I felt confident that something would be done, and I was rarely disappointed. . . .

Richard M. Nixon, *RN: The Memoirs of Richard Nixon*
(New York, 1979), 614–15.

III
The Watergate Break-In

The Burglary

5 Held in Plot to Bug Democrats' Office

By Alfred E. Lewis,
Washington Post Staff Writer

Five men, one of whom said he is a former employee of the Central Intelligence Agency, were arrested at 2:30 a.m. yesterday in what authorities described as an elaborate plot to bug the offices of the Democratic National Committee here.

Three of the men were native-born Cubans and another was said to have trained Cuban exiles for guerrilla activity after the 1961 Bay of Pigs Invasion.

They were surprised at gunpoint by three plainclothes officers of the metropolitan police department in a sixth-floor office at the plush Watergate, 2600 Virginia Ave., N.W. where the Democratic National Committee occupies the entire floor.

There was no immediate explanation as to why the five suspects would want to bug the Democratic National Committee offices or whether or not they were working for any other individuals or organizations.

A spokesman for the Democratic National Committee said records kept in those offices are "not of a sensitive variety" although there are "financial records and other such information."

Police said two ceiling panels in the office of Dorothy V. Bush, secretary of the Democratic Party, had been removed.

Her office is adjacent to the office of Democratic National Chairman Lawrence F. O'Brien. Presumably, it would have been possible to slide a bugging device through the panels in that office to a place above the ceiling panels in O'Brien's office.

All wearing rubber surgical gloves, the five suspects were captured inside a small office within the committee's headquarters suite.

Police said the men had with them at least two sophisticated devices capable of picking up and transmitting all talk, including telephone conversations. In addition, police found lockpicks and door jimmies,

27

almost $2,300 in cash, most of it in $100 bills with the serial numbers in sequence . . .

The five men were identified as:·

• Edward Martin, alias James W. McCord, of New York City and perhaps the Washington metropolitan area. Martin said in court yesterday that he retired from the CIA two years ago. He said he presently is employed as a "security consultant."

• Frank Sturgis of 2515 NW 122d St., Miami. Prosecutors said that an FBI check on Sturgis showed that he had served in the Cuban Military army intelligence in 1958, recently travelled to Honduras in Central America, and presently is the agent for a Havana salvage agency. He has a home and family in Miami. Sturgis also was once charged with a gun violation in Miami, according to FBI records.

• Eugenio R. Martinez of 4044 North Meridian Ave., Miami. Prosecutors said that Martinez violated the immigration law in 1958 by flying a private plane to Cuba. He is a licensed real estate agent and a notary public in Florida.

• Virgilio R. Gonzales of 930 NW 23d Ave., Miami. In Miami yesterday his wife told a Washington Post reporter that her husband works as a locksmith at the Missing Link Key Shop. Harry Collot, the shop owner, said that Gonzales was scheduled to work yesterday but didn't show up. "He's done it before, but it's not a regular thing," Collot said. He said he thought Gonzales came to America about the time Fidel Castro became well-known, and began working for Missing Links sometime in 1959. He described Gonzales as "pro-American and anti-Castro . . . he doesn't rant or rave like some of them do."

• Bernard L. Barker of 5229 NW 4th St., Miami. Douglas Caddy, one of the attorneys for the five men, told a reporter that shortly after 3 a.m. yesterday, he received a call from Barker's wife. "She said that her husband told her to call me if he hadn't called her by 3 a.m.; that it might mean he was in trouble."

All were charged with felonious burglary and with possession of implements of crime. . . .

Washington Post, June 18, 1972.

GOP Security Aide Among 5 Arrested in Bugging Affair

By Bob Woodward and Carl Bernstein,
Washington Post Staff Writers

One of the five men arrested early Saturday in the attempt to bug the Democratic National Committee headquarters here is the salaried security coordinator for President Nixon's re-election committee.

The suspect, former CIA employee James W. McCord Jr., 53, also holds a separate contract to provide security services to the Republican National Committee, GOP national chairman Bob Dole said yesterday.

Former Attorney General John N. Mitchell, head of the Committee for the Re-Election of the President, said yesterday McCord was employed to help install that committee's own security system.

In a statement issued in Los Angeles, Mitchell said McCord and the other four men arrested at Democratic headquarters Saturday "were not operating either in our behalf or with our consent" in the alleged bugging attempt.

Dole issued a similar statement, adding that "we deplore action of this kind in or out of politics." An aide to Dole said he was unsure at this time exactly what security services McCord was hired to perform by the National Committee.

Police sources said last night that they were seeking a sixth man in connection with the attempted bugging. The sources would give no other details.

Other sources close to the investigation said yesterday that there still was no explanation as to why the five suspects might have attempted to bug Democratic headquarters in the Watergate at 2600 Virginia Ave. NW, or if they were working for other individuals or organizations.

"We're baffled at this point . . . the mystery deepens," a high Democratic party source said.

Democratic National Committee Chairman Lawrence F. O'Brien said the "bugging incident . . . raised the ugliest questions about the integrity of the political process that I have encountered in a quarter century.

"No mere statement of innocence by Mr. Nixon's campaign manager will dispel these questions."

The Democratic presidential candidates were not available for comment yesterday.

O'Brien, in his statement, called on Attorney General Richard G. Kleindienst to order an immediate, "searching professional investigation" of the entire matter by the FBI.

A spokesman for Kleindienst said yesterday, "The FBI is already investigating . . . Their investigative report will be turned over to the criminal division for appropriate action."

The White House did not comment.

Washington Post, June 19, 1972.

White House Consultant Tied to Bugging Figure

By Bob Woodward and E. J. Bachinski,
Washington Post Staff Writers

A consultant to White House special counsel Charles W. Colson is listed in the address books of two of the five men arrested in an attempt to bug the Democratic National headquarters here early Saturday.

Federal sources close to the investigation said the address books contain the name and home telephone number of Howard E. Hunt with the notations, "W. House" and "W.H."

In addition a stamped, unmailed envelope containing Hunt's personal check for $6 made out to the Lakewood Country Club in Rockville and a bill for the same amount also were found among the suspects belongings, sources said.

Hunt worked for the Central Intelligence Agency from 1949 to 1970. At least two of the five suspects in what Democratic Party chairman Lawrence F. O'Brien has called an "incredible act of political espionage" have worked for the CIA. The other three are either active in the anti-Castro movement in Florida or are known by leaders of that movement.

In other developments yesterday:

• It was reported that one of the five suspects, Eugenio R. Martinez, contacted University of Miami officials two weeks ago seeking housing for about 3,000 Young Republicans during the Republican National Convention.

• Former CIA employee and FBI agent James W. McCord Jr., a suspect who worked for the Republicans as a security coordinator, served until four months ago in a special 15-member military reserve unit. The Washington-based unit develops lists of radicals and draws up contingency plans for censorship of the news media and U.S. mail.

• White House spokesman Ronald L. Ziegler told reporters in Flordia with the President that he would not comment on "a third-rate burglary attempt." In addition Ziegler said that "certain elements may try to stretch this beyond what it is."

• Senate Democratic leader Mike Mansfield said he didn't think the Republican party had anything to do with the bizarre bugging incident. . . .

"I've looked into the matter very thoroughly and I am convinced that neither Mr. Colson nor anyone else at the White House had any knowledge of, or participation in, this deplorable incident at the Democratic National Committee," Clawson said in a prepared statement.

He said Hunt was put on at the White House because of his CIA expertise. . . .

Washington Post, June 20, 1972.

The Role of the President's Campaign Committee

Former Attorney General John Mitchell, the ostensible head of Nixon's reelection campaign, later admitted that he had possessed knowledge of the break-in plan and by tacit agreement had authorized it. In his testimony to the Senate Select Committee, Mitchell commented on the ideas and peculiar personality of Gordon Liddy, originator of the "Gemstone Plan" that led to the break-in at the Democratic National Committee headquarters in the Watergate.

John Mitchell

Mr. DASH. Were you aware of Mr. Liddy's background—professional background?

Mr. MITCHELL. I was aware because it was described at the time, but I think I had probably heard beforehand that he had previously been an assistant prosecutor in the State of New York, that he had run for Congress, that he had been with the Federal Bureau of Investigation and had been working in the Treasury and at that particular time, was in the White House.

Mr. DASH. Now, were you aware of his duties at the White House?

Mr. MITCHELL. I became aware of his duties in the White House when, I believe it was on the 8th day of December, Mr. Egil Krogh brought him over to my office in connection with a meeting that had to do with the Dale program—that is the drug abuse law enforcement program—of which there were many such meetings going on around the office, around the administration, around the Government.

Mr. DASH. Well, did you know that Mr. Liddy also worked for Mr. Krogh as one of the Plumbers?

Mr. MITCHELL. No; I had not been advised of those activities as of that time.

Mr. DASH. Now, after Mr. Liddy was hired and became counsel to the committee, there came a time when there was a meeting in your office, on January 27, 1972, at the Department of Justice, attended by Mr. Dean, Mr. Magruder, Mr. Liddy, and of course, yourself.

Can you tell us how this meeting came about, who set it up, and why it was in your office?

Mr. MITCHELL. Well, I can't tell you how it came about other than in the normal process of events. Most of the meetings in my office were put on the calendar through individuals who would call up and ask for meetings and my secretary would make notes of that and then somewhere along prior to the time of the request, she would check with me concerning whether I was agreeable to it and it would be put on the permanent calendar for that particular day.

Mr. DASH. Would she tell you as to what the purpose of the meeting would be in determining whether you were agreeable or not?

Mr. MITCHELL. Normally, this would be the case.

Mr. DASH. Do you know what purpose was stated for the meeting of January 27, 1972?

Mr. MITCHELL. I cannot recall that, Mr. Dash. The meeting, of course, as we are well aware now, had two functions. One of them was to discuss the proposed intelligence plan and the other one had to do with the discussion of the election and what, what part of it that she might have discussed with me. I am not aware. . . .

Mr. DASH. Is it your testimony now that you don't recall having any knowledge that you were going to have an intelligence plan discussed prior to that meeting of January?

Mr. MITCHELL. I just don't recall. . . .

Mr. DASH. [W]hat, to your best recollection, was the intelligence plan that Mr. Liddy presented to you as Attorney General or in your role as adviser to the Committee To Re-Elect the President?

Mr. MITCHELL. I think it can be best described as a complete horror story that involved a mish-mash of code names and lines of authority, electronic surveillance, the ability to intercept aircraft communications, the call girl bit and all the rest of it.

Mr. DASH. Do you recall the use of charts in the show and tell operation?

Mr. MITCHELL. I recall the use of charts because this is where the lines were all crossing with the authority, et cetera, et cetera.

Mr. DASH. Do you recall any of the code names that were used, Mr. Mitchell?

Mr. MITCHELL. No, I can't, Mr. Dash. The matter was of such striking content and concept that it was just beyond the pale.

Mr. DASH. When Liddy completed his presentation, what was your reaction?

Mr. MITCHELL. Well, I think it was very simple. As I recall, I told him to go burn the charts and that this was not what we were interested in. What we were interested in was a matter of information gathering and protection against the demonstrators.

Mr. DASH. Mr. Mitchell, if this was the kind of plan that you have described and, as has been described this way by other witnesses before this committee, and since you were the Attorney General of the United States, why didn't you throw Mr. Liddy out of your office?

Mr. MITCHELL. Well, I think, Mr. Dash, in hindsight I not only should have thrown him out of the office, I should have thrown him out of the window. [Laughter.]

Mr. DASH. Well, since you did neither—[laughter] why didn't you at least recommend that Mr. Liddy be fired from his responsible position at the committee since obviously he was presenting to you an irresponsible program?

Mr. MITCHELL. Well, in hindsight I probably should have done that, too. About the belief I had at the time in turning the matter over we would get back to the purpose that was originally intended, and that he was qualified to pursue that particular segment that we had been talking about. . . .

Hearings, Senate Select Committee, 93 Congress, 1 Sess.,
July 10, 1973, Book 4: 160–3.

Fred LaRue

Fred LaRue was John Mitchell's most important aide and confidant in the campaign committee. In a lengthy interview with the BBC some two decades after the events, LaRue revealed that he and Mitchell had known fully of attempts to bug Democratic headquarters. LaRue's revelations came at an opportune time, for they clearly refuted a popular revisionist theory that absolved Mitchell of any involvement and instead blamed the break-in on the machinations of John Dean.

LARUE: [I]n March of '72 the Mitchells decided to take a break from the campaign, decided to go to Key Biscayne for about two weeks and they invited me to go with them.

[T]here were quite a few decisions that had to be made. Jeb Magruder . . . flew to Key Biscayne. I met with Magruder and explained to him that Mrs. Mitchell wasn't too pleased with having her vacation interrupted and that we would have to keep the meeting short, and I asked to see the memos that were to be discussed at the meeting.

One of the memos was concerning the possible electric surveillance of the Democratic National Committee. I distinctly remember putting this at the last of the—putting it at the tail end of the list, and the next morning I asked Magruder, what is this business about this electronic surveillance? He said, well, this has been in the mill for some time and we need a decision on it. He said, I'm getting pushed very strongly on this and I need a decision from Mitchell.

And I told him, I said I put it at the bottom of the list and if we get there we'll discuss it. Otherwise, you'll have to wait until we come back to Washington.

We had the meeting, we did get through all the action memos. We did discuss the electronic surveillance memo. . . . I remember at the time I told Mitchell that in my opinion this was not worth the risk involved. There were too many downside risks and not enough positives in the plan.

Mitchell was very noncommittal on it. My impression was that he just wanted this to go away. He did not want to make a decision about it. We discussed it at some length. Magruder was pushing very hard to get any okay on it. The decision was made that there would be no action taken on the memo at that time. I distinctly remember this and I know that at that meeting, Mitchell did not sign off on the surveillance.

Q: When the idea of doing the surveillance came up, they probably asked your opinion. What did you say?

LaRue: I told him that it was not worth the risk. This is an endeavor that has a lot of down-side risks. If they're caught doing this, we've got a lot of problems, and there's really—I can see nothing that we were going to gain from any surveillance on the Democratic National Committee. It's a scheme that's not worth the time or the money or the investment or the risk. . . .

Magruder admitted he was getting a lot of pressure. I don't specifically remember who this pressure was coming from. I surmised it was coming—if it wasn't coming from Mitchell it must have been coming from the White House. Who, I do not know. . . .

Q: So that was that, as far as you were concerned.

LaRue: The vacation ended, right, and we went back to Washington. [One morning] Magruder and I were having breakfast . . . and he was paged. He went to the phone and he came back and said, Gordon Liddy wants me to go to a secure phone at some Air Force base and call him. I said, I wonder what that could be about, and he said, well, last night was the night they were supposed to go back into the DNC. I said, Jeb, go use the pay phone and let's find out what's going on.

A few minutes later, Magruder came back and he said, I'm afraid we have a problem. Four or five men were apprehended last night in the DNC and one of them was James McCord, who's our security officer. I told Jeb, well, I've got to go talk to Mitchell about this.

Mitchell was in a meeting with some people from California. I got

Mitchell out of the meeting, we went into another room, and I told him. I said, John, last night four or five guys got caught in the DNC and one of them was James McCord. Mitchell looked at me. He said, that's incredible.

We were not able to really discuss this at that time. Governor Reagan was waiting in the lobby for John and we were under—we had a tight schedule. We had a meeting in a very few minutes. He asked me to discuss this with Magruder.

At some point, a suggestion was made, and I don't know who made it, to call Dick Kleindienst, the Attorney General, and see if we could find out what was going on. Evidently that call was made. I don't know who made it. . . . Right after I met with Mitchell and told him about the break-in, I went to the room for something and my wife said, Fred, what's wrong with you? She said, you look strange. You look like you're really upset about something. I said, I just can't talk about it right now but something has occurred that could very well bring down this administration. . . .

Fred LaRue Interview, 1993, courtesy of
Norma Percy, Producer, London, England.

What Did the White House Know?

Gordon Strachan, one of Haldeman's aides, briefed the President's chief of staff for important meetings. An April 4, 1972 "talking paper" that he prepared for Haldeman's upcoming meeting with Mitchell provides valuable evidence that Haldeman had known in advance of the plan to break into the Watergate. Haldeman's diary entry for March 28, 1973 confirms this knowledge. Equally revealing is an excerpt from a taped transcript of a conversation between John Mitchell and John Ehrlichman in the White House on April 14, 1973. At that point, the President and his closest advisers hoped to maneuver Mitchell into accepting full blame for Watergate. Mitchell's response clearly indicates that the White House itself was involved in the origin of the break-in plans.

Strachan to Haldeman, April 4, 1972

Gordon Liddy's intelligence operation proposal . . . has been approved. Now you may want to cover with Mitchell who will be privy to the information. The current system is Magruder and [Robert] Reisner [Magruder's assistant]. Now that Liddy will begin receiving this political intelligence information, you may want to cover with Mitchell, who should be charged with the responsibility of translating the intelligence into an appropriate political response. If it is to be Colson, you may want to lay the groundwork with Mitchell now. Mitchell may suggest [Pat] Buchanan, who enjoys that role.

Strachan to Haldeman, Haldeman Papers,
Dean File, Nixon Papers, National Archives.

John Mitchell

Well, let me [clears throat] tell you where I stand. Uh, there is no way that I'm going to do anything except staying where I am because I'm too far, uh, far out. Uh, the fact of the matter is that, uh, I got euchred into this thing, when I say, by not paying attention to what these bastards were doing, and uh, well you know how far back this goes—this, uh, whole genesis of this thing was over here [in the White House]—as you're perfectly well aware. . . .

Transcript of April 14, 1973 meeting.
Statement of Information, Committee on the Judiciary, 740.

The White House Reacts: Private and Public Comment

The President was in Florida during the Watergate break-in, but on his return to Washington, he demonstrated prompt and intense interest in the caper—and containing the investigation, Chief of Staff Haldeman recorded in his diary. Publicly, a few days later, the President disavowed any White House links to the burglars. At a meeting on June 30, 1972, the President, Haldeman, and Mitchell, agreed that Mitchell would resign but denied that his resignation in any way was linked to Watergate. Their taped conversation of the meeting, however, indicated the necessity of covering-up any involvement in Watergate for fear of exposing "more stuff."

Haldeman,
June 20, 1972

We got back into the Democratic break-in again. I told the P[resident] about it on the plane last night. He was somewhat interested. The more he thought about it, it obviously bothered him more, because he raised it in considerable detail today. I had a long meeting with Ehrlichman and Mitchell. We added Kleindienst for a while and John Dean for quite a while. The conclusion was that we've got to hope the FBI doesn't go beyond what's necessary in developing evidence and that we can keep a lid on that, as well as keeping all the characters involved from getting carried away with any unnecessary testimony.

The P was concerned about what our counterattack is, our PR offensive to top this. He felt we have to hit the opposition with their activities. Also put out the point that the libertarians have created public callousness. Do they justify this kind of thing less than stealing the Pentagon Papers, or the Anderson files, and so on. He feels we should be on the attack for diversion, and not just take it lying down. He raised it again several times during the day, and it obviously is bothering him. He had Colson over to talk about it, and then later called me a couple of times on various specifics. He called at home tonight, saying that he wanted to change the plan for his press conference and have it on Thursday instead of tomorrow, so that it won't look like he's reacting to the Democratic break-in thing.

Haldeman Diary, Nixon Papers, National Archives.

The President's News Conference of
June 22, 1972

Questions
Bugging of Democratic Headquarters
[1.] Q. Mr. O'Brien has said that the people who bugged his headquarters had a direct link to the White House. Have you had any sort of investigation made to determine whether this is true?

The PRESIDENT. Mr. Ziegler and also Mr. Mitchell, speaking for the campaign committee, have responded to questions on this in great detail. They have stated my position and have also stated the facts accurately.

This kind of activity, as Mr. Ziegler has indicated, has no place whatever in our electoral process, or in our governmental process. And, as Mr. Ziegler has stated, the White House has had no involvement whatever in this particular incident.

As far as the matter now is concerned, it is under investigation, as it should be, by proper legal authorities, by the District of Columbia police, and by the FBI. I will not comment on those matters, particularly since possible criminal charges are involved.

Public Papers of the Presidents, Richard Nixon, 1972, 206–7.

The President and His Men

HALDEMAN: Well, there maybe is another facet. The longer you wait the more risk each hour brings. You run the risk of more stuff, valid or invalid, surfacing on the Watergate caper—type of thing—

MITCHELL: You couldn't possibly do it if you got into a—

HALDEMAN: —the potential problem and then you are stuck—

PRESIDENT: Yes, that's the other thing, if something does come out, but we won't—we hope nothing will. It may not. But there is always the risk.

HALDEMAN: As of now there is no problem there. As, as of any moment in the future there is at least a potential problem. . . .

Transcript of June 30, 1972 meeting, Statement of Information, Committee on the Judiciary, H.R., Book II, 514.

IV

Cover-Up!
The
White House
Responds

The "Smoking Gun": Using the CIA

On June 23, 1972, Nixon and Haldeman met to consider means of containing the widening FBI investigation. Together, they devised the idea of using CIA Director Richard Helms and his deputy, General Vernon Walters, to inform Acting FBI Director L. Patrick Gray that the investigation threatened to expose CIA operations and assets in Mexico. These conversations, later known as the "smoking gun" tapes, offered clear indications of the President's efforts to obstruct justice. The scenario Nixon devised never was realized. Helms and Walters, who had initially appeared as willing accomplices, subsequently refused to lend themselves and the Agency to the effort. After the White House meeting, Walters left a substantial paper trail, detailing his further involvement and attempts to distance himself from the White House cover-up scheme.

**Transcript of a recording of a meeting between
the President and H. R. Haldeman,
the Oval Office, June 23, 1972,
from 10:04 a.m. to 11:39 a.m.**

HALDEMAN: O.K.—that's fine. Now, on the investigation, you know, the Democratic break-in thing, we're back to the—in the, the problem area because the FBI is not under control, because Gray doesn't exactly know how to control them, and they have, their investigation is now leading into some productive areas, because they've been able to trace the money, not through the money itself, but through the bank, you know, sources—the banker himself. And, and it goes in some directions we don't want it to go. Ah, also there have been some things, like an informant came in off the street to the FBI in Miami, who was a photographer or has a friend who is a photographer who developed some films through this guy, Barker, and the films had pictures of Democratic National Committee letterhead documents and things. So I guess, so it's things like that that are gonna, that are filtering in. Mitchell came up with yesterday, and John Dean analyzed very carefully last night and concludes, concurs now with Mitchell's recommendation that the only way to solve this, and we're set up beautifully to do it, ah, in that and that . . . the only network that paid any attention to it last night was NBC . . . they did a massive story on the Cuban . . .

PRESIDENT: That's right.

HALDEMAN: . . . thing.

PRESIDENT: Right.

HALDEMAN: That the way to handle this now is for us to have Walters call Pat Gray and just say, "Stay the hell out of this . . . this is, ah, business here we don't want you to go any further on it." That's not an unusual development . . .

PRESIDENT: Um huh.

HALDEMAN: . . . and, uh, that would take care of it.

PRESIDENT: What about Pat Gray, ah, you mean he doesn't want to?

HALDEMAN: Pat does want to. He doesn't know how to, and he doesn't have, he doesn't have any basis for doing it. Given this, he will then have the basis. He'll call Mark Felt in, and the two of them . . . and Mark Felt wants to cooperate because . . .

PRESIDENT: Yeah.

HALDEMAN: . . . he's ambitious.

PRESIDENT: Yeah.

HALDEMAN: Ah he'll call him in and say, "We've got the signal from across the river to, to put the hold on this." And that will fit rather well because the FBI agents who are working the case, at this point, feel that's what it is. This is CIA.

PRESIDENT: But they've traced the money to 'em.

HALDEMAN: Well, they have, they've traced to a name, but they haven't gotten to the guy yet.

PRESIDENT: Would it be somebody here?

HALDEMAN: Ken Dahlberg.

PRESIDENT: Who the hell is Ken Dahlberg?

HALDEMAN: He's, ah, he gave $25,000 in Minnesota and, ah, the check went directly in to this, to this guy Barker.

PRESIDENT: Maybe he's a . . . bum. . . . He didn't get this from the committee though, from Stans.

HALDEMAN: Yeah. It is. It is. It's directly traceable and there's some more through some Texas people in—that went to the Mexican bank which they can also trace to the Mexican bank . . . they'll get their names today. And (pause)

PRESIDENT: Well, I mean, ah, there's no way . . . I'm just thinking if they don't cooperate, what do they say? They, they, they were approached by the Cubans. That's what Dahlberg has to say, the Texans too. Is that the idea?

HALDEMAN: Well, if they will. But then we're relying on more and more people all the time. That's the problem. And, ah, they'll stop if we could, if we take this other step.

PRESIDENT: All right. Fine.

HALDEMAN: And, and they seem to feel the thing to do is get them to stop?

PRESIDENT: Right, fine.

HALDEMAN: They say the only way to do that is from White House instructions. And it's got to be Helms and, ah, what's his name? . . . Walters.

PRESIDENT: Walters.

HALDEMAN: And the proposal would be that Ehrlichman (coughs) and I call them in . . .

PRESIDENT: All right, fine.

HALDEMAN: . . . and say, ah . . .

PRESIDENT: How do you call him in, I mean you just, well, we protected Helms from one hell of a lot of things.

HALDEMAN: That's what Ehrlichman says.

PRESIDENT: Of course, this is a, this is a Hunt, you will—that will uncover a lot of things. You open that scab, there's a hell of a lot of things and that we just feel that it would be very detrimental to have this thing go any further. This involves these Cubans, Hunt, and a lot of hanky-panky that we have nothing to do with ourselves. Well, what the hell, did Mitchell know about this thing to any much of a degree?

HALDEMAN: I think so. I don't think he knew the details, but I think he knew.

PRESIDENT: He didn't know how it was going to be handled though, with Dahlberg and the Texans and so forth? Well, who was the asshole that did? (Unintelligible) Is it Liddy? Is that the fellow? He must be a little nuts.

HALDEMAN: He is.

PRESIDENT: I mean he just isn't well screwed on, is he? Isn't that the problem? . . .

PRESIDENT: I'm not going to get that involved. I'm (unintelligible).

HALDEMAN: No, sir. We don't want you to.

PRESIDENT: You call them in. . . . Good. Good deal. Play it tough. That's the way they play it and that's the way we are going to play it.

HALDEMAN: O.K. We'll do it. . . .

Vernon Walters Memoranda

---

28 June 1972
MEMORANDUM FOR RECORD

On June 23 at 1300 on request I called with Director Helms on John Ehrlichman and Robert Haldeman in Ehrlichman's office at the White House.

Haldeman said that the "bugging" affair at the Democratic National Committee Hqs at the Watergate Apartments had made a lot of noise and the Democrats were trying to maximize it. The FBI had been called in and was investigating the matter. The investigation was leading to a lot of important people and this could get worse. He asked what the connection with the Agency was and the Director repeated that there was none. Haldeman said that the whole affair was getting embarrassing and it was the President's wish that Walters call on Acting FBI Director Patrick Gray and suggest to him that since the five suspects had been arrested that this should be sufficient and that it was not advantageous to have the enquiry pushed, especially in Mexico, etc.

Director Helms said that he had talked to Gray on the previous day and had made plain to him that the Agency was not behind this matter, that it was not connected with it and none of the suspects was working for, nor had worked for the Agency in the last two years. He had told Gray that none of his investigations was touching any covert projects of the Agency, current or ongoing.

Haldeman then stated that I could tell Gray that I had talked to the White House and suggest that the investigation not be pushed further. Gray would be receptive as he was looking for guidance in the matter.

The Director repeated that the Agency was unconnected with the matter. I then agreed to talk to Gray as directed. Ehrlichman implied I could do this soon and I said I would try to do it today.

Vernon A. Walters
Lieutenant General, USA

28 June 1972
MEMORANDUM FOR RECORD

At 1430 on 23 June I called on the Acting Director of the FBI, L. Patrick Gray, at his office in the FBI Building and saw him alone.

I said that I had come to see him after talking to the "White House". I cited no names and he asked for none. I added that I was aware of the Director's conversation with him the previous day and while the further investigation of the Watergate Affair had not touched any current or ongoing covert projects of the Agency, its continuation might lead to some projects. I recalled that the FBI and the Agency had an agreement in this respect and that the Bureau had always scrupulously respected this. Gray said he was aware of this and understood what I was conveying to him. His problem was how to low key this matter now that it was launched. He said that a lot of money was apparently involved and there was a matter of a check on a Mexican bank for 89 thousand dollars. He asked if the name Dahlberg meant anything to me and I said it did not but that that was not really significant as I had only been with the Agency for a few months.

Gray then said that this was the most awkward matter to come up during an election year and he would see what he could do. I repeated that if the investigations were pushed "south of the border" it could trespass upon some of our covert projects and, in view of the fact that the five men involved were under arrest, it would be best to taper the matter off there. He replied that he understood and would have to study the matter to see how it could best be done. He would have to talk to John Dean about it.

Gray said he looked forward to cooperating closely with the Agency. After some pleasantries about J. Edgar Hoover and our past military careers, I left saying that my job had been an awkward one but he had been helpful and I was grateful.

Vernon A. Walters
Lieutenant General, USA

28 June 1972
MEMORANDUM FOR RECORD

On 26 June at about 10:00 a.m. I received a phone call from Mr. John Dean at the White House. He said he wished to see me about the matter that John Ehrlichman and Bob Haldeman had discussed with me on the 23rd of June. I could check this out with them if I wished. I agreed to call on him in his office in Room 106 at the Executive Office Building at 1145 that morning. Immediately after hanging up, I called Ehrlichman to find out if this was alright and after some difficulty I reached him and he said I could talk freely to Dean.

At 1145 I called at Dean's office and saw him alone. He said that the investigation of the Watergate "bugging" case was extremely awkward, there were lots of leads to important people and that the FBI which was investigating the matter was working on three theories:

1. It was organized by the Republican National Committee.
2. It was organized by the CIA.
3. It was organized by some other party.

I said that I had discussed this with Director Helms and I was quite sure that the Agency was not in any way involved and I knew that the Director wished to distance himself and the Agency from the matter. Dean then asked whether I was sure that the Agency was not involved. I said that I was sure that none of the suspects had been on the Agency payroll for the last two years.

Dean then said that some of the accused were getting scared and "wobbling". I said that even so they could not implicate the Agency. Dean then asked whether there was not some way the Agency could pay bail for them (they had been unable to raise bail). He added that it was not just bail, that if these men went to prison, could we (CIA) find some way to pay their salaries while they were in jail out of covert action funds.

I said that I must be quite clear. I was the Deputy Director and as such had only authority specifically delegated to me by the Director and was not in the chain of command but that the great strength of the Agency and its value to the President of the nation lay in the fact that it was apolitical and had never gotten itself involved in political disputes. Despite the fact that I had only been with the Agency a short time, I knew that the Director felt strongly about this.

I then said that big as the troubles might be with the Watergate Affair, if the Agency were to provide bail and pay salaries, this would become known sooner or later in the current "leaking" atmosphere of Washington and at that point the scandal would be ten times greater as such action could only be done upon direction at the "highest level" and that those who were not touched by the matter now would certainly be so.

Dean seemed at first taken aback and then very much impressed by this argument and said that it was certainly a very great risk that would have to be weighed. I repeated that the present affair would be small potatoes compared to what would happen if we did what he wanted and it leaked. He nodded gravely.

I said that, in addition, the Agency would be completely discredited with the public and the Congress and would lose all value to the President and the Administration. Again he nodded gravely.

He then asked if I could think of any way we (CIA) could help. I said I could not think of any but I would discuss the matter with the Director and would be in touch with him. However, I felt that I was fully cognizant of the Director's feelings in this matter. He thanked me and I left.

Vernon A. Walters
Lieutenant General, USA

29 June 1972
MEMORANDUM FOR RECORD

At 1145 on 27 June 1972, I saw John Dean at his office in the Executive Office Building.

I told him that I had spoken to Director Helms and found that what I had said to Dean the previous day did indeed reflect Helms' views accurately. That he felt any involvement of the Agency would be most counter productive and furthermore, we had a legislative constraint about the expenditure of our funds within the United States. We had to clear them with the Chairmen of the CIA Oversight Committee in both House and Senate. This visibly lessened his enthusiasm.

I then repeated my arguments that this caper while presently seeming very large would be overtaken by other spicier developments. Unfortunate though its consequences might be currently, Agency involvement by direction at the highest level would undoubtedly become known sooner or later and would then reach to people who were still uninvolved. He nodded. I said that my mind boggled that such risks as those involved in this caper could have been taken for such an unremunerative target. Involving the Agency would transform what was now a medium-sized conventional explosive into a multi-megaton explosion and simply was not worth the risk to all concerned.

Dean thanked me looking glum and said he agreed with my judgment in all of these matters.

Vernon A. Walters
Lieutenant General, USA

Senate Select Committee Exhibits, Book 7: 2948–49, Book 9: 3815–18.

The Money Trail

The decisive act in the obstruction of justice was the effort to provide hush money to help the burglary defendants with lawyers' fees and family expenses. Maurice Stans, who was in charge of fund-raising for the Committee to Re-elect the President, would recall in later testimony that he provided cash for Herbert Kalmbach, a lawyer and accountant for the President. Kalmbach delivered the funds to the defendants, most extensively through Dorothy Hunt, the wife of E. Howard Hunt, one of those defendants. After Mrs. Hunt was killed in a United Airline crash on December 8, 1972, it was discovered that she had been carrying $10,000 in cash. A taped telephone conversation between Charles Colson and Howard Hunt provided damning evidence of the White House's role in providing funds for the burglars. Colson's conversation is circumspect, but there can be little doubt that he was responding to demands for money: "I'm reading you," he told Hunt. "You don't need to be more specific." John Mitchell's aide, Fred LaRue, who at the time was trying to raise money from Thomas Pappas, a prominent Nixon supporter, in order to further fund the hush money, later provided important corroborating evidence in Senate testimony. In their grand jury testimony, both John Dean and Howard Hunt confirmed the payment of monies. Finally, Dean and the President discussed payments and possible clemency actions in their taped conversation of March 21, 1973, particularly notable for Nixon's off-hand remark that they easily could raise a million dollars.

Maurice Stans Testimony, June 12, 1973

Mr. STANS. On the 29th of June I received an urgent call from Mr. Kalmbach. He said he was in Washington at the Statler-Hilton Hotel, that it was extremely vital that he see me right away, and he wanted me to come over there, and I did. I dropped everything and went over there to see him. He said, "I am on a special mission on a White House project and I need all the cash I can get."

I said, "I don't have any cash to give to you. Will you take a check?"

He said, "No, I can't take a check, it must be in cash, and this has nothing to do with the campaign. But I am asking for it on high authority."

Mr. EDMISTEN. What high authority did he say?

Mr. STANS. He did not say. "I am asking for it on high authority and you will have to trust me that I have cleared it properly."

As I said, I had no cash belonging to the committee at that time because we had closed it all out but I did have two parcels of money that were available, and I gave those to Mr. Klambach. They added up to $75,000 of funds outside the committee.

Mr. EDMISTEN. Now, Mr. Stans, did you not ask him why he wanted this money?

Mr. STANS. Yes, I did.

Mr. EDMISTEN. What did he say?

Mr. STANS. He said, "This is for a White House project and that I have been asked to take care of and I cannot tell you. You will have to trust me."

Mr. EDMISTEN. Would Mr. Kalmbach have been your superior in this organization, campaign organization?

Mr. STANS. No, Mr. Kalmbach was a man I knew very well. He had been my principal deputy in the 1968 fundraising campaign for Richard

Nixon. He subsequently had close affiliation with a number of people in the White House that I was aware of.

He was personal counsel to the President. He was a man that I knew was a man of highest integrity, trustworthiness and honesty, and I had no question to doubt, no reason to doubt, anything he told me and I didn't. . . .

SSC, Book 2: 702–3.

Herbert Kalmbach, Hearings, July 16, 1973

Mr. DASH. Now, did you receive a telephone call from Mr. John Dean on June 28?

Mr. KALMBACH. Yes, I did.

Mr. DASH. And what did he tell you on the telephone?

Mr. KALMBACH. As I remember the telephone conversation, Mr. Dean called me. It was in the early afternoon, midafternoon, on the 28th. He told me that it was a matter of extreme importance that I return to or come back to Washington, preferably by the first available flight, to undertake a very important assignment.

Mr. DASH. And what did you do in response to that call?

Mr. KALMBACH. I took a 10 or 10:15 or 10:30 flight that night.

Mr. DASH. Arriving in Washington when?

Mr. KALMBACH. Arriving in Washington at 6, 6:15, 6:30, the following morning.

Mr. DASH. Now, what did you do next, Mr. Klambach?

Mr. KALMBACH. I then took a cab into town and checked into the Statler-Hilton Hotel.

Mr. DASH. Did you then meet Mr. Dean, either at that time or a later time that day?

Mr. KALMBACH. Yes, after I checked in and changed, I think probably I had some breakfast, I called Mr. Dean around, as I can best recall, around 9 in the morning in his office in the Executive Office Building.

Mr. DASH. And what transpired? What was the call about? What did Dean say, what did you say, and what followed? . . .

Mr. KALMBACH. Well, he indicated that the reason for this call and for my coming back to Washington was that it was necessary to talk to me about a very important assignment, namely that, he said—he used the editorial, "We,"—"We would like to have you raise funds for the legal defense of these defendants and for the support of their families. . . ."

Mr. DASH. These were the seven defendants, Mr. Hunt, Mr. Liddy, Mr. McCord, Mr. Barker, Mr. Sturgis, Mr. Gonzales—

Mr. KALMBACH. That is correct.

Mr. DASH. Now, you knew that they were for all of these defendants?

Mr. KALMBACH. I just remember that he said the Watergate defendants at that time and I was not even certain at that point in time that I even knew their names.

Mr. DASH. All right. Did you ask him any questions about that?

Mr. KALMBACH. Yes, I did. I recall that in my conversation with him, I asked whether or not it would not be perhaps preferable to have a public committee formed to raise funds for these people and for these purposes. And also, I recall that I wondered aloud about whether or not maybe they could mortgage homes or raise funds in that way until a public committee could be established. His answer to that was that there was no time for this, that a public committee might be misinterpreted, and he just waved it aside and pressed on with his request.

Mr. DASH. Did he tell you how much money might be involved?

Mr. KALMBACH. My recollection is that he indicated $50,000 to $100,000 for this assignment.

Mr. DASH. Did he stress, since he had indicated to you that a public effort might be misinterpreted, did he stress that this had to be completely secret?

Mr. KALMBACH. Yes, he made a very strong point that there was absolute secrecy required, confidentiality, indicating that if this became known, it might jeopardize the campaign and would cause misinterpretation as to the reasons for raising these funds and for the help of these people. . . .

Mr. DASH. After meeting with Mr. Dean, what did you do? Did you indicate, first, that you would accept this assignment from Mr. Dean?

Mr. KALMBACH. I did.

Mr. DASH. And you did accept it under the basis that if Mr. Dean was asking you as the President's counsel, that he had authority to ask you for that?

Mr. KALMBACH. Absolutely. I had known Mr. Dean since mid-1970, and I had complete trust in the man and knowing that he was counsel to the President.

Mr. DASH. All right, then, you accepted this assignment. What did you do right after that meeting with Mr. Dean?

Mr. KALMBACH. I walked back to the Statler-Hilton and I think within a matter of minutes after I was back at the hotel I called Mr. Stans.

Mr. DASH. What did you say to Mr. Stans?

Mr. KALMBACH. I told him that I had been given a special assignment requiring as much cash as perhaps he would have available, and I think I mentioned $50,000 to $100,000, and asked him if it would be possible that he could help me in this assignment.

Mr. DASH. What did he say?

Mr. KALMBACH. He said that he would see what he could do. He said that he would have, as I remember it, he said he would have to go to a safe deposit box but that he would meet me at the Statler-Hilton in my room early in the afternoon.

Mr. DASH. Did he meet you early in the afternoon?

Mr. KALMBACH. Yes, sir, he did.

Mr. DASH. Did he have anything with him?

Mr. KALMBACH. Yes, he did. He had—he gave me $75,100. . . .

Mr. DASH. Did Mr. Stans question you as to why you needed the money?

Mr. KALMBACH. Again, Mr. Dash, when I talked to Mr. Stans, we had known each other a number of years, I told him it was for a very important assignment, that I had been advised that it was in complete confidence, that I could not tell him the nature of the assignment, that he would have to trust me, and he said "Of course, I do trust you, Herb", and with that he gave me the funds. . . .

SSC, Book 5: 2097–210.

Accounting for Hush Money,
October 2, 1972

MEMORADUM TO: Mr. William O. Bittman
FROM: Dorothy Hunt
SUBJECT: Accounting of Monies Received

In July, I received and paid out the following amounts:

$5,000	Bail money for Frank Sturgis
$15,000	Income replacement James McCord
$12,000	Bail at $4,000 each for Messrs. Barker, Martinez and Gonzalez
$6,000	Income replacement for Mr. Barker
$4,000	Income replacement for Mr. Sturgis
$30,000	Income replacement for Mr. Hunt and Mrs. Hunt
$3,000	Income replacement for Mr. Martinez
$3,000	Income replacement for Mr. Gonzalez
$10,000	Under table bail money for Mr. Barker

(Note: Income replacement was for a period of July–Nov.)

In August, I gave Mr. Barker a total of $3,000 for expenses of travel for himself and others and for telephone expenses, and for interest paid on pawning of wife's jewelry.

In other words, I received a total of $88,000 and have paid out $91,000 (using the final $3,000 from my own funds)

You already have an accounting of the $53,500 received on September 19th.

Dorothy Hunt Memorandum, SSC, Book 9: 233.

Transcript of Hunt/Colson Conversation, November 1972

C. Before you say anything, let me say a couple of things. One, I don't know what is going on here, other than, I am told that everybody is going to come out alright. That's all I know. I've deliberately not asked any specific questions, for this reason. That I have my own ideas about how things will turn out and I'm not worried about them and you shouldn't be, but I've always thought that if it came to an open trial, that I would want to be free to come into it and character and testimony and etc. etc. This way, the less details I know of what's going on in some ways the better.

H. I appreciate that.

C. If you follow. So, I have tried to stay out of asking specific questions and it's very hard for me to do that for the reason that you're an old and dear friend and I'm sure you regredt [sic] the day I ever recommended you to the White House.

H. Not in the least, Chuck, I'm just sorry that it turned out the way it did.

C. Well, I am too, obviously and I hope to hell you had nothing to do with it and I've clung to that belief and have told people that and if you did have anything to do with it, I'm goddamn sure it's because you were doing what you were told to do.

H. That's exactly right . . .

C. Because you're a loyal soldier obviously and always have been . . .

H. Would you be willing to receive a memorandum from me?

C. Yea . . . the only . . .

H. Because I think it might help you.

C. Except there are things you may not want to tell me.

H. No, there's really nothing I don't want to tell you. I would think that you could receive this memorandum, read it and destroy it.

C. Nope.

H. You couldn't do that?

C. Nope. The reason I can't is the same reason your letter to me, when I got that and then I was asked by Federal authorities, did . . . had I had any communication and I said yea I've received this letter and here it is. I can't and you can't get in the position where you're purguring [sic].

H. No, of course not. And I'm afraid John Mitchell has already done.

C. The problem is, you see, I don't want to get into the position of knowing something that I don't now know for the reason that I want to be perfectly free to help you and the only way I can help you is to remain as completely unknowing as I am. See, my problem . . . let me tell you the problem. Is that . . . I could do you a lot more good by not . . . by honestly being able to testify that I don't know, I just don't know the answer and I don't. And right now I don't know anything about the goddamn Watergate. Now, supposing Teddy Kennedy holds his hearings and I get called up there. Well, I can't refuse to answer and I wouldn't. I'd answer I just don't know. I have no idea what happened and I don't.

H. Of course I'm never going to be put on the stand, as it stands now.

C. That's right. . . .

Jesus Christ, I know it. I hope you're doing some writing to keep yourself busy.

H. Oh, I am. I don't know if anything will ever come of it, but it's a good . . . it keeps my mind from my plight, let's put it that way. So that I was never clear in my own mind, and I'm still not, and . . . that one of the initial outputs that I had read about was that while this is done by a bunch of wild assed guys and so forth . . . well, that's fine for we're protecting the guys who are really responsible, but now that that's . . . and of course that's a continuing requirement, but at the same time, this is a two way street and as I said before, we think that now is the time when a move should be made and surely the cheapest commodity available is money. These lawyers have not been paid, there are large sums of money outstanding. That's the principal thing. Living allowances which are due again on the 31st of this month, we want that stuff well in hand for some months in advance. I think these are all reasonable requests. They're all promised in advance and reaffirmed from time to time to my attorney and so forth, so in turn I've been giving commitments to the people who look to me and. . . .

C. I'm reading you. You don't need to be more specific.

H. I don't want to belabor it.

C. No, it isn't a question of that, it's just that the less speciis [sic] I know, the better off I am . . . we are, you are. . . .

C. I'll tell you one thing I've said to people, and I just want you to know this because I think it's important. I've told people the truth that I've known you for a long time, that I've considered you a personal friend, you're a person in whom I've had a high regard and high confidence, a patriot, real patriot, and that had you ever been the one mastermineding [sic] this, it never would have fallen apart, that the reason that I am convinced, and I told this to the federal authorities on the grand jury, the reason that I'm convinced that you Howard Hunt never had a goddamn thing to do with this or if; you did, it was on the peripheries, is that if you ever did it, you would do it a lot smarter than this and that I've know [sic]. . . .

H. Well, the reason I called you was to make . . . to get back to the beginning here is because of commitments that were made to all of us at the onset, have not been kept, and there's a great deal of unease and concern on the part of 7 defendants [sic] and, I'm quite sure, me least of all. But there's a great deal of financial expense that has not been covered and what we've been getting has been coming in very minor gibs and drabs and Parkison, who's been the go between with my attorney, doesn't seem to be very effective and we're now reaching a point of which. . . .

C. Okay, don't tell me any more. Because I understand and . . .

H. These people have really got to . . . this is a long haul thing and the stakes are very very high and I thought that you would want to know that this thing must not break apart for foolish reasons. . . .

H. I would hope that somewhere along the line the people who were paralyzed initially by this within the White House could now start to give some creative thinking to the affair and some affirmative action for Christ sake.

C. That's true.

H. Very, very hard time.

C. Well, you know, I'll tell you, I find it's only the rough experiences in life and you've had your share of them, god knows, that really harden you and make something out of you, and you learn by them and become a better man for it and we'll talk about that. You'll come out of this fine, I'm positive of that.

H. Well, I want all of us to come out of it, including you.

C. My position, I suppose has been hurt in one sense, that I've been publicly but obviously people around here know I didn't have anything to do with it, but so be it. We'll all come out of it, don't worry about that. That's the last thing to worry about and I understand this message . . .

H. If; you can do anything about it . . . I would think the sooner they can get moving on it the better. Good to talk to you. I'll discuss with Bittman whether he still feels he needs to talk to you.

C. Alright and as soon as I feel that the situation, the future of the thing is clear enough that you and I can get together, we'll damn well do it, but I don't want to do it pre-maturely because it will limit my ability to help you.

H. Chuck, I understand that completely. L [sic] That's why I never tried to get in touch with you.

C. Im [sic] in a better position to help you if I can honestly swear nnder [sic] oath, which I can do, because I don't know a goddamn thing about it and I don't. And as long as I'm in that position then I can say what kind of a guy I think Howard Huhnt [sic] is and why I think this is a bum wrap. . . .

H. I know, I spent a lifetime serving my country and in a sense I'm still doing it.

C. Damn right. Alright, pal, we'll be talking to you.

H. Okay.

SSC Exhibit No. 152, Book 9: 3888–91.

Fred LaRue

LARUE: It was a damage control situation, you know, and this came up, consistently came up in discussions with the prosecutor. When did the coverup start? When did you all sit down and say, we're going to cover this up? There was never any such meeting. . . .

And as far as a conscious planned coverup, I guess it seems that way and there was one, obviously, but it evolved as a consequence of the campaign. It was imperative that this not come out at this time.

The American people are strange. . . . They don't like this kind of thing. And even though Richard Nixon was riding at this point fairly high in the poll, it could have been very damaging, could have cost him the election. . . .

Q: Tell about how Liddy came in and what he did about security first.

LaRue: It was decided that Mardian and I would meet with Liddy in my apartment. I think it was Tuesday afternoon. Liddy came by the apartment. The first thing he did was ask that I turn up the radio. I said, what for? He said, well, in case you have some bugs in the apartment, somebody could overhear the convesation. I said, Liddy, I have this apartment swept once a week. There's not any bugs here. He said, well, just turn the radio up anyway, so I did.

We asked Liddy about the break-in, what he knew about it. He told us about hiring the Cubans, about using McCord.

It was also at this meeting that he told us about some other activities that I had no knowledge of and I'm sure [Robert] Mardian didn't, the break-in in Dr. Fielding's office, the interview with Dita Beard, the proposed firebombing of the Brookings Institute. All these things we found out about at this meeting.

Later that afternoon or that night, Mardian and I met with Mitchell and we told him about the so-called White House horrors. He was incredulous, and this was—I'm sure this is the first he'd ever heard of any of this. . . .

Well, at this meeting one of the subjects that came up was that Liddy informed me that certain commitments had been made to the Cubans and to McCord in case they got caught, which they had. He wanted to know if these commitments would be kept. And I said, Gordon, if the commitments were made I'm sure they'll be kept. . . .

It appears that the Committee to Re-Elect had a fairly substantial amount of cash on hand at the committee for various projects, polling, or anything they perhaps wanted to use cash rather than checks. I think Maury Stans became very nervous about this in face of the ongoing investigation, and at some point, I don't recall exactly when, I think he had Hugh Sloan bring me all the cash they had at the committee—it was some $40,000 or $50,000—and just with the message that this was some cash they had and he wanted to get it out of the finance committee.

I reported this to Mitchell and this was some of the initial cash that was used for the support payments for the bail for the defendants. . . .

And I've reflected on this many times and at the Key Biscayne meeting, or even after that, had I gone to Mitchell and said, John, this is crazy. I mean, this is a hare-brained scheme, it's not going to do a damn thing but get us in trouble. Let's put a stop to it. If you have to, go to the White House and back them off the damn thing. Had I done that and done it forcefully, John would have listened to me and he would have done that and this whole mess could have been avoided. It's one of the real regrets I have about Watergate. . . .

[W]e were under constant demand for money for legal fees, for support for the defendants. The $30,000 or $29,000, it was soon gone. . . .

One day I got a call from Dean. He said he had a demand from Hunt's lawyer for an additional $135,000. I said, well, do you want me to, you know, give him the money? And he said, I'm not going to make that decision. And I said, well, I'm not either. He said, well, maybe you better talk to Mitchell about it.

I talked to Mitchell about it. He was rather indecisive and finally he said, well, I guess you better pay it. . . . I arranged for, I think, $75,000 to be sent, and I think that was probably the last payment made to Hunt. . . .

Fred LaRue Interview, 1993, courtesy of
Norma Percy, Producer, London, England.

John Dean Testimony

Q. Now in about the first week of December, did Mr. Mitchell contact you about using some of the White House cash fund to meet the defendants' demands?

A. Yes, he did.

Q. How did that come about?

A. Well, the demands had reached a crescendo and there was no other money available. There had been earlier discussions with LaRue and [Paul L.] O'Brien about this. It was suggested that they borrow roughly forty or fifty thousand dollars from the White House fund and they would repay these funds.

This was a renewed request of that from Mr. Mitchell directly to me, telling me that I should talk to Mr. Haldeman about getting those funds.

Q. Mr. Mitchell told you that the need was acute?

A. Yes.

Q. And he asked you to see Haldeman to seek his approval to go ahead and use some of the money for this purpose?

A. That's correct. He was quite aware of the fact that the funds were under Mr. Haldeman's control.

Q. Did Mr. Mitchell indicate that the money would be returned sometime?

A. He did.

Q. Did you then consult with Mr. Haldeman about this?

A. Yes, I did.

Q. Can you tell the Grand Jury the substance of whatever conversation you had with Mr. Haldeman about this matter?

A. Well, I told Mr. Haldeman that while I didn't like the procedure,

I had no alternative to offer him because the demands at this point were very acute and Mr. Mitchell had made the request and I didn't have any suggestion to make.

I said, "It's my understanding that they will pay the money back as soon as they have raised additional monies themselves and that the White House fund will then be kept intact."

He said that I should go ahead and tell Strachan to deliver the money to Mr. LaRue.

Q. For this purpose?

A. For this purpose.

Statement of Information, House Judiciary Committee,
Book 4, Part 1, 693–94.

E. Howard Hunt Testimony

Q. Okay. Now, then, you did have a conversation with Mr. O'Brien, Mr. Paul O'Brien, about the middle of March, 1973 did you not?

A. Yes, sir. . . .

Q. During this conversation did you say, in essence, to Mr. O'Brien, first, you apologized for putting him in the middle, and then explained that you only had a certain number of days in which to get your affairs in order and that, again, commitments had been made but had not been kept? Did you say those words, in substance?

A. In substance, yes, sir.

Q. In substance, to Mr. O'Brien?

A. Yes, sir.

Q. And did you say you'd done a number of "seamy" things for the White House?

A. I may very well have, yes, sir.

Q. Well, to the best of your recollection, did you?

A. Yes, sir. In the context that I wanted him and his principals to—to remind him and his principals that Watergate was not the only activity that I had engaged in for them.

Q. And you used the word to describe the nature of those activities, such as "seamy"?

A. Yes, sir. . . .

Q. And you said that your commitments had not been met and you mentioned that you'd done a number of "seamy" things for the White House; and if the commitments weren't met, you might have to review the alternatives. Correct?

A. I would put it a different way, sir, to the best of my recollection. That I said that the commitments had not been kept and, accordingly, if I were suddenly to become a very poor man, that I would no longer have options available to me which were currently available.

Q. And did you mention "seamy" things that you had done for the White House?

A. I had done that previously.

Q. But in the same conversation?

A. Yes. I had done seamy things for the White House, yes, period.

Q. And that if the commitments weren't met, and you would become a poor man, you might have to review the alternatives?

A. And see what other steps could be taken on my behalf.

Q. Now, a few days thereafter, you received a package, didn't you?

A. Yes.

Q. How much was in that package?

A. $75,000. . . .

Statement of Information, House Judiciary Committee,
Book 4, Part 1, 699–703.

"Stonewalling" and Perjury

For the President and his men, obstruction of justice took forms other than hush money. In a taped conversation with Colson on February 14, Nixon told Colson that "the cover-up is the main ingredient. That's where we gotta cut our losses; . . . the President's losses gotta be cut on the cover-up deal." He told other aides a month later to "stonewall it," "plead the Fifth Amendment," do anything to "save the plan." By then, Nixon's aides had taken desperate measures. Jeb Magruder, Mitchell's deputy at the Campaign Committee, and Herbert Porter, who had also worked on the campaign, perjured themselves before the grand jury. On August 29, 1972, the President publicly insisted that he and his staff had "conducted a complete investigation"; a cover-up, he insisted, "really hurts" more than the mistakes of some "overzealous people" in the campaign. Yet on September 15—the same date that the burglars were indicted—H. R. Haldeman, Nixon's chief of staff, ushered John Dean into the Oval Office to explain the progress of the cover-up. The taped conversation offers insight into the cover-up activities of the Administration. Nixon received a battle report and Dean assured him that the cover-up would hold, at least until the election. The conversation is between knowing conspirators and indicates Nixon's state of mind while he was at the top of his game. It is also revealing of the atmosphere of hostility and anger that pervaded the White House. Dean's Senate testimony explains how he helped block the October 1972 hearings before Wright Patman's House Banking and Currency committee. Patman and his staff had made great progress in following the money trail.

Tape Transcript, March 21, 1973, The President, Dean and Haldeman, 10:12–11:55 a.m.

D—. . . Here is what is happening right now. What sort of brings matters to the (unintelligible). One, this is going to be a continual blackmail operation by Hunt and Liddy and the Cubans. No doubt about it. And McCord, who is another one involved. McCord has asked for nothing. McCord did ask to meet with somebody, with Jack Caulfield who is his old friend who had gotten him hired over there. And when Caulfield had him hired, he was a perfectly legitimate security man. And he wanted to talk about commutation, and things like that. And as you know Colson has talked indirectly to Hunt about commutation. All these things are bad, in that they are problems, they are promises, they are commitments. They are the very sort of thing that the Senate is going to be looking most for. I don't think they can find them, frankly.

P—Pretty hard.

D—Pretty hard. Damn hard. It's all cash.

P—Pretty hard I mean as far as the witnesses are concerned.

D—Alright, now, the blackmail is continuing. Hunt called one of the lawyers from the Re-Election Committee on last Friday to leave it with him over the weekend. The guy came in to see me to give a message directly to me. From Hunt to me.

P—Is Hunt out on bail?

D—Pardon?

P—Is Hunt on bail?

D—Hunt is on bail. Correct. Hunt now is demanding another $72,000 for his own personal expenses; another $50,000 to pay attorneys fees; $120,000. . . .

Hunt has now made a direct threat against Ehrlichman. As a result of this, this is his blackmail. He says, "I will bring John Ehrlichman down to his knees and put him in jail. I have done enough seamy things for he and Krogh, they'll never survive it."

P—Was he talking about Ellsberg?

D—Ellsberg, and apparently some other things. I don't know the full extent of it.

P—I don't know about anything else.

D—I don't know either, and I hate to learn some of these things. So that is that situation. Now, where are at [sic] the soft points? How many people know about this? Well, let me go one step further in this whole thing. The Cubans that were used in the Watergate were also the same Cubans that Hunt and Liddy used for this California Ellsberg thing, for the break in out there. So they are aware of that. How high their knowledge is, is something else. Hunt and Liddy, of course, are totally aware of it, of the fact that it is right out of the White House.

P—I don't know what the hell we did that for!

D—I don't know either.

P—What in the (expletive deleted) caused this? (unintelligible)

D—Mr. President, there have been a couple of things around here that I have gotten wind of. At one time there was a desire to do a second story job on the Brookings Institute where they had the Pentagon papers. Now I flew to California because I was told that John had instructed it and he said, "I really hadn't. It [is] a mis-impression, but for (expletive deleted), turn it off." So I did. I came back and turned it off. The risk is minimal and the pain is fantastic. It is something with a (unintelligible) risk and no gain. It is just not worth it. But—who knows about all this now? You've got the Cubans' lawyer, a man by the name of Rothblatt, who is a no good, publicity seeking (characterization deleted), to be very frank with you. He has had to be pruned down and turned off. He was canned by his own people because they didn't trust him. He didn't want them to plead guilty. He wants to represent them before the Senate. So F. Lee Bailey, who was a partner of one of the men representing McCord, got in and cooled Rothblatt down. So that means that F. Lee Bailey has knowledge. Hunt's lawyer, a man by the name of Bittman, who is an excellent criminal lawyer from the Democratic era of Bobby Kennedy, he's got knowledge.

P—He's got some knowledge?

D—Well, all the direct knowledge that Hunt and Liddy have, as well as all the hearsay they have. . . . Mrs. Hunt was the savviest woman in the world. She had the whole picture together. . . . That is the extent of the knowledge. So, where are the soft spots on this. . . .

P—How much money do you need?

D—I would say these people are going to cost a million dollars over the next two years.

P—We could get that. On the money, if you need the money you could get that. You could get a million dollars. You could get in case. I know where it could be gotten. It is not easy, but it could be done. . . . Well, it sounds like a lot of money, a million dollars. Let me say that I think we could get that. . . .

D—There have been a lot of people having to pull oars and not everybody pulls them all the same time, the same way, because they develop self-interests.

H—What John is saying, everybody smiles at Dean and says well you better get something done about it.

D—That's right.

H—Mitchell is leaving Dean hanging out on him. None of us, well, maybe we are doing the same thing to you.

D—That's right.

H—But let me say this. I don't see how there is any way that you can have the White House or anybody presently in the White House involved in trying to gin out this money.

D—We are already deeply enough in that. That is the problem, Bob.

P—I thought you said—

H—We need more money. . . .

Jeb Magruder Testimony,
June 14, 1973

Mr. DASH. Now, Mr. Magruder, you said you needed some of this information to work out a solution. Is it not true that sometime after the time you returned to Washington from California during the months of, say, June, July, or August, that there came a time when you agreed to make up a story about how the break-in and the bugging took place and who was involved? . . .

Mr. MAGRUDER. Well, there were, from the time of the break-in to my second grand jury appearance and then actually into my third grand jury appearance in September, a series of meetings. These meetings do not appear on my calendar because they were ad hoc meetings, they were not planned meetings. They were mainly held in Mr. Mitchell's office. The main participants typically were Mr. Mitchell, Mr. LaRue, Mr. Mardian, and Mr. Dean, athough many other people met in these meetings. Much of the meetings would be on subjects that were perfectly, I think, acceptable to discuss.

You know, it is very hard for me to pinpoint exactly when and how we came up with the coverup story, but it became apparent, when we found out the sums were in the $200,000 range, that we had to come up with a very good story to justify why Mr. Liddy would have spent that amount of money on legal activities.

Mr. DASH. What was that story, Mr. Magruder, that you finally came up with?

Mr. MAGRUDER. What we did was we simply took factual activity that we had asked Mr. Liddy to do and we exaggerated to a great extent the amount of money spent on those activities to the tune of the $230,000.

I asked Mr. Porter to, would he be willing to work with us on this coverup story and, as he has testified, he indicated that he did.

So he took care of, in effect, $100,000 and I took care of, in effect,

$150,000 by indicating that Mr. Liddy had legal projects for us in the intelligence field, and we worked over this story with Mr. Mitchell, Mr. Dean, Mr. LaRue, and Mr. Mardian, although Mr. Mardian has participated to a much lesser extent with me than the others did. My primary contacts on the story were Mr. Dean and Mr. Mitchell.

Mr. DASH. All of these persons that you have named—you finally did arrive at the story and they knew in fact what actually had occurred?

Mr. MAGRUDER. Yes; they did.

Mr. DASH. Could you tell us why the story required that the break-in involvement be cut off at Mr. Liddy and not at you?

Mr. MAGRUDER. Well, there was some discussion about me and I volunteered at one point that maybe I was the guy who ought to take the heat, because it was going to get to me, and we knew that. And I think it was, there were some takers on that, but basically, the decision was that because I was in a position where they knew that I had no authority to either authorize funds or make policy in that committee, that if it got to me, it would go higher. Whereas Mr. Liddy, because of his past background, it was felt that that would be believable that Mr. Liddy was truly the one who did originate it. And, of course, it was true, I think, that Mr. Liddy did originate the plan, was basically the one who did come up with these ideas in specific terms.

We felt that was more believable than somebody like myself who did not have any background in this area authorizing these kinds of sums of money and authorizing this type of program when it was known full well throughout the committee and White House that I had no such authority. . . .

Mr. DASH. You say you were next brought before the grand jury when?

Mr. MAGRUDER. In August, August 18.

Mr. DASH. When you testified to the grand jury that time, did you testify to the false story?

Mr. MAGRUDER. Yes; I did.

Mr. DASH. What role did Mr. Dean play in preparing you for your second grand jury appearance?

Mr. MAGRUDER. On the day before the grand jury appearance, I was aware that I was a target of the grand jury at that time. So, I was briefed by our lawyers and Mr. Mardian. Also, I was interrogated for approximately 2 hours by Mr. Dean and approximately ½ hour in a general way by Mr. Mitchell. . . .

Mr. DASH. Were you again called before the grand jury prior to the trial, the first trial?

Mr. MAGRUDER. Yes.

Mr. DASH. When was that?

Mr. MAGRUDER. That was in September, the middle of September.

Mr. DASH. Did you know why you were being called before that grand jury?

Mr. MAGRUDER. Yes. At that time, they had gotten a copy—they had subpoenaed my diary and my diary contained meetings, primarily the meetings in January and February, with Mr. Liddy that we knew they would be very interested in. So consequently, Mr. Mitchell, Mr. Dean, and I met to try to determine how I would answer—

Mr. DASH. You mean prior to your appearance before the grand jury in September?

Mr. MAGRUDER. Yes, sir.

Mr. DASH. What was the purpose of that meeting?

Mr. MAGRUDER. The purpose was to develop the story in effect of what took place at those meetings. Mr. Dean asked if he could be removed from those meetings, and I said that would not work, because too many people knew he had attended those meetings.

Then Mr. Mitchell and Mr. Dean, and I agreed that we would indicate—I would indicate—that the first meeting never occurred, that we had canceled it and that at the second meeting, we had discussed the new election law, which actually had been passed that week, and I introduced Mr. Liddy to Mr. Mitchell and he had not met Mr. Mitchell. It turned out that he had met Mr. Mitchell, but I was unaware of that.

So I indicated to the grand jury that it was an informal meeting to introduce Mr. Liddy and also to discuss the new election law.

Mr. DASH. Was any suggestion made that you might erase entries in the diary?

Mr. MAGRUDER. Yes; as I recall, one of the individuals indicated that. I think we agreed that erasures could be determined by the Federal Bureau of Investigation if anything was erased. . . .

Senate Select Committee, Book 2: 801–3, 816.

Herbert Porter Testimony, June 7, 1973

Mr. DORSEN. Following the break-in at the Watergate, did you have a conversation with Mr. Jeb Magruder concerning any statements you might make to the Federal Bureau of Investigation?

Mr. PORTER. Yes, sir; I did.

Mr. DORSEN. Where and when did this conversation occur?

Mr. PORTER. I would say that approximately 10 or 11 days, I am not sure of the exact date, whether it was June 28 or the 29th, but in that time frame, Mr. Magruder asked me to come in to his office, which I did. He shut the door and he told me that he had just come from a meeting with Mr. Mitchell, Mr. LaRue, himself, and a fourth party whose name I cannot remember, where my name had been brought up as someone who could be, what was the term he used, counted on in a pinch or a team player or words to that effect.

Mr. DORSEN. You are now recounting what Mr. Magruder told you.

Mr. PORTER. Yes, sir.

Mr. DORSEN. Please continue.

Mr. PORTER. He said that I believe at that time Mr. Liddy had been fired from the campaign. He said it was— "apparent" was the word he used—that Mr. Liddy and others had on their own, illegally participated in the break-in of the Democratic National Committee, and Mr. Magruder swore to me that neither he nor anybody higher than Mr. Liddy in the campaign organization or at the White House had any involvement whatsoever in Watergate, at the Watergate break-in, and reinforced that by saying, "Doesn't that sound like something stupid that Gordon would do?" and you have to know Mr. Liddy, I agreed with that. [Laughter.]

He said, "I want to assure you now that no one did." He said, however, "There is a problem with some of the money. Now, Gordon was authorized money for some dirty tricks, nothing illegal, but nonetheless, things that could be very embarrassing to the President of the United States and to Mr. Mitchell and Mr. Haldeman and others. Now, your name was brought up as someone who we can count on to help in this situation," and I asked what is it you are asking me to do, and he said, "Would you corroborate a story that the money was authorized for something a little bit more legitimate sounding than dirty tricks, even though the dirty tricks were legal, it still would be very embarrassing. You are aware that the Democrats have filed a civil suit against this committee." I said, "Yes, I have read that in the paper." He said, "Do you know what immediate discovery is?" I said, "I do not. They may get immediate discovery, which means they can come in at any moment and swoop in on our committee and take all of the files and subpena all of the records and you know what would happen if they did that." I conjured up in my mind that scene and became rather excitable and knew I didn't want to see that. So I said, "Well, be specific," and he said, "Well, you were in charge of the surrogate campaign, you were very concerned about radical elements disrupting rallies, and so forth," and I said yes, and he said, "Suppose that we had authorized Liddy instead of the dirty tricks, we had authorized him to infiltrate some of these radical groups. How could such a program have cost $100,000?" And I thought very quickly of a conversation I had had with a young man in California in December, as a matter of fact, and I said "Jeb, that is very easy. You could get 10 college-age students or 24- or 25-year-old students, people, over a period of 10 months." Mr. Magruder had prefaced his remark by saying from December on. And I said, "You can pay them $1,000 a month which they would take their expenses out of that, and that is $100,000. That is not very much for a $45 million campaign." And he said, "Now that is right; would you be willing, if I made that statement to the FBI, would you be willing to corroborate that when I came to you in December and asked you how much it would cost, that that is what you said?" That was the net effect, the net of his question. I thought for a moment and I said, "Yes, I probably would do that." I don't remember saying yes, but I am sure I gave Mr. Magruder the impression I would probably do that and that was the end of the conversation.

Mr. DORSEN. Now, Mr. Porter, did the conversation you agreed to tell the FBI actually take place?

Mr. PORTER. Sir?

Mr. DORSEN. Did the conversation which you agreed with Mr. Magruder that you would tell to the FBI actually take place in December of 1971?

Mr. PORTER. No, sir; it did not take place in December.

Mr. DORSEN. Later, did you tell the FBI what Mr. Magruder asked you to tell them?

Mr. PORTER. Yes, sir; I did.

Mr. DORSEN. And subsequent to that, did you appear before a Federal grand jury?

Mr. PORTER. Yes, sir.

Mr. DORSEN. Were you asked about the surrogate candidate program?

Mr. PORTER. Yes, sir.

Mr. DORSEN. What did you tell the Federal grand jury?

Mr. PORTER. The same thing. . . .

SSC, Book 2: 635–36.

President's Press Conference, August 29, 1972

Q: Mr. President, wouldn't it be a good idea for a special prosecutor, even from your standpoint, to be appointed to investigate the contribution situation and also the Watergate case?

The PRESIDENT. With regard to who is investigating it now, I think it would be well to notice that the FBI is conducting a full field investigation. The Department of Justice, of course, is in charge of the prosecution and presenting the matter to the grand jury. The Senate Banking and Currency Committee is conducting an investigation. The Government Accounting Office, an independent agency, is conducting an investigation of those aspects which involve the campaign spending law.

Now, with all of these investigations that are being conducted, I don't believe that adding another special prosecutor would serve any useful purpose.

The other point that I should make is that these investigations—the investigation by the GAO, the investigation by the FBI, by the Department of Justice—have, at my direction, had the total cooperation of the—not only the White House but also of all agencies of Government.

In addition to that, within our own staff, under my direction, counsel to the President, Mr. Dean, has conducted a complete investigation of all leads which might involve any present members of the White House staff or anybody in the Government. I can say categorically that his investigation indicates that no one in the White House staff, no one in this Administration, presently employed, was involved in this very bizarre incident. . . .

What really hurts in matters of this sort is not the fact that they occur, because overzealous people in campaigns do things that are wrong. What really hurts is if you try to cover it up. I would say that here we are, with control of the agencies of the Government and presumably with control of the investigatory agencies of the Government with the exception of GAO, which is independent. We have cooperated completely. We have indicated that we want all the facts brought out and as far as any people who are guilty are concerned, they should be prosecuted.

This kind of activity, as I have often indicated, has no place whatever in our political process. We want the air cleared. We want it cleared as soon as possible.

President's Press Conference, October 5, 1972

Q: Mr. President, don't you think that your administration and the public would be served considerably and that the men under indictment would be treated better, if you people would come through and make a clean breast about what you were trying to get done at the Watergate?

The PRESIDENT: One thing that has always puzzled me about it is why anybody would have tried to get anything out of the Watergate. Be that as it may, that decision having been made at a lower level, with which I had no knowledge, and, as I pointed out—

Q: Surely you know now, sir.

The PRESIDENT: I certainly feel that under the circumstances that we have to look at what has happened and to put the matter into perspective.

Now when we talk about a clean breast, let's look at what has happened. The FBI has assigned 133 agents to this investigation. It followed out 1,800 leads. It conducted 1,500 interviews.

Incidentally, I conducted the investigation of the Hiss case. I know that is a very unpopular subject to raise in some quarters, but I conducted it. It was successful. The FBI did a magnificent job, but that investigation involving the security of this country, was basically a Sunday school exercise compared to the amount of effort that was put into this.

I agree with the amount of effort that was put into it. I wanted every lead carried out to the end because I wanted to be sure that no member of the White House staff and no man or woman in a position of major responsibility in the Committee for Re-election had anything to do with this kind of reprehensible activity. . . .

Meeting: The President, Haldeman and Dean, Oval Office, September 15, 1972. (5:27–6:17 p.m.)

P—Hi, how are you? You had quite a day today, didn't you? You got Watergate on the way, didn't you?

D—We tried.

H—How did it all end up?

D—Ah, I think we can say well at this point. The press is playing it just as we expect.

H—Whitewash?

D—No, not yet—the story right now—

P—It is a big story

H—Five indicted plus the WH former guy and all that.

D—Plus two White House fellows

H—That is good that takes the edge off whitewash really that was the thing Mitchell kept saying that to people in the country Liddy and Hunt were big men. Maybe that is good. . . .

D—The resources that have been put against this whole investigation to date are really incredible. It is truly a larger investigation than was conducted against the after inquiry of the JFK assassination.

P—Oh.

D—Good statistics supported the finding.

H—Isn't that ridiculous—this silly thing.

P—Yes (Expletive deleted). Goldwater put it in context when he said, "(expletive deleted) everybody bugs everybody else. You know that."

D—That was priceless.

P—It happens to be totally true. We were bugged in '68 on the plane and in '62 even running for Governor—(expletive deleted) thing you ever saw.

D—It is a shame that evidence to the fact that that happened in '68 was never around. I understand that only the former Director had that information.

H—No, that is not true.

D—There was evidence of it?

H—There are others who have information.

P—How do you know? Does DeLoache know?

D—DeLoache?

H—I have some stuff too—on the bombing incident and too in the bombing halt stay.

P—The difficulty with using it, of course, is it reflects on Johnson. If it weren't for that, I would use it. Is there any way we could use it without using his name—saying that the DNC did it? No—the FBI did the bugging.

D—That is the problem—would it reflect on Johnson or Humphrey?

H—Johnson. Humphrey didn't do it.

P—Oh, hell no.

H—He was bugging Humphrey, too.

P—(Expletive deleted). . . .

[Telephone call from John Mitchell] Hello. P— comments only from here on until end of call: Well, are you still alive. I was just sitting here with John Dean and he tells me you were going to be sued or something. Good, Good. Yeah. Good. Sure. Well. I tell you just don't let this keep you or your colleagues from concentrating on the big game. This thing is just one of those side issues and a month later everybody looks back and wonders what all the shooting was about. OK, John. Good night. Get a good night's sleep. And don't bug anybody without asking me? OK? Yeah. Thank you."

D—Three months ago I would have had trouble predicting there would be a day when this would be forgotten, but I think I can say that 54 days from now nothing is going to come crashing down to our surprise.

P—That what?

D—Nothing is going to come crashing down to our surprise.

P—Oh well, this is a can of worms as you know a lot of this stuff that went on. And the people who worked this way are awfully embarrassed. But by the way you have handled all this seems to me has been very skillful putting your fingers in the leaks that have sprung here and sprung there. The Grand Jury is dismissed now?

D—That is correct. They have completed and they have let them go so there will be no continued investigation prompted by the Grand Jury's inquiry. . . .

P—We are all in it together. This is a war. We take a few shots and it will be over. Don't worry. I wouldn't want to be on the other side right now. Would you?

D—Along that line, one of the things I've tried to do, I have begun to keep notes on a lot of people who are emerging as less than our friends because this will be over some day and we shouldn't forget the way some of them have treated us.

P—I want the most comprehensive notes on all those who tried to do us in. They didn't have to do it. If we had had a very close election and they were playing the other side I would understand this. No—they were doing this quite deliberately and they are asking for it and they are going to get it. We have not used the power in this first four years as you know. We have never used it. We have not used the Bureau and we have not used the Justice Department but things are going to change now. And they are either going to do it right or go.

D—What an exciting prospect.

P—Thanks. It has to be done. We have been (adjective deleted) fools for us to come into this election campaign and not do anything with regard to the Democratic Senators who are running, et cetera. And who the hell are they after? They are after us. It is absolutely ridiculous. It is not going to be that way any more. . . .

John Dean: Blocking the Patman Committee Hearings

I would next like to turn to the White House efforts to block the Patman committee hearings. As early as mid-August 1972, the White House learned through the congressional relations staff that an investigation was being conducted by the staff of the House Banking and Currency Committee, under the direction of Chairman Patman, into may aspects of the Watergate incident. The focus of the investigation at the outset was the funding of the Watergate incident, and other possible illegal funding that may have involved banking violations. The White House concern was twofold: First, the hearings would have resulted in more adverse preelection publicity regarding the Watergate, and second, they just might stumble into something that would start unraveling the coverup.

The initial dealings with the Patman committee and the reelection committee were handled by Mr. Stans and Mr. Parkinson. However, as the Patman committee proceeded, Stans called for assistance from the White House. I was aware of the fact that the Patman investigators had had numerous conversations with Parkinson and the investigators themselves came to the Republican National Convention to interview Stans on August 25, 1972. Upon Mr. Stans' return from the Republican Convention he met with the investigative staff of the Patman committee, which I believe occurred on August 30. He was accompanied at both these interviews by Mr. Parkinson.

At some point in time during these investigations Mr. Parkinson was put in touch with Congressman Garry Brown, who was a member of the Banking and Currency Committee. To the best of my recollection, this may have resulted from discussions between members of the White House congressional relations staff with the Republican members of the Banking and Currency Committee to determine who would be most helpful on the committee, and Brown indicated his willingness to assist.

On September 8, Congressman Brown sent a letter to the Attorney General regarding the forthcoming appearance of Secretary Stans and others before the Patman committee. I have submitted to the committee a copy of this letter, which was, in fact, drafted by Mr. Parkinson for Congressman Brown.

It is my recollection that Secretary Stans was scheduled to appear before the Patman committee for formal testimony on September 14. Prior to Parkinson's drafting the letter for Congressman Brown, I had been asked to discuss the matter with Henry Petersen, which I did. I told Petersen of the problem and asked him for his feeling about Stans and others appearing before the Patman committee and what effect that might have on either the grand jury or the indicted individuals once the indictments were handed down. I recall that Petersen had very strong feelings that it could be very detrimental to the Government's ability to prosecute successfully the Watergate case, but he said he would have to give some thought to responding to Congressman Brown's letter. I had several additional discussions with Petersen and later with the Attorney General, when Petersen indicated he did not think he could respond before the scheduled appearance of Stans on September 14.

The Justice Department did not feel that it could write such a letter for one individual regarding the Patman hearings and was very reluctant to do so. I also had conversations with Mitchell about this and reported the matter to Haldeman and Ehrlichman. The Justice Department felt that for them to write such a letter would look like a direct effort to block the hearings and I frankly had to agree. Therefore, no response was sent prior to the scheduled September 14 appearance of Stans and Mr. Parkinson himself informed the committee that Stans would not appear because he felt it would be detrimental to the then pending civil and criminal investigations.

It was after my September 15 meeting with the President where this matter had been briefly and generally discussed and, as the subsequent activities on the Patman committee became more intense that the White House became more involved in dealing with the Patman committee. On September 25, Chairman Patman announced that he would hold a vote on October 3 regarding the issuing of subpenas to witnesses. With this announcement the White House congressional relations staff began talking with members of the committee as well as the Republican leadership of the House.

I recall several conversations with Mr. Timmons and Dick Cook regarding this matter as well as conversations with Haldeman. Timmons and Cook informed me that there was a daily change in the list of potential witnesses and the list was ever growing and beginning to reach into the White House itself. In discussing it with Haldeman I asked him how he thought the Patman hearings might be turned off. He suggested that I might talk with Secretary Connally about the matter because Connally would know Patman as well as anybody. I called Secretary Connally and told him the reason I was calling. He said that the only thing he could think of, the only soft spot that Patman might have, was that he had received large contributions from a Washington lobbyist and had heard rumors that some of these contributions may not have been reported.

I discussed this matter with Bill Timmons and we concluded that several Republicans would probably have a similar problem so the matter was dropped. At this time I cannot recall the name of the lobbyist whom Secretary Connally said had made the contributions to Mr. Patman. Timmons and I had also discussed that probably some of the members of the Banking and Currency Committee would have themselves potential campaign act violations and that it probably would be worthwhile to check out their reporting to the Clerk of the House. I told Timmons I would look into it. . . .

A number of people worked on getting the votes necessary to block the Patman committee hearings. Mr. Timmons discussed the matter with the House Republican leaders who agreed to be of assistance by making it a matter for the leadership consideration, which resulted in direction from the leadership to the members of the committee to vote against the hearings. I was informed that Congressman Brown had been working with several members on the Democratic side of the Patman committee to assist in voting against the hearings or as an alternative not to appear for the hearings. Timmons informed me that he was also in direct contact with one of the leaders of the southern delegation who was being quite helpful in persuading the southerners on the committee not to vote for the subpenas or in the alternative not to appear at the meeting on October 3. Also Mitchell reported to me that he had been working with some people in New York to get the New Yorkers on the committee to vote against the hearings. He told me, and I cannot recall now which members of the New York delegation he referred to, that he had assurances that they would either not show up or would vote against the hearings. I in turn passed this information on to Timmons, but I did not tell him the source of my information. On October 3, the vote was held and the subpenas were defeated by a vote of 20 to 15 and another sigh of relief was made at the White House that we had leaped one more hurdle in the continuing coverup.

John Dean Testimony, June 25, 1973, SSC, Book 3: 959–62.

V

The Conspiracy Unravels: Judge Sirica, the Ellsberg Case, the Senate, and the Special Prosecutor

Sirica and McCord

When he was arrested during the Watergate burglary, James McCord was the security director for the Committee to Re-elect the President. He was known to have had CIA ties in the past. In late December 1972, McCord wrote to John Caulfield, an investigator who worked directly for John Ehrlichman, warning if any blame attached to the CIA, he would reveal the Administration's involvement. On March 23, as he prepared to sentence the burglars, presiding Judge John Sirica read a letter from McCord in open court that directly implicated the Administration in the crime and subsequent cover-up. Sirica, the chief judge of the federal district court in Washington, was known as "Maximum John," a tough law-and-order man. Tentatively, he sentenced the burglars to lengthy jail sentences to pressure them to cooperate and name others involved.

McCord to Sirica,
United States v. Liddy et al,
Transcript of Proceedings, March 19, 1973.

Certain questions have been posed to me from your honor through the probation officer, dealing with details of the case, motivations, intent and mitigating circumstances. . . .

Several members of my family have expressed fear for my life if I disclose knowledge of the facts in this matter, either publicly or to any government representative. Whereas I do not share their concerns to the same degree, nevertheless, I do believe that retaliatory measures will be taken against me, my family, and my friends should I disclose such facts. Such retaliation could destroy careers, income, and reputations of persons who are innocent of any guilt whatever.

Be that as it may, in the interests of justice, and in the interests of restoring faith in the criminal justice system, which faith has been severely damaged in this case, I will state the following to you at this time which I hope may be of help to you in meting out justice in this case:

1. There was political pressure applied to the defendants to plead guilty and remain silent.

2. Perjury occurred during the trial in matters highly material to the very structure, orientation and impact of the government's case, and to the motivation and intent of the defendants.

3. Others involved in the Watergate operation were not identified during the trial, when they could have been by those testifying.

4. The Watergate operation was not a CIA operation. The Cubans may have been misled by others into believing that it was a CIA operation. I know for a fact that it was not.

5. Some statements were unfortunately made by a witness which left the Court with the impression that he was stating untruths, or withholding facts of his knowledge, when in fact only honest errors of memory were involved.

6. My motivations were different than those of the others invovled, but were not limited to, or simply those offered in my defense during the trial. This is no fault of my attorneys, but of the circumstances under which we had to prepare my defense.

Following sentence, I would appreciate the opportunity to talk with you privately in chambers. Since I cannot feel confident in talking with an FBI agent, in testifying before a Grand Jury whose U.S. Attorneys work for the Department of Justice, or in talking with other government representatives, such a discussion with you would be of assistance to me. . . .

James W. McCord, Jr.

The Sentencing,
United States v. Liddy et al,
Transcript of Proceedings, March 23, 1973.

THE COURT: All right, let the Defendants be seated.

Now with respect to the five Defendants who have entered guilty pleas, that is, Messrs. Hunt, Barker, Martinez, Sturgis, and Gonzalez, the Court finds that it requires more detailed information before it can make a final determination of the sentences to be imposed. . . .

First, each of you five Defendants now before me are provisionally committed for the maximum sentence of imprisonment prescribed by law for your offenses. . . .

Among other things, I have taken into consideration, and will keep in mind, the fact that each of you voluntarily entered pleas of guilty.

On the other side of the scale is the fact that none of you have been willing to give the Government or other appropriate authorities any substantial help in trying this case or in investigating the activities which were the subject of this case. . . .

Now I want to speak plainly about this matter. You will no doubt be given an opportunity to provide information to the Grand Jury which has been, and still is, investigating the Watergate affair and to the Senate Select Committee on Presidential Campaign Activities.

I sincerely hope that each of you will take full advantage of any such opportunity. . . .

Now I believe that the Watergate affair, gentlemen, the subject of this trial, should not be forgotten. Some good can and should come from a revelation of sinister conduct whenever and wherever such conduct exists. I am convinced that the greatest benefit that can come from this prosecution will be its impact as a spur to corrective action so that the type of activities revealed by the evidence at trial will not be repeated in our nation.

For these reasons I recommend your full cooperation with the Grand Jury and the Senate Select Committee. You must understand that I hold out no promises or hopes of any kind to you in this matter but I do say that should you decide to speak freely I would have to weigh that factor in appraising what sentence will be finally imposed in this case. Other factors will of course be considered but I mention this one because it is one over which you have control and I mean each one of the five of you.

Defections:
Dean and Magruder

Following McCord's letter and the sentencing of the Watergate defendants, involved White House aides hastily sought legal counsel and prepared to talk to the prosecutors. Two important people were John Dean, the President's Counsel, the ringmaster of the cover-up, and Jeb Magruder, ostensibly Mitchell's deputy at the campaign committee, but in reality Haldeman's eyes and ears in the reelection effort. In the first selection, Dean recounts his decision to speak to government prosecutors, and second, Magruder tells Haldeman of his decision to do likewise and his warning that others would follow. By this point—mid-April—the cover-up was fast unraveling, and prosecutors were coming closer to the President's inner circle of aides.

John Dean Testimony, June 25, 1973

I had been in continuous contact since March 25 with my attorney, Tom Hogan, regarding whom he felt was the best available man in the criminal law field that I might discuss this entire matter with. We had talked on several occasions about Charles Shaffer, whom I had met several years ago and regarded highly as a criminal lawyer.

On March 28 and 29, however, I made several other calls to friends to ask them for suggested names of knowledgeable criminal lawyers, but decided on March 30 that I would retain Mr. Shaffer if he were available. Mr. Hogan informed me that he was and we arranged to meet with him.

The President, along with Haldeman and Ehrlichman, were going to be in California for a week or more in connection with the President's meeting with President Thieu of South Vietnam and I felt that this would give me an opportunity to decide how best I could come forward and end this matter. I had decided that I was going to inform the prosecutors of what the case was all about but before I did so I felt that I should consult with counsel to determine the scope of my own problems.

On March 30, shortly after lunch, I met with Mr. Hogan and Mr. Shaffer. I spent 5 hours telling them everything that I could remember and telling them that I was unwilling to continue in the coverup. Mr. Shaffer advised me to avoid further conversations regarding this subject and said that he would like to talk with me again on Monday morning prior to his seeing the prosecutors.

Accordingly, we met again on Monday morning, April 2, and discussed the matter for several hours more. That afternoon, my attorneys went to the Government prosecutors and told them that I was willing to come forward with everything I knew about the case.

From the outset I was confronted with the problems of executive privilege, attorney-client privilege, and national security. Thus, it was agreed until these problems were resolved that I would exclude matters involving the President from these conversations. I was also uncertain of many of the dates and details of the facts that I had general knowledge of so I began reconstructing a chronology of events. As each session progressed, I was able to provide more information, more leads, and more explanations of the interrelationships within the White House and the relationships of persons who were involved.

During the period of April 2 until April 15, the meetings I had with the prosecutors were initially focusing on the activities which had led up to the June 17 break-in at the Democratic National Committee and all the knowledge I had regarding the events before June 17, but as our discussions evolved and I began telling them more and more of the coverup, their interest began to focus more and more in that area.

As I began explaining what I knew, it was evident that the prosecutors had no conception of how extensive the coverup was so I tried to provide them with all the details that I could remember. Also, as the conversations regarding the coverup began to get into more and more specifics, we moved into areas that came closer and closer to the President, but prior to April 15 I did not discuss any of the areas of Presidential involvement. . . .

SSC, Book 3: 1009.

Jeb Magruder Testimony, Transcript of April 14, 1973. Impeachment Inquiry

HALDEMAN: What do you mean said you had to go?

MAGRUDER: That I had to make full disclosure.

HALDEMAN: Oh I see.

MAGRUDER: Okay. You know, so I've said I will.

HALDEMAN: I see. Okay. Well, that, that, uh—

MAGRUDER: You know, I'm not, I'm, I mean there's no—you know, I'm just, you know, I'm going to plead guilty and go to jail, that's all. I mean, that's what it's going to be and I understand that, uh

HALDEMAN: Well,

MAGRUDER: —agreed to accept it.

HALDEMAN: that—You got to work out [coughs] work out with them. I don't know that—Well, I shouldn't get into that with you. Uh—

MAGRUDER: Well, it's, it's not a problem now. I don't think, they—they've talked to [U.S. Attorney Earl] Silbert, and, uh—

HALDEMAN: Oh they have?

MAGRUDER: Yeah. They've talked to Silbert, and, uh—

HALDEMAN: How does, how do they go about that—what happens?

MAGRUDER: Well, you see is that, uh I did not ask for immunity because I didn't think I deserved it. [Laughs] Uh, All I said is I would tell the story and they said—you know, I would tell them the truth. You know.

HALDEMAN: I see.

MAGRUDER: So then they decide how many charges they are going to charge me with, and, uh, it'll be better than the hundred and thirty-five years, I guess, that I should be getting normally.

HALDEMAN: What in the world is that for?

MAGRUDER: Oh, about eight counts of perjury,

HALDEMAN: Oh.

MAGRUDER: a couple counts of conspiracy and a

HALDEMAN: I see.

MAGRUDER: couple of counts of obstruction of justice. [Laughs]

HALDEMAN: What do you do then? Go into the grand jury or just into the attorney or what?

MAGRUDER: Yeah I'll go in—Yeah, well I'll see, uh—go through it with Silbert, uh, and then, uh, they'll decide what they will offer me, which will be something, you know. Uh, I mean, it'll be less than the f—, twelve or fourteen counts I'm facing now. . . .

HALDEMAN: Oh no you don't go to trial, uh, your example'd be to plead guilty to those counts.

MAGRUDER: I, I—See, I'm, I'm, I'm pleading guilty.

HALDEMAN: I see. . . .

MAGRUDER: I mean I've held long enough. Uh, I've, uh, you know, I am in a terrible position because I committed perjury, you know, so many times, at the trial, and at the grand jury. . . . I know what I know and, and, uh I did tell Larry as you know, Bob, it uh, puts Gordon in a spot, and, you know, that's—nothing I can do about that now. . . . I really think, Bob, you should realize that you know, the whole thing is going to go.

HALDEMAN: What do you mean?

MAGRUDER: Well, whatever it is, is going to go. I mean LaRue's going to go, uh—they're all going to go. I mean, there isn't anybody now that is going to hold. Except Mitchell, I think.

HALDEMAN: Okay. . . .

House Judiciary Committee,
Statement of Information, Book 4: 709.

The Ellsberg Case

The publication of the Pentagon Papers in 1971 had infuriated Richard Nixon. Few subjects angered him more than "leaks." Daniel Ellsberg, a former national security bureaucrat, had obtained the Pentagon Papers and, in turn, provided copies to *The*

New York Times and *The Washington Post*. To discredit Ellsberg, the "plumbers" burglarized the offices of Dr. Lewis Fielding, Ellsberg's former psychiatrist. The plumbers were led by Ehrlichman's protégé Egil Krogh and David Young, a former aide to Henry Kissinger. E. Howard Hunt, Gordon Liddy, and some of the Cuban Watergate burglars led the raid on Fielding's office. Ellsberg was on trial in the spring of 1973 for his role in illegally obtaining the Pentagon Papers. When John Dean on March 17, 1973 informed the President of the break-in at Fielding's offices, Nixon feigned surprise. Subsequently, when the Justice Department learned of the event, Nixon desperately tried to persuade Assistant Attorney General Henry Petersen not to investigate the matter, since it involved "national security." In fact, of course, the break-in was designed to obtain damaging information on Ellsberg. When Federal Judge Matthew Byrne, who was presiding at Ellsberg's trial, learned of the event, he dismissed the case on May 11, 1973. During Ellsberg's trial, Ehrlichman had tentatively offered Byrne the Directorship of the FBI. The episode revealed the nature and background of the Plumbers, parting the curtain on another "White House horror" and abuse of power.

The President and Dean,
March 17, 1973. (1:25–2:10 p.m.)

D— . . . The other potential problem is Ehrlichman's and this is—
P—In connection with Hunt?
D—In connection with Hunt and Liddy both.
P—They worked for him?
D—They—these fellows had to be some idiots as we've learned after the fact. They went out and went into Dr. Ellsburg's [sic] doctor's office and they had, they were geared up with all this CIA equipment—cameras and the like. Well they turned the stuff back into the CIA some point in time and left film in the camera. CIA has not put this together, and they don't know what it all means right now. But it wouldn't take a very sharp investigator very long because you've got pictures in the CIA files that they had to turn over to (unintelligible).
P—What in the world—what in the name of God was Ehrlichman having something (unintelligible) in the Ellsberg (unintelligible)?
D—They were trying to—this was a part of an operation that—in

connection with the Pentagon papers. They were—the whole thing—they wanted to get Ellsberg's psychiatric records for some reason. I don't know.

P—This is the first I ever heard of this. I, I (unintelligible) care about Ellsberg was not our problem.

D—That's right.

P—(Expletive deleted)

D—Well, anyway, (unintelligible) it was under an Ehrlichman structure, maybe John didn't ever know. I've never asked him if he knew. I didn't want to know.

P—I can't see that getting into, into this hearing.

D—Well, look. No. Here's the way it can come up.

P—Yeah.

D—In the CIA's files which they—which the Committee is asking for—the material they turned over to the Department of Justice.

P—Yeah.

D—There are all the materials relating to Hunt. In there are these pictures which the CIA developed and they've got Gordon Liddy standing proud as punch outside this doctor's office with his name on it. And (unintelligible) this material it's not going to take very long for an investigator to go back and say, well, why would this—somebody be at the doctor's office and they'd find out that there was a breakin at the doctor's office and then you'd find Liddy on the staff and then you'd start working it back. I don't think they'll ever reach that point. . . .

Testimony of Henry Petersen,
August 7, 1973

Mr. DASH: On April 16, did you receive a memorandum from Mr. Silbert concerning the Ellsberg psychiatrist's break-in?

Mr. PETERSEN: Yes, sir; I did.

Mr. DASH: Was that the first time that you learned of that break-in?

Mr. PETERSEN: To be precise I ought to correct that. The memorandum was dated April 16. I think I received it on the 17th, Mr. Dash.

Mr. DASH: Right. Was that the first time you learned of the break-in?

Mr. PETERSEN: I think Earl told me on the telephone—this is what told us—"I am sending you a memorandum."

Mr. DASH: And what did you do when you received that memorandum?

Mr. PETERSEN: I sent it to Deputy Assistant Attorney General Kevin Marony. I said "Kevin, check this out. Let me know what this is about." Mr. Marony came back with a note from him and a memorandum from one of his staff in which they said we have no such information, nor does the FBI. Then we asked him to check whether or not there was a psychiatrist involved, and what have you. They did and they turned up from the FBI records that an individual by the name of Fielding had been interviewed.

Well, that clicked. That led us to the photographs and then we made the connection. I advised the President of that and kind of in response to his, well, what's new, and I told him that we had received this information.

Mr. DASH: Did he indicate that he knew anything about that break-in when you told him about it?

Mr. PETERSEN: No; he did not, Mr. Dash. I have to be very careful there. I would like to rephrase the question for you, if I can. I suppose it—

Mr. DASH: Please do.

Mr. PETERSEN: The question probably would be did he indicate he knew anything about it rather than anything about the break-in. And the President said when I told him, "I know about that. That is a national security matter. You stay out of that. Your mandate is to investigate Watergate."

Now, he didn't say he knew about the burglary. He said he knew about it—about the report. I think that is a vital distinction to be recognized.

Mr. DASH: When were you reporting this to the President?

Mr. PETERSEN: It was on April 18, sir. And he said stay out of it and after I got off the telephone, why I called up Mr. Silbert and I called up Mr. Marony and said, "Mr. Silbert," I said, "The President said stay out of it, Earl, and that is it." I called up Mr. Marony and said, "Just forget it." . . .

Mr. Kleindienst had rescued himself of Watergate and finally on the 25th I went on up to Mr. Kleindienst's office and said, "Look, you are out of the Watergate but you are not out of Ellsberg. I need some help." And we spent most of the day talking about this and he solicited some independent opinions and concluded that I was right, that indeed it should be disclosed, and so I said, "Well, you know, the President has given me a"—

Mr. DASH: You communicated that to the President?

Mr. PETERSEN: I told Mr. Kleindienst that the President instructed me to forget about it but nonetheless I thought we ought to go to the President and if he was unhappy about it we would simply have to take the consequences and Mr. Kleindienst agreed with that. He went to the President. The President agreed. May I say, Mr. Dash, that I have been distressed by some of the criticism in the press, maybe even other places about the President on that score and I think it is wholly unwarranted. He made—he took a position with me and I think I can count myself as not the most senior but at least a senior official in the administration. We disgreed with it. We went back to him and he finally agreed with us and I think the ultimate thing is that he came out with the right answer. . . .

SSC, Book 9: 3630–31.

Judge Bryne Statement Declaring Mistrial, *U.S.* v. *Ellsberg* (1973)

Commencing on April 26, the Government has made an extraordinary series of disclosures regarding the conduct of several governmental agencies regarding the defendants in this case. It is my responsibility to assess the effect of this conduct upon the rights of the defendants. My responsibility relates solely and only to this case, to the rights of the defendants and their opportunities for a fair trial with due process of law. . . .

The disclosures made by the government demonstrate that governmental agencies have taken an unprecedented series of actions with respect to these defendants. After the original indictment, at a time when the government's rights to investigate the defendants are narrowly circumscribed, White House officials established a special unit to investigate one of the defendants in this case. The special unit apparently operated with the approval of the FBI, the agency officially charged with the investigation of this case.

We may have been given only a glimpse of what this special unit did regarding this case, but what we know is more than disquieting. The special unit came to Los Angeles and surveyed the vicinity of the offices of the psychiatrist of one of the defendants. After reporting to a White House assistant and apparently receiving specific authorization, the special unit then planned and executed the break-in of the pyschiatrist's office in search of the records of one of the defendants. . . .

The Central Intelligence Agency, presumably acting beyond its statutory authority, and at the request of the White House, had provided disguises, photographic equipment and other paraphernalia for covert operations.

The government's disclosure also revealed that the special unit requested and obtained from the CIA two psychological profiles of one of the defendants. . . .

Within the last forty-eight hours, after both sides had rested their case, the government revealed interception by electronic surveillance of one or more conversations of defendant Ellsberg. The government can only state and does only state that the interception or interceptions took place.

Indeed, the government frankly admits that it does not know how many such interceptions took place or when they took place or between whom they occurred or what was said. We only know that the conversation was overheard during a period of the conspiracy as charged in the indictment.

Of greatest significance is the fact that the government does not know what has happened to the authorizations for the surveillance, nor what has happened to the tapes nor to the logs nor any other records pertaining to the overheard conversations. . . . The FBI reports that, while the files did once exist regarding this surveillance, they now apparently have been removed from both the Justice Department and the FBI files. As I stated, it is reported by the FBI that the records have been missing since mid-1971.

There is no way the defendants or the Court or, indeed, the government itself can test what effect these interceptions may have had on the government's case here against either or both of the defendants. A continuation of the government's investigation is no solution with reference to this case. The delays already encountered threaten to compromise the defendants' rights, and it is the defendants' rights and the effect on this case that is paramount, and each passing day indicates that the investigation is further from completion as the jury waits.

Moreover, no investigation is likely to provide satisfactory answers where improper government conduct has been shielded so long from public view and where the government advises the Court that pertinent files and records are missing or destroyed. My duties and obligations relate to this case and what must be done to protect the right to a fair trial. . . . [T]he conduct of the government has placed the case in such a posture that it precludes the fair dispassionate resolution of these issues by a jury. . . .

Under all circumstances, I believe that the defendants should not have to run the risk, present under existing authorities, that they might be tried again before a different jury.

The totality of the circumstances of this case which I have only briefly sketched offend "a sense of justice." The bizarre events have incurably infected the prosecution of this case. . . .

I have decided to declare a mistrial and grant the motion to dismiss. I am of the opinion, in the present status of the case, that the only remedy available that would assure due process and the fair administration of justice is that this trial be terminated and the defendants' motion for dismissal be granted and the jury discharged.

Nixon Responds

In February 1973, the Senate voted unanimously to support the resolution of the North Carolina Democrat Senator Sam Ervin for a committee to investigate Watergate. Before the Senate hearings formally began, as investigators and others pressed more tightly on the White House itself, Nixon attempted to invoke executive privilege to prevent his closest aides from being forced to testify. But a month later, as the Senate Select Committee prepared for public hearings, Nixon relented. On April 17, 1973, he also revealed that he had learned more about the case and urged vigorous prosecution of those involved. That same day, Press Secretary Ronald Ziegler, with one unforgettable word, declared all his previous remarks on Watergate "inoperative."

Press Conference, March 15, 1973

QUESTION: Mr. President, do you plan to stick by your decision not to allow Mr. Dean to testify before the Congress, even if it means the defeat of Mr. Gray's nomination?

The PRESIDENT: . . . Mr. Dean is Counsel to the White House. He is also one who was counsel to a number of people on the White House staff. He has, in effect, what I would call a double privilege, the lawyer-client relationship, as well as the Presidential privilege.

And in terms of privilege, I think we could put it another way. I consider it my constitutional responsibility to defend the principle of separation of powers. I recognize that many Members of the Congress disagree with my interpretation of that responsibility.

But while we are talking on that subject—and I will go on at some length here because it may anticipate some of your other questions—I am very proud of the fact that in this Administration we have been more forthcoming in terms of the relationship between the Executive, the White House and the Congress, than any Administration in my memory. We have not drawn a curtain down and said that there could be no information furnished by members of the White House staff because of their special relationship to the President.

All we have said is that it must be under certain circumstances, certain guidelines, that do not infringe upon or impair the separation of powers that are so essential to the survival of our system. . . .

I have always insisted that we should cooperate with the Members of the Congress and with the committees of the Congress and that is why we have furnished information, but, however, I am not going to have the Counsel to the President of the United States testify in a formal session before the Congress. However, Mr. Dean will furnish information when any of it is requested, provided it is pertinent to the investigation.

QUESTION: Mr. President, would you then be willing to have Mr. Dean sit down informally and let some of the Senators question him, as they have with Dr. Kissinger?

The PRESIDENT: No, that is quite a different thing. In fact, Dr. Kissinger, Mr. Ehrlichman, as you know, not only informally meet with Members of

Congress on matters of substance, the same is true with members of the press, as you know, Dr. Kissinger meets with you ladies and gentlemen of the press and answers questions on matters of substance.

In this case, where we have the relationship that we have with Mr. Dean and the President of the United States, his Counsel, that would not be a proper way to handle it. He will, however, the important thing is, he will furnish all pertinent information. He will be completely forthcoming. Something that other Administrations have totally refused to do until we got here and I am very proud of the fact that we are forthcoming and I would respectfully suggest that Members of the Congress might look at that record as they decide to test it. . . .

QUESTION: Mr. President, does your offer to cooperate with the Ervin committee include the possibility that you would allow your aides to testify before his committee, and if it does not, would you be willing to comply with a court order, if Ervin went to court to get one, that required some testimony from White House aides?

The PRESIDENT: In answer to your first part of the question, the statement that we made yesterday answered that completely—not yesterday, the 12th I think it was, my statement on Executive Privilege. Members of the White House staff will not appear before a committee of Congress in any formal session. We will furnish information under the proper circumstances, we will consider each matter on a case-by-case basis.

With regard to the second point, that is not before us. Let me say, however, that if the Senate feels at this time that this matter of separation of powers, where as I said, this Administration has been more forthcoming than any Democratic Administration I know of, if the Senate feels that they want a court test, we would welcome it. Perhaps this is the time to have the highest court of this land make a definitive decision with regard to this matter.

I am not suggesting that we are asking for it. But I would suggest that if the Members of the Senate, in this wisdom, decide that they want to test this matter in the courts, we will, of course, present our side of the case, and we think that the Supreme Court will uphold, as it always usually has, the great constitutional principle of separation of powers rather than to uphold the Senate.

Public Papers of the Presidents, Richard Nixon, 1973, 202–13.

Press Conference, April 17, 1973

I have two announcements to make. Because of their technical nature, I shall read both of the announcements to the members of the press corps.

The first announcement relates to the appearance of White House people before the Senate Select Committee, better known as the Ervin Committee.

For several weeks, Senator Ervin and Senator Baker and their counsel have been in contact with White House representatives John Ehrlichman and Leonard Garment. They have been talking about ground rules which would preserve the separation of powers without suppressing the facts.

I believe now an agreement has been reached which is satisfactory to both sides. The committee ground rules as adopted, totally preserve the doctrine of separation of powers. They provide that the appearance by a witness may, in the first instance, be in excecutive session, if appropriate.

Second, executive privilege is expressly reserved and may be asserted during the course of the questioning as to any question.

Now, much has been made of the issue as to whether the proceedings could be televised. To me, this has never been a central issue, especially if the separation of powers problem is otherwise solved, as I now think it is.

All members of the White House Staff will appear voluntarily when requested by the committee. They will testify under oath, and they will answer fully all proper questions.

I should point out that this arrangement is one that covers this hearing only in which wrongdoing has been charged. This kind of arrangement, of course, would not apply to other hearings. Each of them will be considered on its merits.

My second announcement concerns the Watergate case directly:

On March 21, as a result of serious charges which came to my attention, some of which were publicly reported, I began intensive new inquiries into this whole matter.

Last Sunday afternoon, the Attorney General, Assistant Attorney General Peterson, and I met at length in the EOB to review the facts which had come to me in my investigation and also to review the progress of the Department of Justice investigation.

I can report today that there have been major developments in the case concerning which it would be improper to be more specific now, except to say that real progress has been made in finding the truth.

If any person in the executive branch or in the Government is indicted by the grand jury, my policy will be to immediately suspend him. If he is convicted, he will, of course, be automatically discharged.

I have expressed to the appropriate authorities my view that no individual holding, in the past or at present, a position of major importance in the Administration should be given immunity from prosecution.

The judicial process is moving ahead as it should, and I shall aid it in all appropriate ways and have so informed the appropriate authorities.

As I have said before and I have said throughout this entire matter, all Government employees and especially White House Staff employees are expected fully to cooperate in this matter. I condemn any attempts to cover up in this case, no matter who is involved.

Thank you.

Public Papers of the Presidents, Richard Nixon, 1973, 298–99.

The President
and His Men:
Taped Conversations,
February–April 1973

For Nixon, the devil was in the details of his taped conversations which eventually became public. From February through the end of April 1973, Nixon regularly met with his chief aides—especially Haldeman, Ehrlichman and Dean—and revealed himself to be as knowledgeable as they and as deeply involved in the cover-up of the Watergate affair. Some of these taped conversations, recounted below, left a lasting imprint when they became public.

The President and Dean, Oval Office, February 28, 1973. (9:12–10:23 a.m.)

At this point, as he and John Dean prepared for the Senate hearings, Nixon still insisted on maintaining distance from the case. Dean warned the President of his vulnerability with Herbert Kalmbach and the money trail.

D—Liddy and McCord, who sat through the trial, will both be on appeal and there is no telling how long that will last. It is one of these things we will just have to watch.

P—My view though is to say nothing about them on the ground that the matter is still in the courts and on appeal. Second my view is to say nothing about the hearings at this point, except that I trust they will be conducted the proper way and I will not comment on the hearings while they are in process. Of course if they break through—if they get muck-raking—It is best not to cultivate that thing here in the White House. If it is done at the White House again they are going to drop the (adjective deleted) thing. Now there, of course, you say but you leave it all to them. We'll see as time goes on. Maybe we will have to change our policy. But the President should not become involved in any part of this case. Do you agree with that?

D—I agree totally, sir. Absolutely. That doesn't mean that quietly we are not going to be working around the office. You can rest assured that we are not going to be sitting quietly.

P—I don't know what we can do. The people who are most disturbed about this (unintelligible) are the (adjective deleted) Republicans. A lot of these Congressmen, financial contributors, et cetera, are highly moral. The Democrats are just sort of saying, "(Expletive deleted) fun and games!" . . .

D—The one thing I think they are going to go after with a ven-geance—and I plan to spend a great deal of time with next week, as a matter of fact a couple of days getting this all in order—is Herb Kalmbach.

P—Yes.

D—Herb—they have subpoenaed his records, and he has records that run all over hell's acres on things. You know Herb has been a man who had been moving things around for Maury [Stans] and keeping things in tow and taking care of—

P—What is holding up his records?

D—They already have gotten to the banks that had them, and what I think we will do is that there will be a logical, natural explanation for every single transaction. It is just a lot of minutia we've got to go through but he is coming in next week and I told him we would sit down and he is preparing everything—all that is available, and we are going to sit down with Frank DeMarco and see if we can't get this whole thing—

P—They can't get his records with regard to his private transac-tions?

D—No, none of the private transactions. Absolutely, that is privi-leged material. Anything to do with San Clemente and the like—that is just so far out of bounds that—

P—Did they ask for them?

D—No. No indication.

P—Kalmbach is a decent fellow. He will make a good witness.

D—I think he will.

P—He is smart.

D—He has been tough thus far. He can take it. His skin is thick now.

Sure it bothered him when all this press was being played up. LA Times were running stories on him all the time and the like. Local stations have been making him more of a personality and his partners have been nipping at him, but Herb is tough now. He is ready and he is going to go through. He is hunkered down and he is ready to handle it, so I am not worried bout Herb at all.

P—Oh well, it will be hard for him. I suppose the big thing is the financing transaction that they will go after him for. How does the money get to the Bank of Mexico, etc.

D—Oh, well, all that can be explained.

P—It can?

D—Yes, indeed! Yes, sir! They are going to be disappointed with a lot of the answers they get. When they actually get the facts—because the Times and the Post had such innuendo—when they get the facts, they are going to be disappointed.

P—The one point that you ought to get to [Senator] Baker. I tried to get it through his thick skull. His skull is not thick but tell [Attorney General] Kleindienst in talking to Baker—and Herb should emphasize that the way to have a successful hearing and a fair one is to run it like a court: no hearsay, no innuendo! Now you know—

D—That's a hell of a good point.

P—(expletive deleted) well, they are not going to but tell them that is the way Nixon ran the Hiss Case. As a matter of fact some innuendo came out, but there was (adjective deleted) little hearsay. We really just got the facts, and tore them to pieces. Say "no hearsay" and "no innuendo." Ervin should sit like a court there: that is hearsay, and the counsel for our people should get up and say, "I object to that, Mr. Chairman," on the basis that it is hearsay.

D—That is a heck of an idea, Mr. President. Some of these early articles said—will Sam Ervin, Constitutional man, be a judge? Will he admit hearsay? We can try to get some think pieces out to try to get a little pressure on him to perform that way, to make it look like partisan when he doesn't. . . .

P—(expletive deleted) Of course, I am not dumb and I will never forget when I heard about this (adjective deleted) forced entry and bugging. I thought, what in the hell is this? What is the matter with these people? Are they crazy? I thought they were nuts! A prank! But it wasn't! It wasn't very funny. I think that our Democratic friends know that, too. They know what the hell it was. They don't think we'd be involved in such.

D—I think they do too.

P—Maybe they don't. They don't think I would be involved in such stuff. They think I have people capable of it. And they are correct, in that Colson would do anything. Well, OK.—Have a little fun. And now I will not talk to you again until you have something to report to me.

D—All right, sir.

P—But I think it is very important that you have these talks will our good friend Kleindienst.

D—That will be done.

P—Tell him we have to get these things worked out. We have to work together on this thing. I would build him up. He is the man who can make the difference. Also point out to him what we have. (expletive deleted) Colson's got (characterization deleted), but I really, really,—this stuff here—let's forget this. But let's remember this was not done by the White House. This was done by the Committee to Re-Elect, and Mitchell was the Chairman, correct?

D—That's correct!

P—And Kleindienst owes Mitchell everything. Mitchell wanted him for Attorney General. Wanted him for Deputy, and here he is. Now, (expletive deleted). Baker's got to realize this, and that if he allows this thing to get out of hand he is going to potentially ruin John Mitchell. He won't. Mitchell won't allow himself to be ruined. He will put on his big stone face. But I hope he does and he will. There is no question what they are after. What the Committee is after is somebody at the White House. They would like to get Haldeman or Colson, Ehrlichman.

D—Or possibly Dean.—You know, I am a small fish.

P—Anybody at the White House they would—but in your case I think they realize you are a lawyer and they know you didn't have a (adjective deleted) thing to do with the campaign.

D—That's right.

P—That's what I think. Well, we'll see you.

D—Alright, sir—Good-bye.

The President, Haldeman and Dean, Oval Office, March 13, 1973. (12:42–2:00 p.m.)

Clearly, the forthcoming Senate hearings preoccupied Nixon. At this point, Nixon was very much aware of significant details of the involvement of numerous aides. In the meantime, he tacitly supported the break-in, lamenting only that the operation had yielded so few fruits.

P—When will the Ervin thing be hitting the fan most any day, thinking from the standpoint of time?

D—Well, I would say the best indications we have now is that public hearings will probably start about the first of May. Now, there will probably be a big bang of interest, initially. We have no idea how they will proceed yet. We do have sources to find that out, other than Baker. Incidentally, Kleindienst had called Ervin again, returned the call. Ervin is going to see him this week with Baker.

P—Public hearings the first of May. Well it must be a big show.

Public hearings. I wouldn't think though, I know from experience, my guess is that I think they could get through about three weeks of those and then I think it would begin to peter out somewhat. Don't you agree? . . .

P—How much of a crisis? It will be—I am thinking in terms of—the point is, everything is a crisis. (expletive deleted) it is a terrible lousy thing—it will remain a crisis among the upper intellectual types, the soft heads, our own, too—Republicans—and the Democrats and the rest. Average people won't think it is much of a crisis unless it affects them. (unintelligible)

D—I think it will pass. I think after the Ervin hearings, they are going to find so much—there will be some new revelations. I don't think that the thing will get out of hand. I have no reason to believe it will.

P—Oh, yes—there would be new revelations.

D—They would be quick (inaudible) They would want to find out who knew—

P—Is there a higher up?

D—Is there a higher up?

P—Let's face it, I think they are really after Haldeman.

D—Haldeman and Mitchell.

P—Colson is not big enough name for them. He really isn't. He is, you know, he is on the government side, but Colson's name doesn't bother them so much. They are after Haldeman and after Mitchell. Don't you think so?

D—Sure. They are going to take a look and try to drag them, but they're going to be able to drag them into the election—

P—In any event, Haldeman's problem is Chapin isn't it?

D—Bob's problem is circumstantial.

P—Why is that? Let's look at the circumstantial. I don't know, Bob didn't know any of those people like the Hunts and all that bunch. Colson did, but Bob didn't. OK?

D—That's right.

P—Now where the hell, or how much [Dwight] Chapin knew I will be (expletive deleted) if I know.

D—Chapin didn't know anything about the Watergate.

P—Don't you think so?

D—Absolutely not.

P—Strachan?

D—Yes.

P—He knew?

D—Yes.

P—About the Watergate?

D—Yes.

P—Well, then, he probably told Bob. He may not have.

D—He was judicious in what he relayed, but Strachan is as tough as nails. He can go in and stonewall, and say, "I don't know anything about what you are talking about." He has already done it twice you know, in interviews.

P—I guess he should, shouldn't he? I suppose we can't call that justice, can we?

D—Well, it is a personal loyalty to him. He doesn't want it any other way. He didn't have to be told. He didn't have to be asked. It just is something that he found was the way he wanted to handle the situation.

P—But he knew? He knew about Watergate? Strachan did?

D—Yes.

P—I will be damned! Well that is the problem in Bob's case. Not Chapin then, but Strachan. Strachan worked for him, didn't he?

D—Yes. They would have one hell of a time proving that Strachan had knowledge of it, though.

P—Who knew better? Magruder?

D—Magruder and Liddy.

P—Oh, I see. The other weak link for Bob is Magruder. He hired him et cetera.

D—That applies to Mitchell, too.

P—Mitchell—Magruder. Where do you see Colson coming into it? Do you think he knew quite a bit and yet, he could know quite a great deal about a lot of other things and not know a lot about this. I don't know.

D—Well I have never—

P—He sure as hell knows Hunt. That we know. Was very close to him.

D—Chuck has told me that he had no knowledge, specific knowledge, of the Watergate before it occurred. There have been tidbits that I have raised with Chuck. I have not played any games with him. I said, "Chuck, I have indications—"

P—What indications? The lawyer has to know everything.

D—That's right. I said, "Chuck, people have said that you were involved in this, involved in that, involved in all of this. He said, "that is not true, etc." I think that Chuck had knowledge that something was going on over there, but he didn't have any knowledge of the details of the specifics of the whole thing.

P—There must have been an indication of the fact that we had poor pickings. Because naturally anybody, either Chuck or Bob, were always reporting to me about what was going on. If they ever got any information they would certainly have told me that we got some information, but they never had a thing to report. What was the matter? Did they never get anything out of the damn thing?

D—I don't think they ever got anything, sir.

P—A dry hole?

D—That's right.

P—(Expletive deleted). . . .

P—How the hell does Liddy stand up so well?

D—He's a strange man, Mr. President.

P—Strange or strong?

D—Strange and strong. His loyalty is—I think it is just beyond the pale. Nothing—

P—He hates the other side too, doesn't he?

D—Oh, absolutely! He is strong. He really is.

The President, Dean and Haldeman, Oval Office, March 21, 1973. (10:12–11:55 a.m.)

John Dean, realizing that Haldeman and Ehrlichman were angling to set him up, informed the President of the "cancer" close to the Oval Office. Nixon later claimed that he knew nothing about Watergate and a cover-up until this moment—conveniently ignoring his own lengthy involvement with Haldeman and his earlier September 15, 1972 conversation with Dean. Curiously, at this point, Dean himself still appeared anxious to distance the President from events.

D—The reason that I thought we ought to talk this morning is because in our conversations, I have the impression that you don't know everything I know and it makes it very difficult for you to make judgments that only you can make on some of these things and I thought that—

P—In other words, I have to know why you feel that we shouldn't unravel something?

D—Let me give you my overall first.

P—In other words, your judgment as to where it stands, and where we will go.

D—I think that there is no doubt about the seriousness of the problem we've got. We have a cancer within, close to the Presidency, that is growing. It is growing daily. It's compounded, growing geometrically now, because it compounds itself. That will be clear if I, you know, explain some of the details of why it is. Basically, it is because (1) we are being blackmailed; (2) People are going to start perjuring themselves very quickly that have not had to perjure themselves to protect other people in the line. And there is no assurance—

P—That that won't bust?

D—That that won't bust. So let me give you the sort of basic facts, talking first about the Watergate; and then about Segretti; and then about some of the peripheral items that have come up. First of all on the Watergate: how did it all start, where did it start? OK! It started with an instruction to me from Bob Haldeman to see if we couldn't set up a perfectly legitimate campaign intelligence operation over at the Re-Election Committee. Not being in this business, I turned to somebody who had been in the business, Jack Caulfield. I don't remember whether you remember Jack or not. He was your original bodyguard before they had the candidate protection, an old city policeman.

P—Yes, I know him.

D—Jack worked for John and then was transferred to my office. I said Jack come up with a plan that, you know—a normal infiltration, buying information from secretaries and all that sort of thing. He did, he put together a plan. It was kicked around. I went to Ehrlichman with it. I went to Mitchell with it, and the consensus was that Caulfield was not the man to do this. In retrospect, that might have been a bad call because he is an incredibly cautious person and wouldn't have put the situation where it is today. After rejecting that, they said we still need something so I was told to look around for someone who could go over to 1701 and do this. That is when I came up with Gordon Liddy. They needed a lawyer. Gordon had an intelligence background from his FBI service. I was aware of the fact that he had done some extremely sensitive things for the White House while he had been at the White House and he had apparently done them well. Going out into Ellsberg's doctor's office—

P—Oh, yeah.

D—And things like this. He worked with leaks. He tracked these things down. So the report that I got from Krogh was that he was a hell of a good man and not only that a good lawyer and could set up a proper operation. So we talked to Liddy. He was interested in doing it. I took Liddy over to meet Mitchell. Mitchell thought highly of him because Mitchell was partly involved in his coming to the White House to work for Krogh. Liddy had been at Treasury before that. Then Liddy was told to put together his plan, you know, how he would run an intelligence operation. This was after he was hired over there at the Committee. Magruder called me in January and said I would like to have you come over and see Liddy's plan.

P—January of '72?

D—January of '72?

D—"You come over to Mitchell's office and sit in a meeting where Liddy is going to lay his plan out." I said I don't really know if I am the man, but if you want me there I will be happy to. So I came over and Liddy laid out a million dollar plan that was the most incredible thing I have ever laid my eyes on: all in codes, and involved black bag operations, kidnapping, providing prostitutes to weaken the opposition, bugging, mugging teams. It was just an incredible thing.

P—Tell me this: Did Mitchell go along—?

D—No, no, not at all, Mitchell just sat there puffing and laughing. I could tell from—after Liddy left the office I said that is the most incredible thing I have ever seen. He said I agree. And so Liddy was told to go back to the drawingboard and come up with something realistic. So there was a second meeting. . . .

The President, Haldeman and Ehrlichman, EOB Office, April 14, 1973. (8:55–11:31 a.m.)

In a series of conversations, Nixon, Haldeman and Ehrlichman tried to project scenarios that would have Jeb Magruder and John Mitchell assume the blame for Watergate. At this point, the three men believed that if Mitchell were implicated, that would satisfy the investigators and the public, leaving them free from any blame. Mitchell subsequently refused to take the responsibility alone.

P—I would, also, though, I'd put a couple of things in and say, Jeb, let me just start here by telling you the President holds great affection for you and for your family. I was just thinking, I was thinking last night, this poor little kid.

H—Yeah, beautiful kids.

P—Lovely wife and all the rest, it just breaks your heart. And say this, this is a very painful message for me to bring—I've been asked to give you, but I must do it and it is that: Put it right out that way. Also, I would first put that in so that he knows I have personal affection. That's the way the so-called clemency's got to be handled. Do you see John?

E—I understand.

H—Do the same thing with Mitchell.

P—Oh, Mitchell? Well you could say to Mitchell, I think you've got to say that this is the toughest decision he's made and its tougher than Cambodia,—May 8 and December 18 put together. And that he just can't bring himself to talk to you about it. Just can't do it. And he directed that I talk to you. You see, what I am doing, John, is putting you in the same position as President Eisenhower put me in with Adams. But John Mitchell, let me say, will never go to prison. I agree with that assumption. I think what will happen is that he will put on the damnest defense that—the point you have, your suggestion is that he not put on a defense. You're suggesting he go in and say look I am responsible here? I had no knowledge but I am responsible? And nobody else had—that's it. Myself. That's it, and I want to. This thing has got to stop. Innocent people are being smeared in this thing. . . .

Appendix 15. Meeting: The President and Haldeman, Oval Office, April 14, 1973. (1:55–2:13 p.m.)

H—LaRue, everybody involved here is going to blow with the exception of John.

P—Mitchell?

H—Unfortunately, I had this conversation just as John Mitchell was driving up the driveway—I held Mitchell—had him go up to John Ehrlichman's office but then Ehrlichman heard all of this before he went into Mitchell. Jeb has not told Mitchell of his decision yet—he said, I want to make my decision and then my lawyers are working it out with Silbert this morning and then my next step is to tell John Mitchell which I want to do.

P—How the hell can John Mitchell deny it? He was right on the (unintelligible) spot.

H—Jeb says unfortunately I will to a degree implicate John Dean and to possibly to some degree Bart and I hate to do it, but he said where I am now there is nothing—I can't pull any punches. He said there is no way that anything I do will get to you.

P—John Dean will have to testify (unintelligible)

H—Well, John Dean—that doesn't trouble me—I don't think it troubles Dean—where he gets John Dean is on his attendance at those meetings.

P—That meeting Saturday night?

H—No—the problem there is that the discussion at those meetings clearly and specifically did involve bugging.

P—Oh, Dean never denied it as it has turned out. That's John Dean's stand—but what about the aftermath? Does the aftermath held on Dean?

H—I don't think Magruder knows about the aftermath.

P—Where does he get to Gordon Strachan?

H—He says he gets Gordon on—

P—Sending material to him—

H—He still implies at least that Gordon know about it before you know—he knew everything they did. Larry tells me he did not.

P—He will testify that he sent materials to the White House?

H—If he is asked, he will, yes.

P—He'll be asked—is that something he will say he sent to the White House. What would Strachan say?

H—Strachan has no problem with that. He will say that after the fact there are materials that I can now surmise were what he is referring to but they were not at the time identified in any way as being the result of wiretaps and I did not know they were. They were amongst tons of stuff. Jeb makes the point. He said, I am sure Gordon never sent them to Bob because they were all trash. There was nothing in them. He said the tragedy of this whole thing is that it produced nothing.

P—Who else did he send reports to—Mitchell?

H—I don't know. The thing I got before was that he sent them either to—that one went to him and one went to Strachan.

P—What our problem there is they claim that the reports came to the White House—basically to your office—what will you say then?

H—They can. This doesn't ever have to come out.

P—I know, but they will ask it in the Grand Jury.

H—If they do ask it in the Grand Jury—the Grand Jury is secret. The only way it will come out is if they decide to indict Strachan and put him up for trial. He, Jeb, is totally convinced that they have no interest in Strachan at all—and they have all this stuff. And I can see how they feel—Strachan is like a secretary—he is useful as a witness.

P—(Unintelligible)

H—Yeah, he implies—or has in earlier stuff—he doesn't now directly. He doesn't say anything now directly—but did in the earlier stuff that Strachan knew about it beforehand. That Strachan knew they were bugging the Watergate. Strachan says he didn't. Jeb has implied a lot of things that I know aren't true, but I know that a lot of things that other people are saying aren't true so I would have no idea whether he believes now that—one of the problems Jeb has is that he's not sure what is true at this point.

P—He tells you this?

H—He tells me that he is sorry about this because it will probably hurt Dean and it may hurt Bart. You see that is the kind of thing—you know—from his judgment—he is looking at things a little different now. . . .

The President, Haldeman and Ehrlichman, Oval Office, April 14, 1973. (2:24–3:55 p.m.)

E—Well, let me tell you what Mitchell said. It was another gigging of the White House. He said, "You know in Bob's office, Magruder said that Haldeman had cooked this whole thing up over here at the White House and—"

P—Had he said that?

E—Well that is what he said, and that he had been sort of—

P—Now wait a minute. Your conversation with Mitchell is the one where—

H—I've got my notes on it.

P—where Mitchell (unintelligible) is one where—Mitchell does—it's good you have the notes, too, but—

E—Mitchell's theory—

P—Whatever his theory is, let me say, one footnote—is that throwing off on the White House won't help him one damn bit.

E—Unless he can peddle the theory that Colson and others were effectively running the Committee through Magruder and freezing him out of the operation which is kind of the story line he was giving me.

H—Did he include me in the others?

E—Yep.

H—That I was freezing him out of the operation?

E—That you, in other words, he didn't say this baldly or flatly, but he accumulated a whole bunch of things: it's Colson, Dean and Bob working with Magruder, and that was sort of the way the line went.

P—No. The White House wasn't running the campaign committee.

H—He's got an impossible problem with that. The poor guy is pretty sad if he gets up there and says that. It is a problem for us, there is no question about it, but there is no way he can prove it. . . .

P—I guess we're not surprised at Mitchell, are we?

H—No. It's partly true.

P—Hmh.

H—What he's saying is partly true. I don't think he did put it together.

P—He shouldn't—he shouldn't throw the burden over here. Bob, on you. Now, frankly, Colson I understand. Colson certainly put the heat on over there. I don't think John seriously (unintelligible) unless you put them up to this thing.

H—(unintelligible) I didn't. He knows I didn't. No question of that.

P—I should think he knows it. (Unintelligible) himself. So his (unintelligible), huh?

H—That's what he says.

P—You know he'll never—he'll never (unintelligible). What do you think about that as a possible thing—does a trial of the former Attorney General of the United States bug him? This damn case!

H—I don't know whether he (unintelligible) or not.

P—He'll have to take the stand at some points. (Unintelligible) all this has happened now.

H—That's exactly the point. He's got no defense witness that can deny it.

P—You know in one sense, Bob, it's better to (unintelligible) a couple of these small things but it's much better to hand it to the Grand Jury. McCord may move on the theory that Mitchell will be sorry and the others too (unintelligible) the damn thing—and the Ervin Committee get credit in the Watergate thing?

H—Yeah.

P—I don't know. Am I seeing something (unintelligible) that really isn't (unintelligible) or am I?

H—No, no. That was the thing I was trying to get at this morning. That what that proves is the President's, in my view, the President's course was right. The President wasn't covering up. The President was cooperating with the proper place and the proper place had come to the proper result, which is to find out in an orderly manner without tarring innocent people, to find out what's going on.

The President and Dean, Oval Office, April 16, 1973. (10:00–10:40 a.m.)

The President and John Dean met for the last time. Dean bluntly told Nixon that Haldeman and Ehrlichman "are in on the obstruction" and needed counsel.

P—So that is their real culpability, both Ehrlichman and Haldeman are in on the obstruction, is that your point?

D—It would be a very good idea if they had counsel.

P—I told them last night they ought to get lawyers so I am one step ahead of you there. Is there anything else you think I should do? You don't think I should—I am not going to let the Justice Department break this case, John.

D—I understand. You've got to break it. You are breaking it. Well, (expletive omitted) that is what we have done.

D—That's right.

P—I could have told you to go to Camp David and concoct a story couldn't I? and you have never heard that said, have you?

D—No, Sir.

P—In fact, I think I covered a little of that (inaudible) But on the other hand, it was your job to tell me, wasn't it?

D—Uh, huh.

P—And you have. Basically what you have done—no, you told me the truth though. You've told me the truth. It was your job to work for the President, the White House staff and they were not involved in the pre-thing. But then you thought the post-thing. You thought about it and that is why you decided, as you said,

D—I thought we should cut the cancer right off because to keep this whole thing—

P—Look, one thing I want to be sure. When you testify, I don't want you to be in a position, and I don't want the President to be in a position, that his Counsel did not level with him. See my point?

D—There is no point that I have not leveled with you, as you should know.

P—Now when they say, "Now Mr. Dean, why didn't you tell the President—did you know about this? Why didn't you tell the President?"

D—That is a PR situation Mr. President. The U.S. Attorneys are not going to ask me questions asking what I said to the President and what I didn't.

P—Well, I frankly think—I would hope you can help on the PR there by saying—

D—I will be happy to help on it.

P—I would like for you to say—and you are free to talk. You are to say, "I told the President about this. I told the President first there was no involvement in the White House. Afterwards, I told the President that I—" And the President said, "Look, I want to get to the bottom of this thing, period." See what I am driving at—not just the White House. You continued your investigation, et cetera, and the President went out and investigated on his own. Which I have done, believe me. I put a little pressure on Magruder and a few of

D—Uh, huh.

P—And as a result of the President's actions this thing has been broken.

D—That's right.

P—Because also I put pressure on the Justice Department—I told Kleindienst—(expletive omitted)

D—No, I think you are in front right now and you can rest assured everything I do will keep you as far as—

P—No, I don't want, understand when I say don't lie. Don't lie about me either.

D—No, I won't sir—you—

P—I think I have done the right thing, but I want you to—if you feel I have done the right thing, the country is entitled to know it. Because we are talking about the Presidency here. . . .

The President, Haldeman and Ehrlichman, Oval Office, April 16, 1973. (10:50–11:04 a.m.)

Nixon met Haldeman and Ehrlichman right after Dean. The President remarked that Dean was "quite the operator." Ehrlichman described his possible course of action before a grand jury, noting he would claim "executive privilege." Nixon must have realized he was talking for posterity as he asked his aides why he had taken certain actions. The conversation ended with an incredible cover story devised by the three for the President.

P—Come in.

H—Do you want John [Ehrlichman] too?

P—Yes, John too.

H—The scenario worked out pretty well. Yeah—

P—Well, John, let me say this is quite the operator. We first talked about the work he did before this began. I said that I wanted him to know that it is national security work. He said I consider it so. I said, "Have you told anybody about it?" He said, "No. I don't intend to. I don't intend to say a thing more than I need to say in answering questions with regard to this matter, and I will not comment on anything else of course. I will not comment on any conversation I have had with the President." So far as he is concerned, that operation will not be discussed. Of course, the problem I suppose is as far as others are concerned or were involved. But if they do John, I would play it straight out. Damn it, of course we do this.

E—Well, I have been thinking about this a little bit. If I ever got a question like that at the Grand Jury I would have to step out and ask the U.S. Attorney to step out and tell him that its under Executive Privilege. Since it is a National Security matter, I can't answer; that I would be happy to refer it to the President for his decision as to whether I should answer that or not, but that I am in no position to respond. If he says, well then we will have to go talk to the Judge, I will say that is what I think we should do.

P—Fine. And then you get to the Judge and say this involved—

E—a highly sensitive national security—

P—national security investigations involving leaks. Would you say that?

E—No.

P—No? You would not tell them what area?

E—No. I am just not at liberty, and the procedure we have in government for a thing like that is for the witness who is put a question like that to refer it to the President for his personal review.

P—That's right.

E—And I would like an opportunity for that to be done.

P—I can see you being asked the question.

E—I kind of think that is right, but that is the process that I would have to follow.

P—I told him [Dean] I would like to have that letter and he said, "What about Haldeman and Ehrlichman?" I said they have already told me that they will resign in case—naturally nobody is going to resign around here until somebody—until I get better information, until I can satisfy myself with Petersen, etc. And he said, "Well, do you mind if I take the letters and I prepare them? I would like to prepare them so that in the event I have to go to trial they won't prejudice me in that." I said, "Fine, fine. Prepare me what you think your letter of resignation should be." So there it is. So he is thinking in both terms, apparently. I am just guessing and I think that it is altogether proper, because he should have a letter of that sort. But I told him, as I told Haldeman and Ehrlichman last night, there is no question about people resigning around here. I've got their letters of resignation in hand anytime I want them. Wasn't that the proper thing to say to him?

E—That's fine.

H—He doesn't give you any indication how he is going to plead?

P—No. He said my lawyers have to work that out. But he also hits this again, John: that his lawyers think that his possible criminal liability is limited. You know what I mean, damn hard to prove. . . .

P—How do I get credit for getting Magruder to the stand?

E—Well it is very simple. You took Dean off of the case right then.

H—Two weeks ago, the end of March.

P—That's right.

E—The end of March. Remember that letter you signed to me?

P—Uh, huh.

E—30th of March.

P—I signed it. Yes.

E—Yes sir, and it says Dean is off of it. I want you to get into it. Find out what the facts are. Be prepared to—

P—Why did I take Dean off? Because he was involved? I did it, really, because he was involved with [Acting FBI Director Pat] Gray.

E—Well there was a lot of stuff breaking in the papers, but at the same time—

H—The scenario is that he told you he couldn't write a report so obviously you had to take him off.

P—Right, right.

E—And so then we started digging into it and we went to San Clemente. While I was out there I talked to a lot of people on the telephone, talked to several witnesses in person, kept feeding information to you and as soon as you saw the dimensions in this thing from the reports you were getting from the staff—who were getting into it—Moore, me, Garment and others.

H—You brought Len Garment in.

E—You began to move.

P—I want the dates of all those—

E—I've got those.

P—Go ahead. And then—

E—And then it culminated last week.

P—Right

E—In your decision that Mitchell should be brought down here; Magruder should be brought in; Strachan should be brought in.

P—Shall I say that we brought them all in?

E—I don't think you can. I don't think you can.

H—I wouldn't name them by name. Just say I brought a group of people in.

E—Personally come to the White House.

P—I will not tell you who because I don't want to prejudice their rights before (unintelligible)

E—But you should say, "I heard enough that I was satisfied that it was time to precipitously move. I called the Attorney General over, in turn Petersen."

P—The Attorney General. Actually you made the call to him on Saturday.

E—Yes.

P—But this was after you heard about the Magruder strategy.

E—No, before.

P—Oh.

E—We didn't hear about that until about three o'clock that afternoon.

P—Why didn't you do it before? This is very good now, how does that happen?

E—Well—

P—Why wasn't he called in to tell him you had made a report, John?

H—That's right. John's report came out of the same place Magruder's report did—

P—No. My point is

E—I called him to tell him that I had this information.

P—Yeah but, why was that? That was because we had heard Magruder was going to talk?

E—No. Oh, I will have to check my notes again.

H—We didn't know whether Magruder was going to talk.

E—That's right.

H—Magruder was still agonizing on what he was going to do.

P—Dean—but you remember you came in and said you have to tell him about it politely. Well, anyway—

H—I will tell you the reason for the hurry up in the timing was that we learned that Hunt was going to testify on Monday afternoon.

E—The President is right. I didn't talk to Kleindienst. Remember, I couldn't get him.

P—Yeah.

E—I didn't talk to him until he got home from Burning Tree, which was the end of the day, and I had already talked to Magruder.

P—Right. But my point is when did we decide to talk to Kleindienst? Before Magruder?

E—Oh, yes. Remember, early in the morning I said I will see these two fellows but I've got to turn this over to the Attorney General. . . .

**The President, Haldeman and Ehrlichman,
EOB Office, April 17, 1973.
(5:20–7:14 p.m.)**

At this fateful meeting, the President, Haldeman, and Ehrlichman reluctantly concluded that the aides would have to leave the White House. Nixon assured them they would be provided with jobs at a future Nixon Foundation. Haldeman vowed to spend the rest of his life destroying people like Dean and Magruder for what they had "done to the President."

E—Well, as I said before. We beat the rap but we're damaged goods.

P—Right, you can't go back in the government, but I will tell you one thing, you are not damaged goods as far as I am concerned. It's one hell of a thing. The point is that let's wait and see what happens before we see where we are.

H—Sure.

P—We ought to expect the worst but I think that what I would like both of you to consider 50% of your time also for editing etc., and so on, with the Foundation. The Foundation is going to be a hell of a big thing, it's bound to be. These first four years are terribly important and so forth. I mean after all, you understand, that looking down the road, looking down the road, as far as—you say your Dad was good at looking down the road?

H—Yep.

P—If you are indicted and tried and found innocent, it washes away.

H—Well—

P—Agree? For government service, I mean.

E—Or for the practice of law.

P—I don't think so. Really?

E—Well, I think so. I think so. Jeanne [Ehrlichman's wife] is furious about it.

H—That's isn't true John.

E—It depends on the circumstances. There is nothing I can be discouraged about at this point. But I think we've just about had it. I think the odds are against it.

H—You can always handle traffic cases—

E—Well I am not too pleased with the traffic cases.

P—The hell with the traffic cases. Well, anyway—

H—Well there's all kinds of things we could do.

P—Well I have a Foundation. I just think it is fair, I don't know whether I can find anybody to do it. I don't know whether you would even do it. Incidentally, it is terribly important that poor Kalmbach get through this thing.

H—I think he is alright.

P—How could he learn? Did you talk to him there? Did Dean call him about the money?

H—Yes, sir.

P—Does he say what said?

E—Dean told me that he told him what it was for. I don't believe him. Herb said that he just followed instructions, that he just went ahead and did it and sent the money back and—

P—They said they need it for?

E—I don't even know if they told him what for. It was an emergency and they needed this money and I don't know whether he can get away with that or if it's more specific than that.

P—You can corroborate then Herb on that one.

E—I can if Dean is the accuser. I can.

P—If Dean is the accuser, you can say that he told you on such and such a date that he did not tell Herb Kalmbach what the money was for.

E—That he has told me—that he has told me—

P—That's right—that's right.

H—If we have to get out of here, I think the Foundation funding—is one thing—but there is a lot of intrigue too—I hope to get funding for the ability to clear my name and spend the rest of my life destroying what some people like Dean and Magruder have done to the President.

Haldeman and Ehrlichman Resign

The pressure on the President to clean house mounted throughout April, a course of action urged not only by critics but by numerous presidential advisers and friends. H. R. Haldeman and domestic policy adviser John Ehrlichman fought hard to retain their positions. Finally, at the end of the month, Nixon accepted the "resignations" of the two men—"two of the finest public servants it has been my privilege to know." He also dismissed Attorney General Richard Kleindienst and White House Counsel John Dean. Dean, as it turned out, was already talking to prosecutors. In an address to the nation, Nixon again tried to distance himself from Watergate, but without his two closest associates to shield him, he was more exposed than ever.

Address to the Nation, April 30, 1973

Last June 17 while I was in Florida trying to get a few days rest after my visit to Moscow, I first learned from news reports of the Watergate break-in. I was appalled at this senseless illegal action and I was shocked to learn that employees of the re-election committee were apparently among those guilty. I immediately ordered an investigation by appropriate government authorities.

On September 15, as you will recall, indictments were brought against seven defendants in this case. As the investigation went forward, I repeatedly asked those that conducted the investigation whether there was any reason to believe that members of my administration were in any way involved. I received repeated assurance there were not. Because of these continuing reassurances, because I believed the reports I was getting, because I had faith in the persons from whom I was getting them, I discounted the stories in the press that appeared to implicate members of my administration or other officials of the campaign committee. Until March of this year, I remained convinced that the denials were true and that the charges of involvement by members of the White House staff were false.

The comments I made during this period, the comments made by my press secretary in my behalf, were based on the information provided to us at the time we made those comments. However, new information then came to me, which persuaded me that there was a real possibility that some of these charges were true and suggesting further there had been an effort to conceal the facts, both from the public—from you—and from me. As a result, on March 21st, I personally assumed the responsibility for coordinating intensive new inquiries into the matter, and I personally ordered those conducting the investigations to get all the facts and to report them directly to me, right here in this office.

I again ordered that all persons in the government, or at the re-election committee, should cooperate fully with the FBI, the prosecutors and the grand jury.

I also ordered that any one who refused to cooperate in telling the truth would be asked to resign from government service. And with ground rules adopted that would preserve the basic Constitutional separation of powers between the Congress and the Presidency, I directed that members of the White House staff should appear and testify voluntarily under oath before the Senate committee which was investigating Watergate, I was determined we should get to the bottom of the matter, and that the truth should be fully brought out no matter who was involved. At the same time, I was determined not to take precipitate action and to avoid if at all possible, any action that would appear to reflect on innocent people. I wanted to be fair. But I knew that in the final analysis, the integrity of this office, public faith in the integrity of this office, would have to take priority over all personal considerations.

Today, in one of the most difficult decisions of my Presidency, I accepted the resignation of two of my closest associates in the White House—Bob Haldeman, John Ehrlichman—two of the finest public servants it has been my privilege to know. I want to stress that in accepting these resignations, I mean to leave no implication whatever of personal wrongdoing on their part. And I leave no implication tonight of implication on the part of others who have been charged in this matter. But in matters as sensitive as guarding the integrity of our democratic process, it is essential not only that rigorous legal and technical standards be observed, but also that the public—you—have total confidence that they are both being observed and enforced by those in authority, and particularly by the President of the United States.

They agreed with me that this move was necessary in order to restore that confidence, because Attorney General Kleindienst, though a distinguished public servant, my personal friend for 20 years, with no personal involvement whatever in this matter, has been a close personal and professional associate of some of those who are involved in this case, he and I both felt it was also necessary to name a new attorney general. The counsel to the President, John Dean, has also resigned. . . .

Who then is to blame for what happened in this case? For specific criminal actions by specific individuals, those who committed those actions must, of course, bear the liability and pay the penalty. For the fact that alleged improper actions took place in the White House or within my campaign organization, the easiest course would be for me to blame those to whom I delegated the responsibility to run the campaign.

But that would be a cowardly thing to do. I will not place the blame on subordinates, on people whose zeal exceed their judgement, and who may have done wrong in a cause they deeply believe in to be right. In any organization, the man at the top must bear the responsibility. That responsibility therefore belongs here, in this office. I accept it. And I pledge to you tonight from this office that I will do everything in my power to insure that the guilty are brought to justice, and that such abuses are purged from our political processes in the years to come, long after I have left this office. . . .

When I was inaugurated for a second term this past January 20, I gave each member of my senior White House staff a special four-year calendar, with each day marked to show the number of days remaining to the Administration.

In the inscription on each calendar, I wrote those words: "The Presidential term which begins today consists of 1,461 days—no more, no less. Each can be a day of strengthening and renewal for America; each can add depth and dimension to the American experience. If we strive together, if we make the most of the challenge and the opportunity that these days offer us, they can stand out as great days for America, and great moments in the history of the world."

I looked at my own calendar this morning up at Camp David as I was working on this speech. It showed exactly 1,361 days remaining in my term. I want these to be the best days in America. . . .

Public Papers of the Presidents, Richard Nixon, 1973, 328–33.

The Special Prosecutor

Richard Nixon appointed his Secretary of Defense, Elliot Richardson, to be Attorney General, succeeding the dismissed Richard Kleindienst. Although the President had resisted the idea of naming a Special Prosecutor and removing the case from Department of Justice jurisdiction, Richardson at the outset sided to appoint one. Fulfilling that promise proved difficult. More than a dozen prospective prosecutors indicated that they would not be interested. Finally, Richardson settled on Archibald Cox, a Harvard Professor and John F. Kennedy's Solicitor General. Richardson pledged to the Senate that Cox would have complete independence. The President regarded the new prosecutor as a "partisan viper." Nevertheless, Richardson during his confirmation hearing committed himself to Cox, and Cox expressed his satisfaction.

Nomination of Archibald Cox

Testimony of Elliot Richardson

Secretary RICHARDSON: . . . I am very pleased to have the privilege of presenting to the committee this morning the man whom you have confirmed to important office in the Department of Justice. [Archibald Cox] served, as you know, for 5 years by appointment of President Kennedy in 1961 as Solicitor General of the United States. I feel confident in saying that all those who are aware of his career as Solicitor General would say that he fulfilled the responsibilities of that office with great distinction, with sound legal scholarship and effectiveness and responsibility as an advocate in behalf of the United States.

He has served in other public responsibilities, starting as an attorney in the Department of Labor in the late 1940's. He later became Associate Solicitor of the Department of Labor.

He had been Selectman of his hometown of Wayland, Mass., a position which any New Englander will tell you demands great fairness and impartiality.

He has shown that quality also as chairman of the Wage Stablization Board by appointment of President Truman in 1952 and arbitrator in many types of labor disputes.

Recently, his sensitivity to human problems and these same qualities of fairness and impartiality have been called upon to deal with student disorders on the campuses of Columbia University and Harvard University.

These are qualities which I know can very effectively be brought to bear upon the grave, difficult, and delicate issues surrounding the Watergate case and related matters. I know that it will represent a very substantial sacrifice for Professor Cox to undertake these responsibilities and that it is only out of a strong sense of public duty that he has agreed, with the Senate's approval, to undertake this assignment.

He is aware, of course, that his experience as a lawyer does not embrace criminal prosecutions or very much trial experience, but he authorized me to say in announcing the appointment on Friday that he plans to name as his own principal deputy a man who has had wide litigation experience.

The CHAIRMAN: What you are saying is he is going to select his own staff.

Secretary RICHARDSON: He will select his own staff in its entirety, in any case, Mr. Chairman, but he did want it understood from the outset that he wished to supplement or complement his own background of experience by seeking an experienced trial attorney as his own principal deputy.

I am very pleased that he has agreed to undertake this assignment and, as you know, he would be doing so on a basis of full independence and with complete authority to carry out all aspects of the assignment, to pursue every lead wherever it may take him, to determine when and under what circumstances grand jury proceedings should be brought, what indictments should issue, and what other actions in aid of a full, fair, and impartial investigation of all these matters should be undertaken.

Duties and Responsibilities of the Special Prosecutor

The Special Prosecutor

There will be appointed by the Attorney General, within the Department of Justice, a Special Prosecutor to whom the Attorney General shall delegate the authorities and provide the staff and other resources described below.

The Special Prosecutor shall have full authority for investigating and prosecuting offenses against the United States arising out of the unauthorized entry into Democratic National Committee Headquarters at the Watergate, all offenses arising out of the 1972 Presidential Election for which the Special Prosecutor deems it necessary and appropriate to assume responsibility, allegations involving the President, members of the White House staff, or Presidential appointees, and any other matters *which he consents to have* assigned to him by the Attorney General.

In particular, the Special Prosecutor shall have full authority with respect to the above matters for:

> conducting proceedings before grand juries and any other investigations he deems necessary;
>
> reviewing all documentary evidence available from any source, as to which he shall have full access;
>
> determining whether or not to contest the assertion of "Executive Privilege" or any other testimonial privilege;
>
> determining whether or not application should be made to any Federal court for a grant of immunity to any witness, consistently with applicable statutory requirements, *or for warrants, subpoenas, or other court orders;*
>
> deciding whether or not to prosecute any individual, firm, corporation or group of individuals;
>
> initiating *and conducting* prosecutions, framing indictments, filing informations, and handling all aspects of any cases within his jurisdiction (whether initiated before or after his assumption of duties), including any appeals;
>
> coordinating and directing the activities of all Department of Justice personnel, including United States Attorneys;
>
> *dealing with and appearing before* Congressional committees having jurisdiction over any aspect of the above matters *and determining what documents, information, and assistance shall be provided to such committees.*

In exercising this authority, the Special Prosecutor will have the greatest degree of independence that is consistent with the Attorney General's statutory accountability for all matters falling within the jurisdiction of the Department of Justice. The Attorney General will not countermand or interfere with the Special Prosecutor's decisions or actions. *The Special Prosecutor will determine whether and to what extent he will inform or consult with the Attorney General about the conduct of his duties and responsibilities.* The Special Prosecutor will not be removed from his duties except for extraordinary improprieties on his part. . . .

The CHAIRMAN: Mr. Cox, stand up, please, sir.

Do you solemnly swear the testimony you are about to give is the truth, the whole truth, and nothing but the truth, so help you God?

Mr. COX: I do.

The CHAIRMAN: You have studied the guidelines?

Testimony of Archibald Cox

Mr. COX: Yes, I have, Mr. Chairman.

The CHAIRMAN: Are you satisfied with them?

Mr. COX: I am. I discussed them first with Secretary Richardson over the telephone and there were a number of points—I think we talked for almost 2 hours—that we worked out together. Then I saw them in the New York Times again and went over them, and of course, I have seen this last draft. I am satisfied that they give the special prosecutor all the formal power to be independent that anyone could possibly ask for, and I shall certainly intend to be independent and to take full responsibility to the best of my ability. . . .

Committee on the Judiciary, U.S. Senate, May 21, 1973, 143–46.

The Special Prosecutor: Nixon's Reaction

Publicly, Nixon welcomed the appointment of Cox and pledged his cooperation. In a statement to the press on May 22, 1973, he again summarized the Watergate case and his relationship—or lack of one—to it. But his version of events was at variance with what witnesses such as John Dean already were telling the prosecutors or Senate investigators.

Statement, May 22, 1973

. . . I wanted justice done with regard to Watergate; but in the scale of national priorities with which I had to deal—and not at that time having any idea of the extent of political abuse which Watergate reflected—I also had to be deeply concerned with ensuring that neither the covert operations of the CIA nor the operations of the Special Investigations Unit should be compromised. Therefore, I instructed Mr. Haldeman and Mr. Ehrlichman to ensure that the investigation of the break-in not expose either an unrelated covert operation of the CIA or the activities of the White House investigations unit—and to see that this was personally coordinated between General Walters, the Deputy

Director of the CIA, and Mr. Gray of the FBI. It was certainly not my intent, nor my wish, that the investigation of the Watergate break-in or of related acts be impeded in any way. . . .

It now seems that later, through whatever complex of individual motives and possible misunderstandings, there were apparently wide-ranging efforts to limit the investigation or to conceal the possible involvement of members of the administration and the campaign committee.

I was not aware of any such effort at the time. Neither, until after I began my own investigation, was I aware of any fund raising for defendants convicted of the break-in at Democratic headquarters, much less authorize any such fund raising. Nor did I authorize any offer of executive clemency for any of the defendants.

In the weeks and months that followed Watergate, I asked for, and received, repeated assurances that Mr. Dean's own investigation (which included reviewing files and sitting in on FBI interviews with White House personnel) had cleared everyone then employed by the White House of involvement.

(1) I had no prior knowledge of the Watergate bugging operation, or of any illegal surveillance activities for political purposes.

(2) Long prior to the 1972 campaign, I did set in motion certain internal security measures, including legal wiretaps, which I felt were necessary from a national security standpoint and, in the climate then prevailing, also necessary from a domestic security standpoint.

(3) People who had been involved in the national security operations later, without my knowledge or approval, undertook illegal activities in the political campaign of 1972.

(4) Elements of the early post-Watergate reports led me to suspect, incorrectly, that the CIA had been in some way involved. They also led me to surmise, correctly, that since persons originally recruited for covert national security activities had participated in Watergate, an unrestricted investigation of Watergate might lead to and expose those covert national security operations.

(5) I sought to prevent the exposure of these covert national security activities, while encouraging those conducting the investigation to pursue their inquiry into the Watergate itself. I so instructed my staff, the Attorney General and the acting director of the FBI.

(6) I also specifically instructed Mr. Haldeman and Mr. Ehrlichman to ensure that the FBI would not carry its investigation into areas that might compromise these covert national security activities, or those of the CIA.

(7) At no time did I authorize or know about any offer of executive clemency for the Watergate defendants. Neither did I know until the time of my own investigation, of any efforts to provide them with funds.

With hindsight it is apparent that I should have given more heed to the warning signals I received along the way about a Watergate cover-up and less to the reassurances.

With hindsight, several other things also become clear.

With respect to campaign practices, and also with respect to campaign finances, it should now be obvious that no campaign in history has ever been subjected to the kind of intensive and searching inquiry that has been focused on the campaign waged in my behalf in 1972.

It is clear that unethical, as well as illegal, activities took place in the course of that campaign.

None of these took place with my specific approval or knowledge. To the extent that I may in any way have contributed to the climate in which they took place, I did not intend to; to the extent that I failed to prevent them, I should have been more vigilant. . . .

It now appears that there were persons who may have gone beyond my directives, and sought to expand on my efforts to protect the national security operations in order to cover up any involvement they or certain others might have had in Watergate. The extent to which this is true, and who may have participated and to what degree, are questions that it would not be proper to address here. The proper forum for settling these matters is in the courts. . . .

The truth about Watergate should be brought out—in an orderly way, recognizing that the safeguards of judicial procedure are designed to find the truth, not to hide the truth.

With his selection of Archibald Cox—who served both President Kennedy and President Johnson as Solicitor General—as the special supervisory prosecutor for matters, related to the case, Attorney General designate Richardson has demonstrated his own determination to see the truth brought out. In this effort he has my full support. . . .

Public Papers of the Presidents, Richard Nixon, 1973, 547–55.

The Special Prosecutor Takes Over

Until May 1973, prosecution and primary investigation of the Watergate affair had been under control of the United States Attorney's office in the District of Columbia. Attorneys had secured convictions of the burglars, but publicly they were criticized for not pursuing the case more actively. In fact, the office operated vigorously, but its lack of concern for publicity cost the prosecutors dearly in media support. As they passed control of the case to Special Prosecutor Cox, Principal Assistant U.S.

Attorney Earl Silbert prepared for Cox an eighty-seven page summary of the case that indicated they had pursued the case diligently and as a result of interrogating Dean and Magruder already had substantial knowledge. In his summary, Silbert discussed with remarkable prescience twenty-seven principals and their standing in the affair. Silbert raised significant questions regarding President Nixon. In the margin of the report, Cox noted he was "incline[d] to lay off for now." Pursuing the President of the United States, after all, was no small matter.

Records of the Watergate Special Prosecution Force, Silbert to Cox, June 7, 1973

27. President Nixon: Were he not President, there is no question but that President Nixon would have to be questioned about a number of matters. One is the critical June 23rd meeting between Haldeman and Ehrlichman and Helms and Walters. Other post-Watergate conversations with Haldeman, Ehrlichman, and Dean could be vital in determining the truth. Still another would be his contact with John Wilson, the attorney for both Haldeman, and Ehrlichman. In this regard, his May 22nd statement, rather than answering all the questions, raises a host of others. This is obviously a matter of such extreme sensitivity, raising Constitutional questions, that whatever steps are taken can only be by you.

National Archives, Record Group 460.

Senate Select Committee: John Dean

The Senate's decision to hold public hearings fatefully brought the Watergate affair into the full glare of national attention. Senator Sam Ervin, a southern conservative on racial matters, nevertheless had a good record on a variety of civil liberties issues. He was highly respected and the Democratic majority gave him ample support for a large legal and investigative staff. Before the Senate vote, the Republicans unsuccessfully tried to have the committee investigate campaign practices in previous elections. The hearings began on May 17, 1973. Committee Chief Counsel Samuel Dash structured the first days around minor officials of the Committee to Re-elect the President. This seemed rather dull fare, particularly for the national television audience, but Dash shrewdly allowed these people to testify that the White House had controlled them and that White House officials had manipulated Committee funds for the break-in scheme. A month later, the Committee presented its star witness, former White House Counsel John W. Dean. Dean read for nearly seven hours from a prepared 245-page statement. His matter-of-fact presentation did not mask the seriousness of his charges of persistent White House attempts to pursue its enemies illegally and the President's awareness of a cover-up. Ranking Republican member Howard Baker (R-TN), who had been in regular contact with the White House, worked valiantly during his cross-examination to discredit Dean, focusing on the question, "what did the President know, and when did he know it," realizing that it was Dean's word against Nixon's.

John Dean Testimony,
June 27, 1973

Senator BAKER: I was about to say, Mr. Dean, that you have been a very patient witness, and very thorough. You presented us with a great mass of information, almost 250 pages in your written statement of voluminous testimony in response to the interrogation of members of this committee, and we are very grateful.

Some of the specific allegations that you make in your testimony are at least prima facie extraordinarily important. The net sum of your testimony is fairly mind-boggling. It is not my purpose in these questions that are about to follow to do what would ordinarily be the expected function of a committee member, to try to test your testimony. I think that you have been subjected to a rather rigid examination by my colleagues on the committee thus far and, of course, your testimony and its credibility, its importance and relevance, will fall into place not only in terms of its own significance but in terms of its relationship to the testimony of other witnesses. . . .

It occurs to me that at this point, the central question, and in no way in derrogation of the importance of the great volume of material and the implications that flow from it, but the central question at this point is simply put. What did the President know and when did he know it?

Mr. DEAN: Mr. Vice Chairman, I might say this, in preparing my testimony I made a very conscious effort to not write a brief against any man but merely to state facts sequentially as close as I could. By sequentially some things it was necessary to follow forward to explain a given sequence of events to bring the matter into a time sequence but I did not by design try to write a brief or a document that focused in on any individual or any set of circumstances surrounding any individual. Rather, laid them out in the totality of their context.

Senator BAKER: I understand that, Mr. Dean, and I really do hope you understand that what I am saying to you is not a criticism of you nor any implication of criticism. Rather instead you have presented us with a sequential presentation, and I am trying to convert it into an organized presentation, according to categories and to the quality and scope of the information that you possess. So please believe me, I am not trying to attack your testimony but rather to organize it for our own committee purpose.

Now, there is one other thing I would like to say and it may or may not be possible to do this, and again I am not being critical of you as a witness. As I said just a moment ago I think you have been a very remarkable witness. When I used to practice law, I used to call on the trial judge from time to time to instruct the witness to first answer the question and then to explain it. So I hope I can keep my questions brief and I hope you might preface your answers with a yes or no, if that is possible, and then whatever explanation you wish.

Mr. DEAN: Certainly.

Senator BAKER: It is not meant to be an entrapment, nor a "do you still beat your wife" question, answer yes or not. But it is meant to try to advance the cause of factfinding.

Under the heading of what did the President know and when did he know it falls into several subdivisions. The first one is the break-in at the Democratic National Committee headquarters of the Watergate complex on the morning of June 17, 1972.

Do you know what the President knew of that in advance?

Mr. DEAN: I do not.

Senator BAKER: Do you have any information that he did know of it?

Mr. DEAN: I only know that I learned upon my return to the office that events had occurred that indicated that calls had come from Key Biscayne to Washington to Mr. Strachan to destroy incriminating documents in the possession of Mr. Haldeman.

Senator BAKER: The question is, I hope, not impossibly narrow but your testimony touches many people. It touches Mr. Ehrlichman, Mr. Haldeman, Mr. Colson, Mr. Mitchell, Mr. Dean, and many others. But I am trying to focus on the President.

Mr. DEAN: I understand.

Senator BAKER: What did the President know and when did he know it?

Is it possible for you, based on direct knowledge or circumstantial information, and you have given us an indication of circumstances, or even hearsay, to tell us whether or not you can shed any further light on whether the President knew or, in the parlance of tort law, should have known of the break-in at the Watergate complex on June 17?

Mr. DEAN: You mean, could he have prior knowledge of it?

Senator BAKER: Yes.

Mr. DEAN: I cannot testify of any firsthand knowledge of that. I can only testify as to the fact that anything that came to Mr. Haldeman's attention of any importance was generally passed to the President by Mr. Haldeman, and if Mr. Haldeman had advance knowledge or had received advance indications it would be my assumption that that had been passed along but I do not know that for a fact.

Senator BAKER: So that would fall into category 2 of my organization.

Mr. DEAN: Yes, sir.

Senator BAKER: That is an inference that you do draw from the arrangements of the organization of the White House and your knowledge of the relationships, the relationship of Mr. Haldeman and the President.

Mr. DEAN: That is correct.

Senator BAKER: But it does not fall in category 1 or 3 which is to say direct knowledge or hearsay information from other parties.

Mr. DEAN: That is correct.

Senator BAKER: The coverup is the second heading and, of course, the coverup embraces and involves so many things and so many people over such a span of time that it is difficult really to place it in a single category but I would like to try.

What did the President know and when did he know it about the coverup . . . ?

Mr. DEAN: I would have to start back from personal knowledge and that would be when I had a meeting on Sepember 15 when we discussed what was very clear to me in terms of coverup. We discussed in terms of delaying lawsuits, compliments to me on my efforts to that point. Discussed timing and trials, because we didn't want them to occur before the election. That was direct conversation that I testified to.

Now, going back from September 15, back to the June 17 time, I believe that I have testified to countless occasions in which I have—I reported information to Mr. Haldeman and Mr. Ehrlichman, made recommendations to them regarding Mr. Magruder, I was aware of the fact that often Mr. Haldeman took notes, I know that Mr. Haldeman met daily with the President, I was quite aware of the fact that this was one of the most important and virtually the only issue that was really developing at all, and given the normal reporting channels I worked through it was my assumption, without questioning, that this was going in to the President.

Now, at what point in time this was that Mr. Haldeman discussed this with the President, I have no idea. . . .

Senator BAKER: I am going to try now to focus entirely on the meeting of September 15.

Mr. DEAN: Right.

Senator BAKER: And I have an ambition to focus sharply on it in order to disclose as much information as possible about the September 15 meeting. What I want to do is to test, once again, not the credibility of your testimony, but the quality of the evidence, that is, is it direct evidence? . . .

Mr. DEAN: During the morning of the 15th the indictments had been handed down. I think there was a general sigh of relief at the White House. I had no idea that I was going to be called to the President's office. Mr. Haldeman was quite aware of the fact that I had spent a great deal of time; he had spent a great deal of time, that Mr. Ehrlichman had spent a great deal of time, on this matter. In the late afternoon I received a call requesting I come to the President's office. . . .

As I tried to describe in my statement, the reception was very warm and very cordial. There was some preliminary pleasantries, and then the next thing that I recall the President very clearly saying to me is that he had been told by Mr. Haldeman that he had been kept posted or made aware of my handling of the various aspects of the Watergate case and the fact that the case, you know, the indictments had now been handed down, no one in the White House had been indicted, they had stopped at Liddy.

Senator BAKER: Stop, stop, stop just for one second. Let's examine those particular words just for a second.

That no one in the White House had been indicted. Is that as near to the exact language—I don't know so I am not laying a trap for you, I just want to know.

Mr. DEAN: Yes, there was a reference to the fact the indictments had been handed down and it was quite obvious that no one in the White House had been indicted on the indictments that had been handed down.

Senator BAKER: Did he say that, though?

Mr. DEAN: Did he say that no one in the White House had been handed down? I can't recall it. I can recall a reference to the fact that the indictments were now handed down and he was aware of that and the status of the indictments and expressed what to me was a pleasure to the fact that it had stopped at Mr. Liddy.

Senator BAKER: Tell me what he said.

Mr. DEAN: Well, as I say, he told me I had done a good job—. . . .

Yes, I can recall he told me that he appreciated how difficult a job it had been for me.

Senator BAKER: Is that close to the exact language?

Mr. DEAN: Yes, that is close to the exact language. That stuck very clearly in my mind because I recall my response to that was that I didn't feel that I could take credit. I thought that others had done much more difficult things and by that I was referring to the fact that Mr. Magruder had perjured himself. [Laughter.] There was not an extended discussion from there as to any more of my involvement. I had been complimented. I told him I couldn't take the credit, and then we moved into a discussion of the status of the case.

Senator BAKER: Stop, before you get to the status, and let's lay that aside just for a second because I do want to hear about that, too, but this really, and I don't mean to be melodramatic, but this is really a terribly important moment in history. As you know, this meeting was in the afternoon in the oval office in Washington on September 15, 1972, and you were there, the President was there, and Mr. Haldeman.

Mr. DEAN: Mr. Haldeman was there.

Senator BAKER: What was the President's demeanor, what was his attitude, what was the expression on his face, the quality of his voice?

Mr. DEAN: Well, as I said, when I walked in it was very warm, very cordial. They were smiling, they were happy, they were relaxed. The President, I think I said earlier this morning, was about to go somewhere and I think that actually was delaying his departure to have this conversation with me. The fact that I had not been in to see the President other than on a rather mechanical activity before the dealing with his testamentary papers, indicated so clearly that Haldeman had thought that the President should compliment me for my handling of this matter, and that that was one of the reasons I probably had been called over, and the President had done it at Mr. Haldeman's request. . . .

SSC, Book 4:1465–88.

Senate Select Committee: Ehrlichman and Haldeman

The appearances of Nixon's chief aides, John Ehrlichman and H. R. Haldeman, provided high moments during the hearings. Ehrlichman, combative and openly contemptuous of the Senators and the hearings, clashed repeatedly with his questioners. Haldeman was surprisingly docile, contrary to his reputation, and apparently cooperative. His testimony offered a variation of

Nixon's "everybody does it" defense, recounting alleged incidents of dirty tricks by the McGovern opposition. What he did not offer was any corroborating evidence. Both men, despite their dismissal by the President, said little to implicate Nixon in the cover-up. Committee Chair Sam Ervin, Herman Talmadge (D-GA), Lowell Weicker (R-CT), Committee Counsel Samuel Dash, and minority counsel, Fred Thompson, led the questioning.

John Ehrlichman Testimony, July 24, 1973

Mr. EHRLICHMAN: Mr. Chairman, and members of the committee, at the time of my resignation I assured the President that I intended to spend such time and personal resources as I had in the statement of the truth of these matters now before this committee. . . .

Because I sincerely do not believe I am guilty of any wrongdoing, I have not invokved the Fifth Amendment, nor have I attempted to negotiate "immunity" for myself from anyone. . . .

I am here to refute every charge of illegal conduct on my part which has been made during the course of these hearings, including material leaked to the news media. What I say here will not be new but it may be different from what you have been reading in the papers. . . .

It has been repeatedly said that this is not a trial; that the committee will recommend legislation, not assess guilt or innocence. At the same time, the soundness and integrity of the President, his staff and many close associates have been impugned and directly put in issue here. Many important questions about the White House, the Presidency, and its staff system have also been asked here, but not answered. I hope and believe I can contribute a few of those answers and also perhaps some measure of perspective.

Mr. Dean began his statement with a somewhat superficial but gallery-pleasing repetition of the old story about fear and paranoia in the Nixon White House. Why, Mr. Dean wondered, was there all that overplayed concern about hippies coming to Washington to march peacefully down Pennsylvania Avenue? Mr. Dean's explanation is simply that we were all suffering from some advanced forms of neurosis, and nothing else—some strange White House madness. He suggests he was the only sane one in the bunch. . . .

John Dean said one thing in his testimony false than all the other falsehoods there, when he said:

[The Watergate] "was probably the major thing that was occurring at this point in time," meaning, in the context of Senator Baker's question in the White House between June 17 and September 15, 1972.

As liaison to the domestic operating departments and agencies I frequently carried to them the President's expressions of criticism and suggestions for change. To the uninformed this undoubtedly would appear to create tensions between a Cabinet secretary and me. But, actually, I think I maintained a good and frequent contact and good relations with our domestic secretaries, including the several Attorneys General, over my three years in this position. I confess I did not always bring them good news, but then that was not my job. They and I shared a mutual objective, I think, and that was to do all we could to help the President accomplish his stated goals. . . .

From June to September, 1972, my staff and I put in long days, the [Republican] Convention Platform having imposed additional burdens on some of us. After the convention, the speeches, position papers and political statements and releases kept the pressure on us. It was a very busy time.

John Dean, on the other hand, never found things so quiet and he planned the most expensive honeymoon in the history of the White House staff right along this period.

The committee has had the log of how I spent my office time over the years. As it shows, the vast percentage of my time was devoted to domestic policy issues. . . .

The logs for these two offices, Mr. Haldeman and mine, demonstrate clearly the frequency of my meetings with Mr. Dean.

Remember: Dean testified that keeping Watergate covered up was a tremendous drain of my time and told of all the conferences and meetings I was having with him about it. Let's be clear: I did not cover up anything to do with Watergate. Nor were Mr. Dean and I keeping steady company during all these weeks. . . .

Mr. DASH: Who is Mr. Krogh?

Mr. EHRLICHMAN: Bud Krogh, Egil Krogh Jr., was a member of the Domestic Council staff, and he was asked by the President to form this special unit, I was designated as one to whom Mr. Krogh could come with problems in connection with it, and the President said also that he could come to him with problems.

Mr. DASH: Were you in at the beginning of the setting up of this plan?

Mr. EHRLICHMAN: Yes, I was.

Mr. DASH: And you knew what the unit was to do?

Mr. EHRLICHMAN: Yes.

Mr. DASH: What was the unit to do?

Mr. EHRLICHMAN: The unit as originally conceived was to stimulate the various departments and agencies to do a better job of controlling leaks and the theft or other exposure of national security secrets from within their departments. It was a group which was to bring to account, so to speak, the various security offices of the Departments of Defense and State and Justice and CIA, to get them to do a better job. . . .

Mr. DASH: Is this the special investigations unit that later became, began to be known popularly as the plumbers?

Mr. EHRLICHMAN: Yes.

Mr. DASH: . . . Now, you did become aware at some point in time—at this point, I don't want to go into this specifically—of the activities of staff members of the special investigation unit, Mr. Hunt and Mr. Liddy, with regard to the office of Mr. Ellsberg's psychiatrist?

Mr. EHRLICHMAN: Yes, I did.

Mr. DASH: And that took place when, the so-called break-in of Ellsberg psychiatrist's?

Mr. EHRLICHMAN: I have heard two dates, but it was around Labor Day of 1971. . . .

Mr. DASH: Are you telling the committee that additional information, that these former White House staffers working under your direction had broken into Mr. Ellsberg's psychiatrist's office, would not have created an even more serious embarrassing situation for the campaign?

Mr. EHRLICHMAN: I would not think so, Mr. Dash, for several reasons. No. 1, that episode was a part of a very intensive national security investigation which had been impressed with a very high security classification. The likelihood of that being disclosed was very slight.

No. 2, those people were operating, at least I believe they were operating, under express authorization—

Mr. DASH: Express authorization to break in?

Mr. EHRLICHMAN: Yes, sir. Under a national security situation, under a situation of considerable moment to the nation in the theft of top secret documents, and their apparent delivery to the Soviet Embassy. It never was my view that Hunt and Liddy, as individuals, had done something that was completely irrational in that break-in. In other words, they were operating in a national security setting and pursuant to either instructions or authorization and, that being the case, that had never been a subject which I considered to be seriously embarrassing.

Mr. DASH: . . . I am not trying to probe into any other secrets; but certainly at the time in June, 1972, right after the break-in you were aware of, and I take it, he [President Nixon] was aware of the break-in?

Mr. EHRLICHMAN: . . . I cannot speak for the President on that. I can only say that I was aware of it.

Mr. DASH: Did Mr. Young and Mr. Krogh call you while you were in Cape Cod after Mr. Hunt and Mr. Liddy came back, and tell you that they had established that it was feasible that they could get access and that you said, "Ok, go ahead and let them do it."

Do you recall that call that Mr. Krogh and Mr. Young made to you in Cape Cod?

Mr. EHRLICHMAN: No. . . .

Mr. DASH: Would you be surprised if I told you that Mr. Young would so testify?

Mr. EHRLICHMAN: Yes, I would. . . .

*   *   *

Senator ERVIN: . . . You said something about the burglarizing of the office of the psychiatrist of Ellsberg was justified by the President's inherent power under the Constitution, did you not?

Mr. EHRLICHMAN: Yes, sir.

Senator ERVIN: And you referred to a certain statute.

Mr. EHRLICHMAN: I referred to a statute in which the Congress in 1968 made a recognition of that inherent power.

Senator ERVIN: Is that 18 U.S. Code 2511?

Mr. EHRLICHMAN: Yes, sir.

Senator ERVIN: Will you please tell me—now, this statute has nothing to do with burglary . . . This has to do with the interception or disclosure of wire or oral communications prohibited.

Mr. EHRLICHMAN: No, sir, it also has to do with the Congress' recognition of what the Constitution provides with relation to the powers of the President.

Senator ERVIN: Is there a single thing in there that says that the President can authorize burglaries?

Mr. EHRLICHMAN: Well, let us read it, Mr. Chairman.

Senator ERVIN: . . . It says here that this statute, which makes it unlawful to intercept and disclose wire or other communications, says that this shall not interfere with the constitutional power of the President to—

Mr. EHRLICHMAN: To do anything.

Senator ERVIN: —to do anything necessary to protect the country against five things . . . The first says actual or potential attacks or other hostile acts of a foreign power. You do not claim that burglarizing Dr. Ellsberg's psychiatrist's office to get his opinion, his recorded opinion, of intellectual or psychological state of his patient is an attack by a foreign power, do you?

Mr. EHRLICHMAN: Well, we could have a lot of fun with all four of these until we get to the operative one, Mr. Chairman.

Senator ERVIN: Well, Mr. Ehrlichman, the Constitution specifies the President's powers to me in the Fourth Amendment. It says: "The right of the people to be secure in their persons, houses, papers, and effects, against unreasonable searches and seizures, shall not be violated, and no warrant shall issue, but upon probable cause, supported by oath or affirmation, and particularly describing the place to be searched, and the person or things to be seized."

Nowhere in this does it say the President has the right to suspend the Fourth Amendment.

Mr. EHRLICHMAN: No, I think the Supreme Court has said the search or seizure or whatever it is has to be reasonable and they have said that a national security undertaking can be reasonable and can very nicely comply with the Fourth Amendment.

But, Mr. Chairman, the Congress in 1968 has said this: "Nothing contained in this Chapter or in Section 605 of the Communications Act," and so forth, "shall limit the constitutional power of the President to take such measures as he deems necessary to protect the nation against", and then it goes on, "to protect national security information against foreign intelligence activities."

Now, that is precisely what the President was undertaking. He was not undertaking it under this statute. He was undertaking it under that constitutional power which you gentlemen and other members of the Congress recognized in this section.

Senator ERVIN: Yes, I have studied that statute . . . And there is not a syllable in there that says the President can suspend the Fourth Amendment or authorize burglary. It has no reference to burglary. It has reference only for interception and disclosure of—interception of wire or oral communications. . . .

*   *   *

Senator TALMADGE: You are a lawyer, and I understand you are a good one.

Mr. EHRLICHMAN: Well, I am certainly not a constitutional lawyer, Senator. Far from it.

Senator TALMADGE: Do you remember when we were in law school, we studied a famous principle of law that came from England and also is well known in this country, that no matter how humble a man's cottage is, that even the King of England cannot enter without his consent.

Mr. EHRLICHMAN: I am afraid that has been considerably eroded over the years, has it not?

Senator TALMADGE: Down in my country we still think it is a pretty legitimate principle of law. [Applause.]

Now, you authorized this in the name of national security, I believe.

Mr. EHRLICHMAN: We believe that we had a serious national security problem at that time; yes, sir.

Senator TALMADGE: What relationship did Dr. Fielding have with national security?

Mr. EHRLICHMAN: Well, the CIA has perfected a technique, as I understand it, and again I am not your best witness on this, in which they can find out a lot about a foreign agent, a foreign official, someone who is the object of their investigation through the device of what they call a psychiatric profile. Two people in this special unit, Mr. Young and Mr. Hunt, had both had experience with the use of these profiles in the past, and they felt strongly that in this case, where there were so many unknowns, we did not know whether we were dealing here with a spy ring or just an individual kook, or whether we were dealing with a serious penetration of the Nation's military and other secrets, in such an uncertain situation that a profile of this kind might, certainly, not positively, but might, add some important additional ingredient which would help to understand the dimensions of the problem.

Senator TALMADGE: You do not think—

Mr. EHRLICHMAN: Sir, I cannot vouch for this. I have a kind of inherent personal doubt about the psychiatry in general, but I cannot second-guess, I cannot second-guess the investigation experts who have used this technique; and, as I say, the CIA maintains a staff, and they do this thing on a regular basis, and it is used in our Government.

Now, I understand from testimony before the McClellan committee that the CIA's position is that they have not ever used it before in a case of espionage involving a U.S. citizen. I do not know whether that is so or not. But in any event, the people involved here were very concerned about what they were dealing with, and they felt that this would be a helpful technique.

Senator TALMADGE: You did not think that Dr. Fielding was a security risk to the country, did you?

Mr. EHRLICHMAN: Of course not, no.

SSC, Book 6: 2509, 2522–53, 2601.

H. R. Haldeman Testimony, July 31, 1973

Mr. THOMPSON: Mr. Haldeman, let me ask you one more line of questions. You have in your statement on page 28 the following paragraph where you make some allegations yourself. You say—

Moreover, the pranksterism that was envisioned would have specifically excluded such actions as the following: violent demonstrations and disruptions, heckling or shouting down of speakers, burning or bombing campaign headquarters, physical damage or trashing of headquarters and other buildings, harassment of candidates' wives and families by obscenities, disruption of the national convention by splattering dinner guests with eggs and tomatoes, indecent exposure, rock throwing, assaults on delegates, slashing bus tires, smashing windows, setting trash fires under the gas tank of a bus, knocking policemen from their motorcycles.

Do you have any basis for these allegations?

Mr. HALDEMAN: These have all, as I understand it, been documented as specific events and this is not an attempt to make a complete list. It says "such as," and there were a number of others—

Mr. THOMPSON: Did you personally—

Mr. HALDEMAN: Including one I would have loved to put in here but my lawyers made me take it out for the tender mercies of the television audience, but all of these I have been told are documented incidents that took place. Some of them are incidents which I personally observed so—

Mr. THOMPSON: Go down the list, if you will and tell us about the ones of which you have personal knowledge.

Mr. HALDEMAN: Well, the violent demonstrations and disruption I have substantial knowledge of because there was a fairly extensive program of violent demonstration and disruption during President Nixon's campaign at a number of campaign stops. That one of the more notable examples was in San Francisco at a luncheon appearance at the Palace Hotel, I believe it was, where the violence and activity was such that the entire block in which the Palace Hotel is situated had had to be cordoned off by police and with mounted police. It was in a state of complete siege with men with guns and I believe bayonets, and mounted policemen wearing gas masks. It was quite a scene. I had been widely reported as a movie fan and I took some movies of that because it was sort of a remarkable situation. . . .

There was almost invariably heckling or shouting down of speakers and specifically the President of the United States, at virtually every public campaign rally during the campaign. There was also an organized group of demonstrators with very unpleasant signs and very vocal lungs that would try to shout down the President as he spoke. . . .

The harassment of candidates' wives and families by obscenities. Mrs. Nixon and Tricia and Julia were subjected to such harassment in very crude form in a number of their public appearances. As you know, they traveled on independent schedules, campaigning on behalf of the President's reelection, and all of these incidents have been, I understand, put together in a document form and this question—I referred to some of these things at the time I met with the committee staff the first time and I was asked at that time, by the staff, to provide more information than the general comments that I had to make, and I indicated that I would do so. I requested that this be done and I assume that it has and that the committee—I trust that the staff has received some documentation.

Mr. THOMPSON: Mr. Haldeman, I think we have what we need available. I wanted to know what you knew from personal knowledge and recollection and you are one witness who can address this subject matter. Obviously it is relevant.

Mr. HALDEMAN: I didn't cover the national convention things but I can testify to that, too, as can any of the people who were at the Republican Convention and remember the problems that delegates had in getting to the convention hall because of the slashing of bus tires, threats of violence to delegates, the trash fires under—these were mostly covered, most of them covered on television, so I don't think they are events that are unfamiliar with the American people.

Mr. THOMPSON: You make the statement on page 29. "So far there has been no investigation of these activities and very little publicizing of them." You are in error on the first part. They are being investigated.

Mr. HALDEMAN: I am happy to hear that I am in error and welcome being corrected.

Mr. THOMPSON: You say some of these instances took place with the clear knowledge and consent of the opposing candidates in the last election. Do you have any basis for that statement?

Mr. HALDEMAN: I understand that there is some in the documentation. The one specific that comes immediately to mind on that is the occasion of a trip to Los Angeles to the Century Plaza Hotel at which there was a very large demonstration staged out in front. The handbills to notify people of this demonstration, of this planned demonstration, where to be, at what time, and that sort of thing, were handed out by the McGovern headquarters and I understand there was a phone call program set up in the McGovern headquarters there for calling people to urge them to come and attend this demonstration.

Mr. THOMPSON: Mr. Haldeman, thank you.

Mr. Chairman, I will reserve any further questions I have until after the members of the committee have questioned the witness. Thank you.

Senator ERVIN: Ervin. Were you at the McGovern headquarters?

Mr. HALDEMAN: Pardon me, sir?

Senator ERVIN: Were you at the McGovern headquarters at that time?

Mr. HALDEMAN: No, I was not. This was reported in the newspapers and the manager or one of the officials of the McGovern headquarters issued an apology, an acknowledgment and an apology for that having been done.

Senator ERVIN: Did he acknowledge that he had instigated it?

Mr. HALDEMAN: The manager had?

Senator ERVIN: Yes.

Mr. HALDEMAN: I don't know that he had. . . .

SSC, Book 8: 3079–81.

Senate Select Committee: Revelation of the Tapes

Few congressional investigations have matched the high drama of Alexander Butterfield's testimony on July 16, 1973, revealing the existence of the White House taping system. That Nixon had taped conversations finally offered a conclusive answer to Senator Baker's question, "what did the President know, and when did he know it?" Now, tapes of his conversations perhaps made it possible to know for sure; the only question was whether the Committee and the nation could secure access to the tapes. After July, the major questions of Watergate all swirled around this matter of access.

Alexander Butterfield Testimony, July 16, 1973

Mr. THOMPSON: And what were your duties at the White House?

Mr. BUTTERFIELD: My duties were many and varied, as a matter of fact, Mr. Thompson. I will try to state them briefly.

I was in charge of administration—that is to say that the staff secretary, who is the day-to-day administrator at the White House, reported directly to me. And, of course, I reported to Mr. Haldeman, as did everyone.

In addition to administration, I was responsible for the management and ultimate supervision of the Office of the Presidential Papers and the Office of Special Files. Both of those offices pertained to the collection of documents which will eventually go to the Nixon library.

Third, I was in charge of security at the White House insofar as liaison with the Secret Service and the Executive Protective Service is concerned and insofar as FBI background investigations for prospective Presidential appointees is concerned.

A fourth duty was that I was the secretary to the Cabinet and had that duty not from January 21, 1969, but from November, I believe November 4, 1969, through until the day I departed, March 14 of this year.

I was additionally the liaison between the President and the Office of the President and all of the various support units. By that I mean the Office of the Military Assistant to the President and the Office of White House Visitors, again the Secret Service, the Executive Protective Service, the residence staff, Mrs. Nixon's staff—I served as sort of a conduit between all those elements and the Office of the President.

Finally, I was in charge of the smooth running of the President's official day, both in Washington, D.C., and the western White House in San Clemente. I had nothing to do with the smooth running of his day in Florida or in Camp David, but I was responsible for the smooth implementation of the official events on his calendar in Washington and the western White House.

That pretty well sums it up, sir.

Mr. THOMPSON: You were employed on January 29, 1969, and continued to be employed until March 14 of this year, is that correct?

Mr. BUTTERFIELD: That is correct.

Mr. THOMPSON: Mr. Butterfield, are you aware of the installation of any listening devices in the Oval Office of the President?

Mr. BUTTERFIELD: I was aware of listening devices; yes, sir.

Mr. THOMPSON: When were those devices placed in the Oval Office?

Mr. BUTTERFIELD: Approximately the summer of 1970. I cannot begin to recall the precise date. My guess, Mr. Thompson, is that the installation was made between—and this is a very rough guess—April or May of 1970 and perhaps the end of the summer or early fall 1970. . . .

Mr. THOMPSON: So far as the Oval Office and the EOB office are concerned, would it be your testimony that the device would pick up any and all conversations no matter where the conversations took place in the room and no matter how soft the conversations might have been?

Mr. BUTTERFIELD: With regard to the Oval and EOB offices?

Mr. THOMPSON: Yes, sir.

Mr. BUTTERFIELD: Yes, sir, it is my—

Mr. THOMPSON: Was it a little more difficult to pick up in the Cabinet room?

Mr. BUTTERFIELD: Yes, sir, it was a great deal more difficult to pick up in the Cabinet room.

Mr. THOMPSON: All right. We have talked about the rooms, now if we could move on to telephones; are you aware of the installation of any devices on any of the telephones, first of all, the Oval Office?

Mr. BUTTERFIELD: Yes, sir. . . .

Mr. THOMPSON: All right. You alluded to a reason for the installation of these devices. Would you state why, as far as your understanding is concerned, these devices were installed in these rooms?

Mr. BUTTERFIELD: There was no doubt in my mind they were installed to record things for posterity, for the Nixon library. The President was very conscious of that kind of thing. We had quite an elaborate setup at the White House for the collection and preservation of documents, and of things which transpired in the way of business of state.

Mr. THOMPSON: On whose authority were they installed, Mr. Butterfield?

Mr. BUTTERFIELD: On the President's authority by way of Mr. Haldeman and Mr. Higby.

Mr. THOMPSON: Did the President instruct Mr. Haldeman and Mr. Haldeman instruct Mr. Higby who, in turn, instructed you?

Mr. BUTTERFIELD: Mr. Haldeman instructed Mr. Higby to tell me and as I said earlier, I was the liaison with the Secret Service and it would be proper for me to give the instruction to the Secret Service.

Mr. THOMPSON: During your tenure at the White House as far as your own knowledge is concerned, who else knew about the presence of these recording devices?

Mr. BUTTERFIELD: The President, Mr. Haldeman, Mr. Higby, and I, plus the Secret Service people who I would prefer not to name in this public hearing in that this kind of thing is a part of their profession, and I am not sure of the correctness of that statement and the propriety of refusing. . . .

SSC, Book 5:2073–81.

VI

The Tapes and the Saturday Night Massacre

The Battle
for the Tapes

The tapes dramatically altered the struggle over Watergate and the President's place in it. Immediately following Butterfield's revelations, both Special Prosecutor Cox and Senator Ervin requested access. In his replies to both men, Nixon invoked "executive privilege" and the need to maintain confidentiality. Cox and Ervin secured subpoenas on July 23, requiring Nixon to produce tape recordings and other documents. Cox's action proved the more significant. The controversy over Nixon's refusal to surrender the tapes heightened the political fury. In July, Nixon went to Bethesda Naval Hospital with a severe case of viral pneumonia. Addressing the White House staff upon his return, he laughed off reports that he would resign because of ill health or the burdens of office. Such an idea, he asserted, "is just plain poppycock." Referring to the whole affair, he said: "Let others wallow in Watergate; we are going to do our job."

Charles Alan Wright, the President's lawyer, told Judge Sirica in August that one of the subpoenaed tapes had national security material "so highly sensitive" that the President would not even hint at its contents to Wright. Wright also argued that impeachment was the only remedy for checking and balancing the President in such cases. But Sirica rejected the President's argument and ordered that the tapes be produced for his examination *in camera*. He held that there could be "no exception whatever" to the compulsory process of the courts. Rather than defy Sirica, Nixon resorted to traditional court appellate procedures.

Statement of Information

J. Fred Buzhardt, Esquire
Counsel to the President
The White House
Washington, D.C.

Dear Mr. Buzhardt:

I am writing to request access to the recordings of certain conversations between the President and various members of the White House staff and others whose conduct is under investigation in connection with the alleged cover-up of the break-in at the Democratic National Committee offices. The conversations are listed below.

May I emphasize three essential aspects of this request:

First, the request is part of an investigation into serious criminal misconduct—the obstruction of justice. The tapes are material and important evidence—quite apart from anything they show about the involvement or non-involvement of the President—because the conversations recorded in all probability deal with the activities of other persons under investigation. Indeed, it is not implausible to suppose that the reports to the President on these occasions may themselves have been made pursuant to a conspiracy and as part of a cover-up.

Second, furnishing the tapes in aid of an investigation into charges of criminal conspiracy plainly raises none of the separation-of-powers issues you believe to be involved in furnishing so-called "Presidential Papers" to the Select Committee. The Select Committee is seeking information—as I understand the position—solely in order to recommend legislation. Whatever fears you may entertain that furnishing the tapes in aid of the Select Committee's legislative function would set a precedent for furnishing Presidential papers to other legislative committees are plainly irrelevant to my request. For my request involves only a grand jury investigation resulting from highly extraordinary circumstances. No question of precedent arises because the circumstances almost surely will never be repeated.

Third, I would urge that the tapes be furnished for use in my investigation without restriction. This procedure strikes me as the method of establishing the truth which is most fair to everyone concerned, including the President. It is proper to point out, however, that if you thought it essential to furnish the papers only to the grand jury under the rules pertaining to grand jury documents, an appropriate procedure could be devised. This is an additional circumstance distinguishing the present investigation from the situation before the Select Committee. . . .

You will realize that as the investigation proceeds it may be necessary to request additional recordings.

Sincerely,
ARCHIBALD COX
Special Prosecutor

House Judiciary Committee, Book 9: 390–92.

Statement of Information

July 17, 1973

Dear Mr. President:

Today the Select Committee on Presidential Campaign Activities met and unanimously voted that I request that you provide the Committee with all relevant documents and tapes under control of the White House that relate to the matters the Select Committee is authorized to investigate under S. Res. 60. I refer to the documents mentioned in my letter to Mr. Leonard Garment of June 21, 1973, and the relevant portions of the tapes alluded to by Mr. Alexander Butterfield before the Committee on July 16, 1973.

If your illness prevents our meeting to discuss these issues in the next day or two, I should like to suggest that you designate members of your staff to meet with members of the Select Committee staff to make arrangements for our access to White House documents and tapes pertinent to the Committee's investigation.

I should like respectfully to relate that the Committee's investigation is on-going and that access to relevant documents should not be delayed if the Committee is to perform its mission. May we hear from you at your earliest convenience?

The Committee deeply regrets your illness and hopes for you a speedy recovery.

Sincerely,
Sam J. Ervin, Jr.
Chairman, Select Committee on
Presidential Campaign Activities
United States Senate
Washington, D.C.

House Judiciary Committee, Book 3:1060.

Statement of Information

July 23, 1973

Dear Mr. Chairman:*

I have considered your request that I permit the Committee to have access to tapes of my private conversations with a number of my closest aides. I have concluded that the principles stated in my letter to you of July 6th preclude me from complying with that request, and I shall not do so. Indeed the special nature of tape recordings of private conversations is such that these principles apply with even greater force to tapes of private Presidential conversations than to Presidential papers.

If release of the tapes would settle the central questions at issue in the Watergate inquiries, then their disclosure might serve a substantial public interest that would have to be weighed very heavily against the negatives of disclosure.

The fact is that the tapes would not finally settle the central issues before your Committee. Before their existence became publicly known, I personally listened to a number of them. The tapes are entirely consistent with what I know to be the truth and what I have stated to be the truth. However, as in any verbatim recording of informal conversations, they contain comments that persons with different perspectives and motivations would inevitably interpret in different ways. Furthermore, there are inseparably interspersed in them a great many very frank and very private comments, on a wide range of issues and individuals, wholly extraneous to the Committee's inquiry. Even more important, the tapes could be accurately understood or interpreted only by reference to an enormous number of other documents and tapes, so that to open them at all would begin an endless process of disclosure and explanation of private Presidential records totally unrelated to Watergate, and highly confidential in nature. They are the clearest possible example of why Presidential documents must be kept confidential.

Accordingly, the tapes, which have been under my sole personal control, will remain so. None has been transcribed or made public and none will be. . . .

Sincerely,
[s/Richard Nixon]

House Judiciary Committee, Book 6: 2478–79.

Statement of Information

Dear Mr. Cox:

Mr. Buzhardt has asked that I respond to your letters to him of June 20, July 18, and July 20* in which you made certain requests with regard to tape recording of or about conversations between the President and various members of the White House staff and others.

The President is today refusing to make available to the Senate committee material of a similar nature. Enclosed is a copy of his letter of this date to Senator Ervin stating his position about the tapes. I am instructed by the President to inform you that it will not be possible to make available to you the recordings that you have requested.

In general the reasons for the President's decision are the same as those that underlay his response to the Senate committee. But in your letter of July 18 you state that furnishing the tapes in aid of an investigation into charges of criminal conspiracy raises none of the separation-of-powers issues that are raised by the request from the Senate committee. You indicated a similar position when we met on June 6. At that time you suggested that questions of separation of powers did not arise since you were within the Executive Branch, though, as I recall, you then added that your position is a little hard to describe since, in your view, you are not subject to direction by the President or the attorney general.

I note that in your subsequent letters, and particularly that of July 18 in which you argue that the separation-of-powers argument is inapplicable, there is no suggestion that you are a part of the Executive Branch. Indeed, if you are an ordinary prosecutor and thus part of the Executive Branch as well as an officer of the court, you are subject to the instructions of your superiors, up to and including the President, and can have access to presidential papers only as and if the President sees fit to make them available to you.

But quite aside from the consideration just stated, there is an even more fundamental reason why separation-of-powers considerations are fully as applicable to a request from you as to one from the Senate committee. It is clear, and your letter of the 18 specifically states, that the reason you are seeking these tapes is to use some or all of them before grand juries or in criminal trials. Production of them to you would lead to their use in the courts, and questions of separation of powers are in the forefront when the most confidential documents of the presidency are sought for use in the Judicial Branch.

Indeed most of the limited case law on executive privilege has arisen in the contest of attempts to obtain executive documents for use in the courts.

The successful prosecution of those who have broken the laws is a very important national interest, but it has long been recognized that there are other national interests that, in specific cases, may override this. When Congress provided in the Jencks Act, 18 U.S.C. [U.S. Code], Section 3500 (d), that the United States may choose to refuse to disclose material that the court has ordered produced, even though in some instances this will lead to a mistrial and to termination of the prosecution, it was merely recognizing that, as the courts had repeatedly held, there are circumstances in which other legitimate national interests requiring that documents be kept confidential outweigh the interest in punishing a particular malefactor.

Similarly in civil litigation the United States may feel obliged to withhold relevant information, because of more compelling governmental issues, even though this may cause it to lose a suit it might otherwise have won. The power of the President to withhold confidential documents that would otherwise be material in the courts comes from "an inherent executive power which is protected in the constitutional system of separation of power." *United States* v. *Reynolds*, 345 U.S. 1, 6n.9 (1953).

In your letter to Mr. Buzhardt of July 10 you quoted Mr. [Elliot L.] Richardson's statement to the Senate Judiciary Committee in which he concluded that it was the President's intention "that whatever should be made public in terms of the public interest in these investigations should be disclosed . . ."

That is, of course, the President's view, but it is for the President, and only for the President, to weigh whether the incremental advantage that these tapes would give you in criminal proceedings justifies the serious and lasting hurt that disclosure of them would do to the confidentiality that is imperative to the effective functioning of the presidency. In this instance the president has concluded that it would not serve the public interest to make the tapes available.

Sincerely,
Charles Alan Wright

House Judiciary Committee, Book 9: 390–92.

Statement of Information

Dear Mr. Chairman:

White House counsel have received on my behalf the two subpoenas issued by you, on behalf of the select committee on July 23. . . .

You will understand, however, I am sure, that it would simply not be feasible for my staff and me to review thousands of documents to decide which do and which do not fit within the sweeping but vague terms of the subpoena.

It continues to be true, as it was when I wrote you on July 6, that my staff is under instructions to cooperate fully with yours in furnishing information pertinent to your inquiry. I have directed that executive privilege not be invoked with regard to testimony by present and former members of my staff concerning possible criminal conduct or discussions of possible criminal conduct. I have waived the attorney-client privilege with regard to my former counsel. In my July 6 letter I described these acts of cooperation with the select committee as 'genuine, extensive and, in the history of such matters, extra-ordinary.' That cooperation has continued and it will continue. Executive privilege is being invoked only with regard to documents and recordings that cannot be made public consistent with the confidentiality essential to the functioning of the office of the President.

I cannot and will not consent to giving any investigatory body private presidential papers. To the extent that I have custody of other documents or information relevant to the work of the select committee and that can properly be made public, I will be glad to make these available in response to specific requests.

Sincerely,
Richard Nixon

House Judiciary Committee, Book 7: 2657–58.

Statement of Information

Dear Judge Sirica:

White House counsel have received on my behalf a subpoena duces tecum issued out of the United States District Court for the District of Columbia on July 23 at the request of Archibald Cox. The subpoena calls on me to produce for a grand jury certain tape recordings as well as certain specified documents. With the utmost respect for the court of which you are chief judge, and for the branch of government of which it is a part, I must decline to obey the command of that subpoena. In doing so I follow the example of a long line of predecessors as President of the United States who have consistently adhered to the position that the President is not subject to compulsory process from the courts.

The independence of the three branches of our government is at the very heart of our constitutional system. It would be wholly inadmissible for the President to seek to compel some particular action by the courts. It is equally inadmissible for the courts to seek to compel some particular action from the President.

That the President is not subject to compulsory process from the other branches of government does not mean, of course, that all information in the custody of the President must forever remain unavailable to the courts. Like all of my predecessors I have always made relevant material available to the courts except in those rare instances when to do so would be inconsistent with the public interest. The principle that guides my actions in this regard was well stated by Attorney General Speed in 1865:

"Upon principles of public policy there are some kinds of evidence which the law excludes or dispenses with . . . the official transactions between the heads of departments of the government and their subordinate officers are, in general, treated as 'privileged communications.' The President of the United States, the heads of the great departments of the government, and the governors of the several states, it has been decided, are not bound to produce papers or disclose information communicated to them where, in their own judgment, the disclosure would, on public considerations, be inexpedient. These are familiar rules laid down by every author on the law of evidence."

A similar principle has been stated by many other attorneys general, it has been recognized by the courts, and it has been acted upon by many Presidents. . . .

Sincerely,
Richard Nixon

House Judiciary Committee, Book 9: 390–92.

**Judge Sirica and the Subpoena;
In re Grand Jury Subpoena Duces Tecum Issued
to Richard M. Nixon, U.S. Dist. Ct., D.C.,
August 29, 1973.**

On July 23, 1973, Watergate Special Prosecutor Archibald Cox acting on behalf of the June 1972 grand jury empanelled by this court, caused to be issued a subpoena duces tecum to the President of the United States, Richard M. Nixon. The subpoena required the President, or any appropriate subordinate official, to produce for the grand jury certain tape recordings and documents enumerated in an attached schedule. . . . In a letter to the Court dated July 25, 1973, the President advised that the tape recordings sought would not be provided. . . .

Thereafter, the grand jury instructed Special Prosecutor Cox to apply for an order requiring production of the recordings. On July 26, the Special Prosecutor petitioned this Court for a show cause order directed to the President. At the time of this application a quorum of the grand jury was polled in open court, and each juror expressed his or her desire that the Court order compliance. Subsequently, the Court ordered that the President or any appropriate subordinate official show cause "why the documents and objects described in [the subpoena] should not be produced as evidence before the grand jury."

In response to the show cause order, the President, by his attorneys, filed a special appearance contesting the Court's jurisdiction to order the President's compliance with the grand jury subpoena. The Court allowed for the filing of a response by the Special Prosecutor and reply by the President, and the matter came on for hearing on August 22nd.

The parties to the controversy have briefed and argued several issues including the Court's jurisdiction in the matter of compulsory process, the existence and scope of "executive privilege" generally, applicability of "executive privilege" to the tape recordings subpoenaed, and waiver of privilege. The Court has found it necessary to adjudicate but two questions for the present: (1) whether the Court has jurisdiction to decide the issue of privilege, and (2) whether the Court has authority to enforce the subpoena *duces tecum* by way of an order requiring production for inspection *in camera*. . . .

I

A search of the Constitution and the history of its creation reveals a general disfavor of government privileges, or at least uncontrolled privileges. Early in the Convention of 1787, the delegates cautioned each other concerning the dangers of lodging immoderate power in the executive department. This attitude persisted throughout the Convention, and executive powers became a major topic in the subsequent ratification debates. The Framers regarded the legislative department superior in power and importance to the other two and felt the necessity of investing it with some privileges and immunities, but even here an attitude of restraint, as expressed by James Madison, prevailed:

> Mr. Pinkney moved a clause declaring "that each House should be the judge of the privilege of its own members."
>
> *   *   *
>
> Mr. Madison distinguished between the power of Judging of privileges previously & duly established, and the effect of the motion which would give a discretion to each House as to the extent of its own privileges. He suggested that it would be better to make provision for ascertaining by *law*, the privileges of each House, than to allow each House to decide for itself. He suggested also the necessity of considering what privileges ought to be allowed to the Executive. (Emphasis in original)

The upshot of Madison's final suggestion regarding a definition of executive privileges was that none were deemed necessary, or at least that the Constitution need not record any. As Charles Pinckney [said]: "They therefore determined to set the example, in merely limiting privilege to what was necessary and no more," constitute[s] an apt description of the Convention's purpose and outlook. Are there, then, any rights or privileges consistent with, though not mentioned in, the Constitution which are necessary to the Executive? One answer may be found in the Supreme Court decision, United States v. Reynolds, 345 U.S. 1, 73 S.Ct. 528, 97 L.Ed. 727 (1953). The Court recognized an executive privilege, evidentiary in nature, for military secrets. *Reynolds* held that when a court finds the privilege is properly invoked under the appropriate circumstances, it will, in a civil case at least, suppress the evidence. Thus, it must be recognized that there can be executive privileges that will bar the production of evidence. The Court is willing here to recognize and give effect to an evidentiary privilege based on the need to protect Presidential privacy.

The Court, however, cannot agree with Respondent that it is the Executive that finally determines whether its privilege is properly invoked. The availability of evidence including the validity and scope of privileges, is a judicial decision. . . .

In all the numerous litigations where claims of executive privilege have been interposed, the courts have not hesitated to pass judgment. . . .

II

If after judicial examination *in camera,* any portion of the tapes is ruled not subject to privilege, that portion will be forwarded to the grand jury at the appropriate time. To call for the tapes *in camera* is thus tantamount to fully enforcing the subpoena as to any unprivileged matter. Therefore, before the Court can call for production *in camera,* it must have concluded that it has authority to order a President to obey the command of a grand jury subpoena as it relates to unprivileged evidence in his possession. The Court has concluded that it possesses such authority. . . .

III

In deciding whether these tape recordings or portions thereof are properly the objects of a privilege, the Court must accommodate two competing policies. On the one hand, as has been noted earlier, is the need to disfavor privileges and narrow their application as far as possible. On the other hand, lies a need to favor the privacy of Presidential deliberations; to indulge a presumption in favor of the President. To the Court, respect for the President, the Presidency, and the duties of the office, gives the advantage to this second policy. This respect, however, does not decide the controversy. Such a resolution on the Court's part, as Chief Justice Marshall observed, "would deserve some other appellation than the term respect." Nevertheless, it does not hurt for the courts to remind themselves often that the authority vested in them to delimit the scope and application of privileges, particularly the privileges and immunities of government, is a trust. And as with every trust, an abuse can reap the most dire consequences. This Court, then, enters upon its present task with care and with a determination to exercise the restraint that characterizes the conduct of courts. . . .

The President Retreats

On August 15, 1973, President Nixon issued a lengthy statement that again contradicted a number of his earlier positions. Nevertheless, he indicated a hard-line position on his view that executive privilege protected his confidential tapes. At a press conference a week later, Nixon complained that the press was obsessed with Watergate. He noted that all the questions involved only that controversy and not "the business of the people." But the press conference continued for another thirty minutes, exclusively preoccupied with Watergate.

**President's Statement,
August 15, 1973**

I said on May 22 that I had no prior knowledge of the Watergate operation. In all the testimony, there is not the slightest evidence to the contrary. Not a single witness has testified that I had any knowledge of the planning for the Watergate break-in.

It is also true, as I said on May 22, that I took no part in, and was not aware of, any subsequent efforts to cover up the illegal acts associated with the Watergate break-in.

In the summer of 1972, I had given orders for the Justice Department and the FBI to conduct a thorough and aggressive investigation of the Watergate break-in, and I relied on their investigation to disclose the facts. My only concern about the scope of the investigation was that it might lead into CIA or other national-security operations of a sensitive nature. Mr. Gray, the Acting Director of the FBI, told me by telephone on July 6 that he had met with General Walters, that General Walters had told him the CIA was not involved, and that CIA activities would not be compromised by the FBI investigation. As a result, any problems that Mr. Gray may have had in co-ordinating with the CIA were moot. I concluded by instructing him to press forward vigorously with his own investigation. . . .

. . . [T]he grand jury on September 15, indicted only the five persons arrested at the Watergate, plus Messrs. Liddy and Hunt.

Those indictments also seemed to me to confirm the validity of the reports that Mr. Dean had been providing to me, through other members of the White House staff—and on which I had based my August 29 statement that no one then employed at the White House was involved. It was in that context that I met with Mr. Dean on September 15, and he gave me no reason at that meeting to believe any others were involved.

Not only was I unaware of any cover-up, but at that time, and until March 21, I was unaware that there was anything to cover-up. . . .

When I received this disturbing information on March 21, I immediately began new inquiries into the case and an examination of the best means to give the grand jury or Senate Committee what we then knew and what we might later learn.

My consistent position from the beginning has been to get out the facts about Watergate, not to cover them up.

On May 22, I said that at no time did I authorize any offer of executive clemency for the Watergate defendants, nor did I know of any such offer. I reaffirm that statement. Indeed, I made my view clear to Mr. Ehrlichman in July, 1972, that under no circumstances could executive clemency be considered for those who participated in the Watergate break-in. I maintained that position throughout.

On May 22, I said that "it was not until the time of my own investigation that I learned of the break-in at the office of Mr. Ellsberg's psychiatrist, and I specifically authorized the furnishing of this information to Judge Byrne." After a very careful review, I have determined that this statement of mine is not precisely accurate. It was on March 17 that I first learned of the break-in at the office of Dr. Fielding, and that was four days before the beginning of my own investigation on March 21. I was told then that nothing by way of evidence had been obtained in the break-in.

On April 18, I learned that the Justice Department had interrogated or was going to interrogate Mr. Hunt about this break-in. I was gravely concerned that other activities of the special-investigations unit might be disclosed, because I knew this could seriously injure the national security. Consequently, I directed Mr. Petersen to stick to the Watergate investigation and stay out of national-security matters.

On April 25, Attorney General Kleindienst came to me and urged that the fact of the break-in should be disclosed to the court, despite the fact that, since no evidence had been obtained, the law did not clearly require it. I concurred, and authorized him to report the break-in to Judge Byrne.

In view of the incident of Dr. Fielding's office, let me emphasize two things:

First, it was and is important that many of the matters worked on by the special-investigations unit not be publicly disclosed because disclosure would unquestionably damage the national security. This is why I have exercised executive privilege on some of these matters in connection with the testimony of Mr. Ehrlichman and others. . . .

Second, I at no time authorized the use of illegal means by the special-investigations unit, and I was not aware of the break-in of Dr. Fielding's office until March 17, 1973.

Many persons will ask why, when the facts are as I have stated them, I do not make public the tape recordings of my meetings and conversations with members of the White House staff during this period.

I am aware that such terms as "separation of powers" and "executive privilege" are lawyers' terms, and that those doctrines have been called "abstruse" and "esoteric." Let me state the common sense of the matter.

Every day, a President of the United States is required to make difficult decisions on grave issues. It is absolutely essential, if the President is to be able to do his job as the country expects, that he be able to talk openly and candidly with his advisers about issues and individuals, and that they be able to talk in the same fashion with him. Indeed, on occasion, they must be able to "blow off steam" about important public figures. This kind of frank discussion is only possible when those who take part in it can feel assured that what they say is in the strictest confidence. . . .

I shall therefore vigorously oppose any action which would set a precedent that would cripple all future Presidents by inhibiting conversations between them and the persons they look to for advice.

This principle of confidentiality in presidential communications is what is at stake in the question of the tapes. I shall continue to oppose any efforts to destroy that principle, which is indispensable to the conduct of the Presidency.

Public Papers of the Presidents, Richard Nixon, 1973, 698–703.

Press Conference, August 22, 1973

Q. Mr. President—

A. Just a moment. We've had 30 minutes of this press conference. I have yet to have, for example, one question on the business of the people. Which shows you are—how we're consumed with it.

I'm not criticizing the members of the press; because you naturally are very interested in this issue. But let me tell you, years from now people are going to perhaps be interested in what happened in terms of the efforts of the United States to build a structure of peace in the world. They are perhaps going to be interested in the efforts of this Administration to have a kind of prosperity that we haven't had since 1955—that is, prosperity without war and without inflation.

Because, throughout the Kennedy years and throughout the Johnson years, whatever prosperity we had was at the cost of either inflation or war, or both.

I don't say that critically of them. I'm simply saying, we've got to do better than that.

Now our goal is to move forward then—to move forward to build a structure of peace. And when you say, have I—do I consider resigning: the answer is no. I shall not resign. I have three and a half years to go, or almost three and a half years, and I'm going to use every day of those three and a half years trying to get the people of the United States to recognize that whatever mistakes we have made that in the long run this Administration, by making this world safer for their children, and this Administration, by making their lives better at home for themselves and their children, deserves high marks rather than low marks. . . .

Public Papers of the Presidents, Richard Nixon, 1973, 698–703.

October:
The Cruelest Month

October 1973 was a defining moment for Nixon's presidency. Vice President Spiro Agnew resigned following his plea of *nolo contendere* to charges of bribery and failure to pay income taxes. Agnew had demanded impeachment for himself, contending that like a sitting President he was immune to criminal prosecution. But Nixon and his aides simply did not want an impeachment precedent. Impeaching Agnew, however, might have saved Nixon, for a trial undoubtedly would have dragged out, possibly exhausting the country and turning it away from any further impeachments. Agnew's resignation, coupled with Nixon's selection of House Republican Leader Gerald R. Ford as Vice President, tightened the vise around the President. For now, in Ford, he had created a viable alternative to himself. Nixon's bitterest opponents would have recoiled at any prospect of impeachment

or resignation if it meant an Agnew presidency. But Ford as a
member of the Washington establishment, and well-liked in
congressional circles, clearly was an acceptable alternative to
Nixon. Also in October, the grand jury handed down indictments
of Egil Krogh, head of the plumbers and John Dean, who had
been so much a part of the cover-up conspiracy. But the most
significant moment came in mid-month when Nixon ordered
Attorney General Richardson to fire Special Prosecutor Cox to
prevent any further court challenges to the President's refusal to
surrender the tapes. Nixon's order precipitated Richardson's
resignation, as well as his deputy's, William Ruckelshaus, in what
came to be known as the "Saturday Night Massacre." Solicitor
General Robert Bork, next in the chain of Justice Department
command, became Attorney General and dismissed Cox.

Excerpts From Grand Jury Criminal Information Against Agnew.

I. The Relationship of Mr. Agnew, I. H. Hammerman II and Jerome B. Wolff.

In the spring of 1967, shortly after Mr. Agnew had taken office as
Governor of Maryland, he advised Hammerman that it was customary
for engineers to make substantial cash payments in return for engineering contracts with the state of Maryland. Mr. Agnew instructed Hammerman to contact Wolff, then the new chairman-director of the
Maryland State Roads Commission, to arrange for the establishment of
an understanding pursuant to which Wolff would notify Hammerman
as to which engineering firms were in line for state contracts so that
Hammerman could solicit and obtain from those engineering firms
cash payments in consideration therefore.

Hammerman, as instructed, discussed the matter with Wolff, who
was receptive but who requested that the cash payments to be elicited
from the engineers be split in three equal shares among Agnew, Hammerman and Wolff. Hammerman informed Mr. Agnew of Wolff's attitude; Mr. Agnew informed Hammerman that the split of cash monies
would be 50 per cent for Mr. Agnew, 25 per cent for Hammerman and
25 per cent for Wolff. Hammerman carried that message to Wolff, who
agreed to that split.

The scheme outlined above was then put into operation. Over the
course of the approximately 18 months of Mr. Agnew's remaining tenure
as Governor of Maryland, Hammerman made contact with approxi-

mately eight engineering firms. Informed periodically by Wolff as to which engineering firms were in line to receive state contracts, Hammerman successfully elicited from seven engineering firms substantial cash payments pursuant to understandings between Hammerman and the various engineers to whom he was talking that the substantial cash payments were in return for the state work being awarded to those engineering firms. The monies collected in that manner by Hammerman were split (among Hammerman, Agnew and Wolff) in accordance with the understanding earlier reached. . . .

Wolff, as chairman-director of the Maryland State Roads Commission, made initial tentative decisions with regard to which engineering firms should be awarded which state contracts. These tentative decisions would then be discussed by Wolff with Governor Agnew. Although Governor Agnew accorded Wolff's tentative decisions great weight, the Governor always exercised the final decision-making authority. . . .

Hammerman also successfully solicited, at Governor Agnew's instruction, a substantial cash payment from a financial institution in return for that institution's being awarded a major role in the financing of a large issue of state bonds.

II. The Relationship between Mr. Agnew and Allen Green.

Shortly after Mr. Agnew's election in November 1966 as Governor of Maryland, he complained to Allen Green, principal of a large engineering firm, about the financial burdens to be imposed upon Mr. Agnew by his role as Governor. Green responded by saying that his company had benefited from state work and had been able to generate some cash funds from which he would be willing to provide Mr. Agnew with some financial assistance. Mr. Agnew indicated that he would be grateful for such assistance.

Beginning shortly thereafter, Green delivered to Mr. Agnew six to nine times a years an envelope containing between $2,000 and $3,000 in cash. Green's purpose was to elicit from the Agnew administration as much state work for his engineering firm as possible. That purpose was clearly understood by Governor Agnew. . . .

Green continued to make cash payments to Vice President Agnew three or four times a year up to and including December 1972. These payments were usually about $2,000 each. The payments were made both in Mr. Agnew's vice presidential office and at his residence in the Sheraton-Park Hotel, Washington, D.C. The payments were not discontinued until after the initiation of the Baltimore County investigation by the United States Attorney for the District of Maryland in January 1973.

III. The Relationship between Mr. Agnew and Lester Matz.

Lester Matz, a principal in another large engineering firm, began making corrupt payments while Mr. Agnew was County Executive of Baltimore County in the early 1960s. In those days, Matz paid 5 per cent of his fees from Baltimore County contracts in cash to Mr. Agnew through one of Mr. Agnew's close associates.

After Mr. Agnew became Governor of Maryland, Matz decided to make his payments directly to Governor Agnew. He made no payments until that summer of 1968 when he and his partner calculated that they owed Mr. Agnew approximately $20,000 in consideration for the work which their firm had already received from the Governor's administration. The $20,000 in cash was generated in an illegal manner and was given by Matz to Governor Agnew in a manila envelope in Governor Agnew's office on or about July 16, 1968. . . .

Matz made no further corrupt payments to Mr. Agnew until shortly after Mr. Agnew became Vice President, at which time Matz calculated that he owed Mr. Agnew approximately $10,000 more from jobs and fees which the Matz firm had received from Governor Agnew's administration since July 1968. After generating $10,000 in cash in an illegal manner, Matz met with Mr. Agnew in the Vice President's office and gave him approximately $10,000 in cash in an envelope. . . .

In or around April 1971, Matz made a cash payment to Vice President Agnew of $2,500 in return for the awarding by the General Services Administration of a contract to a small engineering firm in which Matz had a financial ownership interest. An intermediary was instrumental in the arrangement for that particular corrupt payment.

In re Spiro Agnew, U.S. Dist. Ct. (Md.) proceedings, September 28, 1973.

Agnew Resigns;
New York Times, **October 11, 1973.**

Dear Mr. President:

As you are aware, the accusations against me cannot be resolved without a long, divisive and debilitating struggle in the Congress and in the Courts. I have concluded that, painful as it is to me and to my family, it is in the best interests of the Nation that I relinquish the Vice Presidency.

Accordingly, I have today resigned the Office of Vice President of the United States. A copy of the instrument of resignation is enclosed.

It has been a privilege to serve with you. May I express to the American people, through you, my deep gratitude for their confidence in twice electing me to be Vice President.

Sincerely,
Spiro T. Agnew

Dear Ted:

The most difficult decisions are often those that are the most personal, and I know your decision to resign as Vice President has been as difficult as any facing a man in public life could be. Your departure from the Administration leaves me with a great sense of personal loss. You have been a valued associate throughout these nearly five years that we have served together. However, I respect your decision, and I also respect the concern for the national interest that led you to conclude that a resolution of the matter in this way, rather than through an extended battle in the Courts and the Congress, was advisable in order to prevent a protracted period of national division and uncertainty.

As Vice President, you have addressed the great issues of our times with courage and candor. Your strong patriotism, and your profound dedication to the welfare of the Nation, have been an inspiration to all who have served with you as well as to millions of others throughout the country.

I have been deeply saddened by this whole course of events, and I hope that you and your family will be sustained in the days ahead by a well-justified pride in all that you have contributed to the Nation by your years of service as Vice President.

Sincerely,
Richard Nixon

Statement,
October 20, 1973

Throughout this week, the Attorney General, Elliot Richardson, at my instance, has been holding discussions with Special Prosecutor Archibald Cox, looking to the possibility of a compromise that would avoid the necessity of Supreme Court review. With the greatest reluctance, I have concluded that in this one instance I must permit a breach in the confidentiality that is so necessary to the conduct of the Presidency. Accordingly, the Attorney General made what he regarded as a reasonable proposal for compromise, and one that goes beyond what any President in history has offered. It was a proposal that would comply with the spirit of the decision of the Court of Appeals. It would have allowed justice to proceed undiverted, while maintaining the principle of an independent executive branch. It would have given the Special Prosecutor the information he claims he needs for use in the grand jury. It would also have resolved any lingering thought that the President himself might have been involved in a Watergate coverup.

The proposal was that, as quickly as the materials could be prepared, there would be submitted to Judge Sirica, through a statement prepared by me personally from the subpoenaed tapes, a full disclosure of everything contained in those tapes that has any bearing on Watergate. The authenticity of this summary would be assured by giving unlimited access to the tapes to a very distinguished man, highly respected by all elements in American life for his integrity, his fairness, and his patriotism, so that that man could satisfy himself that the statement prepared by me did indeed include fairly and accurately anything on the tapes that might be regarded as related to Watergate.

In return, so that the constitutional tensions of Watergate would not be continued, it would be understood that there would be no further attempt by the Special Prosecutor to subpoena still more tapes or other Presidential papers of a similar nature.

I am pleased to be able to say that Chairman Sam Ervin and Vice Chairman Howard Baker of the Senate Select Committee have agreed to this procedure and that at their request, and mine, Senator John Stennis has consented to listen to every requested tape and verify that the statment I am preparing is full and accurate. Some may ask why, if I am willing to let Senator Stennis hear the tapes for this purpose, I am not willing merely to submit them to the court for inspection in private. I do so out of no lack of respect for Judge Sirica, in whose discretion and integrity I have the utmost confidence, but because to allow the tapes to be heard by one judge would create a precedent that would be available to 400 district judges. Further, it would create a precedent that Presidents are required to submit to judicial demands that purport to override Presidential determinations on requirements for confidentiality.

To my regret, the Special Prosecutor rejected this proposal. Nevertheless, it is my judgment that in the present circumstances and existing international environment, it is in the overriding national interest that a constitutional confrontation on this issue be avoided. I have, therefore, instructed White House counsel not to seek Supreme Court review from the decision of the Court of Appeals. At the same time, I will voluntarily make available to Judge Sirica—and also to the Senate Select Committee—a statement of the Watergate-related portions of the tapes, prepared and authenticated in the fashion I have described.

I want to repeat that I have taken this step with the greatest reluctance, only to bring the issue of Watergate tapes to an end and to assure our full attention to more pressing business affecting the very security of the nation. Accordingly, though I have not wished to intrude upon the independence of the Special Prosecutor, I have felt it necessary to direct him, as an employee of the executive branch, to make no further attempts by judicial process to obtain tapes, notes, or memoranda of Presidential conversations. I believe that with the statement that will be provided to the court, any legitimate need of the Special Prosecutor is fully satisfied and that he can proceed to obtain indictments against those who may have committed any crimes. And I believe that by these actions I have taken today America will be spared the anguish of further indecision and litigation about tapes.

Our constitutional history reflects not only the language and inferences of that great document, but also the choices of clash and accommodation made by responsible leaders at critical moments. Under the Constitution it is the duty of the President to see that the laws of the Nation are faithfully executed. My actions today are in accordance with that duty, and in that spirit of accommodation.

Public Papers of the Presidents, Richard Nixon, 1973, 890–91.

Richardson's Resignation;
New York Times, October 21, 1973.

Dear Mr. President:

It is with deep regret that I have been obliged to conclude that circumstances leave me no alternative to the submission of my resignation as Attorney General of the United States.

At the time you appointed me, you gave me the authority to name a special prosecutor if I should consider it appropriate. A few days before my confirmation hearing began, I announced that I would, if confirmed, "appoint a special prosecutor and give him all the independence, authority, and staff support needed to carry out the tasks entrusted to him." I added, "Although he will be in the Department of Justice and report to me—and only to me—he will be aware that his ultimate accountability is to the American people."

At many points throughout the nomination hearings, I reaffirmed my intention to assure the independence of the special prosecutor, and in my statement of his duties and responsibilities, I specified that he would have "full authority" for "determining whether or not to contest the assertion of 'Executive Privilege' or any other testimonial privilege." And while the special prosecutor can be removed from office for "extraordinary improprieties," I also pledged that "The Attorney General will not countermand or interfere with the Special Prosecutor's decisions or actions."

While I fully respect the reasons that have led you to conclude that the Special Prosecutor must be discharged, I trust that you understand that I could not in the light of these firm and repeated commitments carry out your direction that this be done. In the circumstances, therefore, I feel that I have no choice but to resign.

In leaving your Administration, I take with me lasting gratitude for the opportunities you have given me to serve under your leadership in a number of important posts. It has been a privilege to share in your efforts to make the structure of our own government more responsive. I believe profoundly in the rightness and importance of those efforts, and I trust that they will meet with increasing success in the remaining years of your Presidency.

> Respectfully,
> Elliot L. Richardson

Dear Elliot:

It is with the deepest regret and with an understanding of the circumstances which brought you to your decision that I accept your resignation.

> Sincerely,
> Richard Nixon

The Saturday Night Massacre

The Saturday Night Massacre resulted in a firestorm of criticism. Most notably, it sparked significant suspicion of Nixon's behavior and motives by members of his own party. The top three Republican leaders in the House said it was necessary for the President to turn over the tapes if he wanted Republicans to defend him. A Republican congressman probably spoke for many Americans when he said, "Damn all this executive privilege. People are saying the tapes have to be turned over." The events of October 20 witnessed a sharp increase in public opposition to Nixon. Congressmen were inundated with unprecedented numbers of telegrams, calls, and letters demanding the President's impeachment. Shortly thereafter, the House voted its first authorization of an Impeachment Inquiry. The public attitudes toward Nixon resulted in *Time* magazine's first-ever editorial that called for the President's resignation. The magazine had been a staunch supporter of Nixon, dating back to the 1940s.

"The President Should Resign;"
***Time*, November 12, 1973.**

Richard Nixon and the nation have passed a tragic point of no return. It now seems likely that the President will have to give up his office: he has irredeemably lost his moral authority, the confidence of most of the country, and therefore his ability to govern effectively.

157

The most important decision of Richard Nixon's remarkable career is before him: whether he will give up the presidency rather than do further damage to his country. If he decides to fight to the end, he faces impeachment by the House, for he has indeed failed his obligation under the Constitution to uphold the law. Whether two-thirds of the Senate would vote to convict him cannot be certain. But even if he were to be acquitted, the process would leave him and the country devastated. Events have achieved an alarming momentum: additional facts that would be brought out under subpoena power at an impeachment trial could strike in many unforeseen and dangerous directions.

Moreover, a trial would take at least several months, during which the country would be virtually leaderless. The White House would be paralyzed while the U.S. and the world awaited the outcome. The Republic would doubtless survive. But the wise and patriotic course is for Richard Nixon to resign, sparing the country and himself this agony. . . .

In the almost daily rush of revelations, it is not easy for the numbed citizen to keep in mind the full enormity of "Watergate." Despite ample instances of past Government corruption, nothing can be found in U.S. history even remotely approaching the skein of events that the word Watergate no longer defines or contains. A Vice President, twice personally chosen by Nixon, forced to resign to escape jail. A former Attorney General and intimate adviser to Nixon under indictment. Another former Cabinet member under indictment. One of the two most powerful presidential aides under indictment. Six other White House aides or Administration officials indicted, convicted or having pleaded guilty; seven more fired or resigned. Most of them shown to have been either in charge of, or aware of, illegal operations. The whole White House pervaded by an atmosphere of aggressive amorality—amorality almost raised to a creed. A ruthless determination to hide as much of this as possible from the public and investigators.

The question that once seemed so important—Did the President know about the cover-up?—was always somewhat beside the point. Whatever he knew or did not know, he must be held accountable for the actions of his top aides and the standards he established. To the extent that the question had meaning, it was almost impossible from the start to answer it in the President's favor: the men involved were too close to him to make his ignorance plausible: after initial indignant denials, each of his later explanations gradually admitted more knowledge, thereby conceding each previous explanation to have been at least partly false. One cannot think of any organization, public or private—including some dictatorships—where a Chief Executive could survive in office after such a performance. . . .

It was just one year ago this week that Richard Nixon was celebrating his fabulous electoral sweep and seemed to stand at the very summit of power and opportunity. Hard-core Nixon haters may gloat over his fall from those heights: for most Americans it is a matter of profound disappointment. The editors of Time Inc., speaking on the editorial page of TIME's sister publication LIFE, have endorsed Nixon for President three times, in 1960, 1968 and 1972. We did so with acknowledgments that aspects of the Nixon record and temperament were troubling, but we believed that his strenghts of intellect and experience and his instinct for political leadership equipped him well for the office. In endorsing Nixon in 1972, following on his first-term achievements in foreign policy, we expressed hope that by the end of his second term we could "salute him as a great President." Thus we come with deep reluctance to our conclusion that he must leave office. We consider the situation so unprecedented, the issue so crucial to the country that we publish this first editorial in TIME's 50-year history. . . .

There are legitimate fears about the precedent that would be set by the President's resignation or impeachment. In two centuries, no American President has been removed from office other than by death or the voters' will. Once the spell is broken, would it become too easy for political opponents of any future President to oust him? We think not. Watergate is unique. In fact, the really dangerous precedent would be the opposite: to allow a President with Nixon's record to continue in office. This would be a terrible circumstance to lodge in our history, a terrible thing to explain to our children and their children.

In recent decades, the American presidency has assumed an almost sacrosanct aura. It is time to remember that quite literally, and not as a flourish of speech, the sovereign in America is not the President but the people. It is true that the people elect him, which gives him his unique mandate, but to conclude from this that a President must be preserved in all circumstances, at any cost, is the first unwitting step toward dictatorship.

As Watergate and related events emerged in congressional hearings and in the press, many patriotic Americans were nagged by a sense of disproportion. Crookedness and corner cutting? Yes. Crimes? No doubt—but after all, as the phrase went, "No one was killed." How could these acts, however shady or offensive, be weighed against the life-and-death responsibilities of the President? This rationalization will not stand: a President's "big decisions" cannot be put into a compartment separate from his other actions, his total behavior. His integrity and trustworthiness are perhaps the most important facts about him to his country and to the world. And these Nixon has destroyed.

The nightmare of uncertainty must be ended. A fresh start must be made. Some at home and abroad might see in the President's resignation a sign of American weakness and failure. It would be a sign of the very opposite. It would show strength and health. It would show the ability of a badly infected political system to cleanse itself. It would show the true power of popular government under law in America.

The President Succumbs

Three days after Cox's firing, presidential Chief of Staff Alexander Haig acknowledged the mistake and Nixon's decision to comply with Judge Sirica's subpoena for the tapes. "This President does not defy the law," Nixon's lawyer said. When Charles Alan Wright appeared in the Circuit Court for the President, he confronted eleven former Cox aides at the prosecution table. The Special Prosecutor's role remained intact—even without a Special Prosecutor—and Nixon had been stymied in his effort to rid himself of his persecutors.

Haig and the "Firestorm;"
October 23, 1973

I thought I would try to do this afternoon is try to put some perspective on what one journalist has referred to as the firestorm. . . .

[W]e learned here in the White House that Professor Cox was convening a press conference for 1 o'clock Saturday afternoon. Now, on Friday night, when these events drew to a conclusion, we all assumed that Professor Cox had three options, or four, depending on the variance that you care to discuss.

First, he could have said, "I have acquired the information which I have subpoenaed which is necessary in my view to bring these cases to litigation."

Secondly, he could have determined that the prohibition which would not grant him carte blanche to request further tapes or personal Presidential memoranda was not acceptable. Had he chosen that option, he could have resigned, with all the implications that that would have had for the participants and for the American people to digest and make their own judgment with respect to the validity of that course of action and the course of action pursued by the President.

An option of that is, he could have delayed. He could have waited, and perhaps waited until further justification developed for a resumption of his needs, should they have developed.

Or, as he finally selected to do, he could appear before the Washington press corps and directly rebut and challenge the President of the United States.

Having done that, I think few Americans will argue that any President faced with this kind of a dilemma can only act as President Nixon did and that is to fire the individual in the executive branch who refused to obey a legitimate order, and that is precisely what ensued.

Now, as Elliot Richardson said this morning, it was in the face of this action, and the personal dilemmas that he, himself, was then faced with—that is, being the instrument of the separation of Professor Cox—that he informed the President on Saturday afternoon that he could not serve as that instrument. A similar situation, with somewhat different background, justified Mr. Ruckelshaus' parallel decision.

Now, gentlemen, that is the sequence of events that led us through the firestorm of this weekend. And this morning, after assessing all of the considerations and the outcome of those actions, which were not pre-planned, not desired, and indeed, I think probably not very well visualized on Friday morning by all participants, this is the setting in which the President entered the Oval Office this morning.

I don't have to describe for you some of the backdrop of this morning's atmosphere, but that being true, and having experienced an additional week of some fairly high tensions in our international business, the President concluded, after very painful and anguishing discussion with me, with his counsel, that the circumstances were sufficiently grave in the context of our national attitudes on this issue, which I must say in my view have been subject to a great deal of misunderstanding, a great deal of misinformation over the past weekend, but in the light of this situation, the President decided that he would abandon, on this occasion, these very strongly held and long held convictions that he, as President of these United States, has the obligation, indeed, to protect the rights and prerogatives of this office not only for himself but for subsequent Presidents in our upcoming history.

Having made that decision, he instructed Professor Wright, sometime around noon today, to prepare to inform Judge Sirica at 2 p.m. this afternoon, at Judge Sirica's hearing, that the President would indeed comply with Judge Sirica's decision, as modified by the appellate court, and turn over the tapes for *in camera* inspection to Judge Sirica. . . .

Presidential Documents, Richard Nixon, 9:1275–78.

Press Conference,
October 26, 1973

Also, in consultations that we have had in the White House today, we have decided that next week the Acting Attorney General, Mr. Bork, will appoint a new special prosecutor for what is called the Watergate matter. The special prosecutor will have independence. He will have total cooperation from the Executive Branch, and he will have as a primary responsibility to bring this matter which has so long concerned the American people, bring it to an expeditious conclusion, because we have to remember that under our Constitution it has always been held that justice delayed is justice denied. It is time for those who are guilty to be prosecuted, and for those who are innocent to be cleared. I can assure you ladies and gentlemen, all of our listeners tonight, that I have no greater interest than to see that the new special prosecutor has the cooperation from the Executive Branch and the independence that he needs to bring about that conclusion.

Public Papers of the Presidents, Richard Nixon, 1973, 896–906.

The New Special Prosecutor

Cox's firing accelerated demands for a new Special Prosecutor, and one possessing firmer guarantees of independence. At his press conference of October 26, 1973, Nixon abjectly surrendered on this point, athough he indicated continued resistance to surrendering any taped presidential conversations. Four days later, Acting Attorney General Robert Bork announced the appointment of Leon Jaworski as Special Prosecutor. In May, Richardson had encountered difficulty in convincing numerous prominent lawyers and judges, including Jaworski, to accept the position. But now the case had become more compelling, clearer, and attractive. Unlike Cox, Jaworski had impeccable establishment and conservative credentials. A former war crimes prosecutor and adviser to Lyndon Johnson, he had recently been president of the American Bar Association, and in 1972 had headed Texas Democrats for Nixon. A combination of Cox's firing and Jaworski's reputation enabled him to secure from the White House a grudging guarantee of independence. Bork provided the Senate Judiciary Committee the guarantee and Jaworski elaborated on his understanding to the Senators. Within six weeks of his appointment, and after examining the evidence, Jaworski visited Al Haig in the White House and suggested that it was time for the President to secure a criminal lawyer.

Press Conference, October 26, 1973

Role of New Prosecutor

Q: Mr. President, would the new special prosecutor have your go-ahead to go to court if necessary to obtain evidence from your files that he felt were vital?

A. Mr. Cormier, I would anticipate that that would not be necessary. I believe that as we look at the events which led to the dismissal of Mr. Cox, we find that these are matters that can be worked out and should be worked out in cooperation and not by having a suit filed by a special prosecutor within the Executive Branch against the President of the United States.

This, incidentally, is not a new attitude on the part of a President. Every President since George Washington has tried to protect the confidentiality of Presidential conversations and you remember the famous case involving Thomas Jefferson where Chief Justice Marshall, then sitting as a trial judge, subpoenaed the letter which Jefferson had written which Marshall thought or felt was necessary evidence in the trial of Aaron Burr. Jefferson refused to do so but it did not result in a suit. What happened was, of course, a compromise in which a summary of the contents of the letter which was relevant to the trial was produced by Jefferson and the Chief Justice of the United States, acting in his capacity as Chief Justice, accepted that.

That is exactly, of course, what we tried to do in this instant case.

I think it would be well if I could just take a moment, Mr. Cormier, in answering your question to point out what we tried to do and why we feel it was the proper solution to a very aggravating and difficult problem.

The matter of the tapes has been one that has concerned me because of my feeling that I have a Constitutional responsibility to defend the Office of the Presidency from any encroachments on confidentiality which might affect future Presidents in their abilities to conduct the kind of conversations and discussions they need to conduct to carry on the responsibilities of this Office. And, of course, the special prosecutor felt that he needed the tapes for the purpose of his prosecution. . . .

Now we come to a new special prosecutor. We will cooperate with him, and I do not anticipate that we will come to the time when he would consider it necessary to take the President to court. I think our cooperation will be adequate. . . .

Tapes: No Public Disclosure

Q: Mr. President, after the tapes are presented to Judge Sirica and they are processed under the procedure outlined by the U.S. Court of Appeals, will you make those tapes public?

A: No, that is not the procedure that the court has ordered, and it would not be proper. Judge Sirica, under the Circuit Court's order, is to listen to the tapes, and then is to present to the Grand Jury the pertinent evidence with regard to its investigation. Publication of the tapes has not been ordered by the Circuit Court of Appeals, and Judge Sirica, of course, would not do anything that would be in contravention of what the Circuit Court of Appeals has ordered.

Public Papers of the Presidents, Richard Nixon, 1973, 896–906.

Remarks of Acting Attorney General Robert H. Bork Announcing His Appointment of Leon Jaworski, November 1, 1973

Ladies and gentlemen, in my capacity as Acting Attorney General, I am announcing today that I have appointed Leon Jaworski as Special Prosecutor for the investigation of the Watergate matter and related subjects.

Mr. Jaworski is a distinguished member of the Bar, and he has a long record of outstanding public service. He has extensive prosecutorial experience. Born and raised in Texas, he personally prosecuted the first major war crime trials in the European theater during World War II. He later served as Special Assistant to the Attorney General in the Kennedy and Johnson Administrations, and as adviser to President Johnson.

In 1971 and 1972, Mr. Jaworski was president of the American Bar Association. He is also a past president of the American College of Trial Lawyers. Today, he is a senior partner in a Houston law firm, a position which he is relinquishing, of course, as he takes on this assignment.

As Special Prosecutor, Mr. Jaworski's jurisdiction will be defined in the same terms as those first established for his predecessor. He has been promised the full cooperation of the executive branch in the pursuit of his investigations. Should he disagree with a decision of the Administration with regard to the release of Presidential documents, there will be no restrictions placed on his freedom of action.

There is no expectation whatever that the President will ever have an occasion to exercise his constitutional right to discharge the Special Prosecutor or that it would ever be necessary in any way to limit the independence that he is being given. Should that expectation prove to be ill-founded, the President has given his personal assurance that he will not exercise his constitutional powers with regard to the Special Prosecutor without first consulting the majority and minority leaders and chairmen and ranking members of the Judiciary Committees of the Senate and the House and ascertaining that their consensus is in accord with his proposed action.

I want to point out that the decision to name Mr. Jaworski to this post is one I made personally. . . .

Presidential Documents, Richard Nixon, 1973, page 1303.

Jaworski's Understanding, November 20, 1973

Mr. JAWORSKI. Mr. Chairman, the call originally came from General Haig. He called me at my office in Houston.

And I told General Haig that I did not think there was any purpose in my coming to Washington to pursue the matter. He had suggested that I at least come and discuss it with him. And I told him that I had been approached, I imagine, some 2 or 3 weeks before Mr. Cox was employed, and the matter had been discussed with me by a gentleman who identified himself as the general counsel of then Secretary Elliot Richardson, a gentleman by the name of Hastings, I believe.

That had been a rather lengthy discussion over the telephone. And I had thought that the framework within which I was to operate was not one that gave me the independence that I wanted, that I thought I should have, that I thought was necessary in order to pursue the endeavor. And accordingly, I indicated no interest in the matter. And I did discuss with him others that might be interested, but cautioned him that I thought that the caliber of individual that was obtained would have direct relationship to the independence that was given to the Special Prosecutor.

General Haig told me that he thought that I could proceed on a different basis. And I mentioned to him—and I am trying to mention all of the highlights—that I felt unless there was such an independence as really reached the maximum within the President's power to give in connection with the appointment, that I first felt that I should not accept, and second, that I did not think it would be acceptable to the American people.

Whereupon General Haig suggested to me that the least I could do was come to Washington and discuss the matter with him.

I finally agreed to do this. And when I came to Washington I first met with General Haig for probably an hour or an hour and a half, during which time this matter was discussed in detail. And as a result of that discussion, there eventuated the arrangement that we have mentioned.

General Haig assured me that he would go and talk with the President, place the matter before him. And he came back and told me after a while, after maybe a lapse of 30 minutes or so, that it had been done, and that the President had agreed.

The CHAIRMAN. You are absolutely free to prosecute anyone; is that correct?

Mr. JAWORSKI. That is correct. And that is my intention.

The CHAIRMAN. And that includes the President of the United States?

Mr. JAWORSKI. It includes the President of the United States.

The CHAIRMAN. And you are proceeding that way?

Mr. JAWORSKI. I am proceeding that way.

Hearings: Special Prosecutor, Committee on the Judiciary,
U.S. Senate, 93 Cong., 1 Sess. , 569ff.

Jaworski Visits Haig

It was snowing as I rode to the White House. It was December 21 and I was going home for a few days, but Haig had called. We met in the Map Room, a private place where Franklin Roosevelt had charted the course of history during World War II.

We began talking about the tapes, the March 21 tape in particular, and Haig said it was terrible beyond description. I told him it was almost unbelievable. But, Haig said, the White House lawyers had told him there was no criminal offense involved as far as the President was concerned.

I shook my head. "I can't agree, Al. Based on what I heard—and what we already knew—I'm afraid the President engaged in criminal conduct."

Haig was upset. But he said he felt I was looking at the picture from the wrong perspective, that some of the facts were different from what I thought they were. He said he had a transcript of the tape that his people had spent long hours in obtaining. "I think it's better than yours," he said, "and I think you ought to look at it." This was an offer I wasn't about to turn down; if it were accurate, it would be better evidence than our own. He said I could have the transcript when I returned to Washington.

Haig continued to say that I was wrong, that he believed the White House lawyers. I told him, "Al, we have other evidence, but I don't have to go beyond what the recording says. It wouldn't be proper to discuss the other evidence, but it corroborates what's on the tape. The recording itself is an alarming thing, and the reason is because it shows conduct that is not only unethical and unprincipled and wrong, but I think suggests criminal culpability."

He shook his head, saying, "This is not what the lawyers say. Not at all what they say."

I said, "Al, I want to tell you something. I think you should get the finest criminal lawyer you can find—someone not connected with the White House in any way—and let him study the tapes."

We walked from the Map Room to the Diplomatic Entrance. I always entered and left this way so as not to attract attention. My car was brought to the door. The snow had blanketed the White House grounds. Haig was silent, thoughtful. "It's important, Al," I said. "Get that laywer, the best you can find."

Leon Jaworski, *The Right and the Power: The Prosecution of Watergate*
(New York, Reader's Digest Press, 1976), 53–54.

The 18½-Minute Tape Gap

In November, the country learned that one of the President's tapes contained a gap of eighteen-and-one-half minutes. Appearing before Judge Sirica to explain the matter, Chief of Staff Haig said that White House lawyers had first attributed the buzzing sound to "some outside source of energy," and not a malfunction of the machines. Haig thought that "perhaps some sinister force had come in and applied the other energy source and taken care of the information on the tape." Then Haig blamed the President's secretary, referring to the "alleged propensity of women to talk on the telephone for far longer periods than they either realize or admit," suggesting that she had held the erasure button down while on the telephone. In January 1974 an advisory panel examined the tape and reported to Sirica that it had been deliberately and methodically erased. The *National Review*, the pre-eminent conservative publication, realized that the tape gap made it more difficult for Nixon's defenders and further diminished his credibility.

Statement of Information

January 15, 1974
Report to Chief Judge John J. Sirica
From the Advisory Panel on the White House Tapes

In response to your request we have made a comprehensive technical study of the White House tape of June 20, 1972, with special attention to a section of buzzing sounds that lasts approximately 18.5 minutes. Paragraphs that follow summarize our findings and indicate the kinds of tests and evidence on which we base the findings.

Magnetic signatures that we have measured directly on the tape show that the buzzing sounds were put on the tape in the process of erasing and re-recording at least five, and perhaps as many as nine, separate and contiguous segments. Hand operation of keyboard controls on the Uher 5000 recorder was involved in starting and again in stopping the recording of each segment. The magnetic signatures observed on the tape show conclusively that the 18.5-minute section could not have been produced by any single, continuous operation. Further, whether the footpedal was used or not, the recording controls must have been operated by hand in the making of each segment.

The erasing and recording operations that produced the buzzing section were done directly on the tape we received for study. . . .

A Uher 5000 recorder, almost surely the one designated as Government Exhibit #60, was used in producing the 18.5-minute section. Support for this conclusion includes recorder operating characteristics that we measured and found to correspond to signal characteristics observed on the evidence tape.

The buzzing sounds themselves originated in noise picked up from the electrical power line to which the recorder was connected. Measurements of the frequency spectrum of the buzz showed that it is made up of a 60 cycles per second fundamental tone, plus a large number of harmonic tones at multiples of 60. Especially strong are the third harmonic at 180 and the fifth harmonic at 300 cycles per second. As many as forty harmonics are present in the buzz and create its "raucous" quality. Variations in the strength of the buzz, which during most of the 18.5-minute section is either "loud" or "soft," probably arose from several causes including variations in the noise on the power line, erratic functioning of the recorder, and changes in the position of the operator's hand while running the recorder. The variations do not appear to be caused by normal machine operations.

Can speech sounds be detected under the buzzing? We think so. At three locations in the 18.5-minute section, we have observed a fragment of speech-like sound lasting less than one second. Each of the fragments lies exactly at a place on the tape that was missed by the erase head during the series of operations in which the several segments of erasure and buzz were put on the tape. Further, the frequency spectra of the sounds in these fragments bear a reasonable resemblance to the spectra of speech sounds.

Can the speech be recovered? We think not. We know of no technique that could recover intelligible speech from the buzz section. Even the fragments that we have observed are so heavily obscured that we cannot tell what was said. . . .

HJC 79:1 Advisory Panel Report.

National Review,
December 21, 1973

Someone, it is clear, erased those 18 minutes of conversation on the White House tape, the segment between Nixon and Haldeman that happened to contain all references to Watergate on that reel.

Miss Rose Mary Woods, who has been Richard Nixon's personal secretary for over twenty years, and also an intimate of the Nixon family, first said that she had erased the portion accidentally while transcribing the reel. She later drew back a bit from that explanation: "People keep telling me I must have." She also expressed the view that she did not see how she could have been responsible for erasing the entire 18-minute segment. The tape is now being examined by technicians in New York but, whatever such examination shows, few at this point would disagree with the following statement: The accidental erasure of just that 18-minute sequence would require an extraordinary combination of mechanical and other coincidences (believers in the accidental theory could gather for lunch in a phone booth).

Isolated, the accidental theory is not, at least pending the technical analysis, impossible. In the realm of history, very strange things actually do occur.

The trouble is that this item is not isolated, but part of a sequence of such items in the Watergate epic, the improbability of the most recent item enhanced still further by all that has gone before. Miss Wood's initial account would be more believable if two other presumptively important tapes had not been found to be nonexistent. This, in turn, would have been more believable if, in an otherwise efficient White House, the records regarding possession of the tapes had not been remarkably sloppy, and if various reels had not circulated among an undetermined number of aides. The sloppy records, in themselves, would not have been all that suspicious, though suspicious, if the White House had not for so long argued the supreme importance of the confidentiality of the tapes. The effect of these events is cumulative. Someone remarked recently that if Richard Nixon tomorrow said his middle name was "Milhous," hardly anyone is left who would believe him. Nixon's defenders are hard put.

VII
The
Final Agony:
Impeachment,
Resignation,
Pardon

Nixon Embattled

By 1974, Nixon was confronting a variety of issues, including probes into his financial affairs. He had used government funds illegally to improve his residences, backdated his gift of his vice-presidential papers to qualify for a special deduction, and left unpaid more than $400,000 in income taxes. "I am not a crook," Nixon publicly proclaimed. Nevertheless, these revelations proved painfully embarrassing to an Administration and a President committed to law and order. In private, Nixon persisted in his resolve to "fight."

At the beginning of March, the Watergate grand jury returned indictments against Mitchell, Haldeman, Ehrlichman, and others for conspiracy and perjury. A week later, it indicted Ehrlichman, Colson, Liddy, and others for their role in the break-in of the offices of Daniel Ellsberg's psychiatrist. But new demands for tapes from both the Special Prosecutor and the House Impeachment Inquiry proved most threatening. On April 11, Jaworski told the President's lawyer, James D. St. Clair, that he would subpoena more tapes in order to prepare for the trial of Mitchell, Haldeman, and Ehrlichman. Five weeks later, Judge Sirica granted the subpoena, which set the stage for the subsequent Supreme Court hearing on the matter. In the meantime, Nixon, in response to the House Inquiry, released tape transcripts on April 29, 1974. Again, however, he refused to surrender certain specified items, provoking what Peter Rodino, the House Committee Chairman, called a "grave matter." The public reaction to the tape transcripts proved even graver for Nixon. The language, the scheming, and the lack of concern alarmed even the President's most ardent supporters. A *Chicago Tribune* editorial urged the President to resign and avoid impeachment.

"Fight!"

Fight because if I am forced to resign the press will become a much too dominant force in the nation, not only in this administration but for years to come. Fight because resignation would set a precedent and result in a permanent and very destructive change in our whole constitutional system. Fight because resignation could lead to a collapse of our foreign policy initiatives. . . .

Decision to fight:
    1. Resign sets precedent—admits guilt.
    2. Lets down friends.
    3. Fight now makes possible fight for future as a man of principle.
    4. Only substance, not politics, must affect this decision.
Priorities:
    1. Press conference and media meetings.
    2. Organize our hard core in the House, Senate, among top governors and our friends like Kendall, etc., who were working under Flanigan's direction.
    3. Mobilize the Cabinet.
    4. Buck up the staff.
Substantive areas:
    1. Rodino, Jaworski, et al.
    2. Foreign policy initiatives.
    3. Run the shop well on the domestic front (energy, et al.).
Style:
    1. Confidence.
    2. Compassion.
    3. Color—the necessity for the interesting.
Be *strong* against unprecedented adversity but avoid intemperate remarks or conduct. . . .

Above all else: Dignity, command, faith, head high, no fear, build a new spirit, drive, act like a President, act like a winner. Opponents are savage destroyers, haters. Time to use full power of the President to fight overwhelming forces arrayed against us.

Richard M. Nixon, *Memoirs* (New York, 1978), 970–71.

Statement of Information,
March 1, 7, 1974

MARCH 1, 1974

THE FOLLOWING INDICTMENT WAS HANDED DOWN BY A FEDERAL GRAND JURY IN WASHINGTON TODAY:

NAMES:
Charles Colson, 42, McLean, Virginia
John Ehrlichman, 48, Seattle, Washington
Harry R. Haldeman, 47, Los Angeles, California
Robert C. Mardian, 50, Phoenix, Arizona
John Mitchell, 60, New York, New York
Kenneth W. Parkinson, 46, Washington, D.C.
Gordon Strachan, 30, Salt Lake City, Utah

CHARGES:
All defendants were charged with one count of conspiracy (Title 18, USC, §S371).

The following defendants were indicted on additional charges:

MITCHELL: One count of violation of 18, USC, §1503 (Obstruction of Justice), two counts of violation of 18, USC, §1623 (Making false declaration to Grand Jury or Court), one count of violation of 18, USC, §1621 (Perjury) and one count of violation of 18, USC, §1001 (Making false statement to agents of the Federal Bureau of Investigation).

EHRLICHMAN: One count of violation of 18, USC, §1503 (Obstruction of Justice), one count of violation of 18, USC, §1001 (Making false statement to agents of the Federal Bureau of Investigation) and two counts of violation of 18, USC, §1623 (Making false declaration to Grand Jury or Court).

HALDEMAN: One count of violation of 18, USC, §1503 (Obstruction of Justice), three counts of violation of 18, USC, §1621 (Perjury).

STRACHAN: One count of violation of 18, USC, §1503 (Obstruction of Justice), one count of violation of 18, USC, §1623 (Making false declaration to Grand Jury or Court).

MARCH 7, 1974

THE FOLLOWING INDICTMENT WAS HANDED DOWN BY A FEDERAL GRAND JURY IN WASHINGTON TODAY:

NAMES:
John Ehrlichman, 48, Seattle, Washington
Charles Colson, 42, McLean, Virginia
G. Gordon Liddy, 43, Oxon Hill, Maryland
Bernard L. Barker, 56, Miami, Florida

Felipe De Diego, 45, Miami, Florida
Eugenio Martinez, 51, Miami, Florida
CHARGE:
Each defendant was charged with a single count of violation of Title 13, USC, Section 241, Conspiracy against rights of citizens. *

Ehrlichman was also charged with one count of violation of Title 18, USC, Section 1001, making false statement to agents of the Federal Bureau of Investigation, and three counts of violation of Title 18, USC, Section 1623, making false declaration to grand jury or court.

*Named as co-conspirators, but not indicted, were the following: Egil Krogh, Jr., E. Howard Hunt, Jr., and David R. Young. Krogh pleaded guilty on November 30, 1973, to a charge of violation of Title 18, USC, Section 241. Hunt was granted immunity by order of U.S. District Court Chief Judge John J. Sirica on March 28, 1973. Young was granted immunity by Chief Judge Sirica on May 16, 1973.

Statement of Information, House Judiciary Committee, Watergate Special Prosecution Force Press Releases, March 1, 7, 1974, pp. 960–62.

Statement of Information, April 11, 1974

April 11, 1974
James D. St. Clair, Esq.
Special Counsel to the President
The White House
Washington, D.C.

Dear Mr. St. Clair:

On March 12, 1974, I wrote to you requesting access to certain taped conversations and related documents that must be examined and analyzed as the Government prepares for trial in *United States* v. *Mitchell*. If the President declines to produce these materials, which we deem necessary for trial, I am compelled by my responsibilities to seek appropriate judicial process. As I indicated in my letter, any judicial proceedings, if they are necessary, must be initiated promptly in order to avoid unnecessary trial delays.

I have conferred with you several times during the last month about this matter. I have delayed seeking a subpoena in the hope that the President would comply with our request voluntarily. Indeed, I have sought no more at this time than an assurance that the materials would be provided sufficiently in advance of trial to allow thorough preparation. Your latest communication to this office was that we would receive any materials the President produces to the Committee on the Judiciary of the House of Representatives. As to other materials requested by my letter, you have said you would not consider our request until the

President decided what to provide the House Judiciary Committee. I have emphasized repeatedly that our request is in no way tied to the requests of the House Judiciary Committee. The requests are distinguishable both factually and legally. Nevertheless, you have refused to consider them separately, and you have been unable to tell us the criteria that will govern the President's response to our request or to assure us when we will receive a definitive response.

Under these circumstances, in accordance with my responsibilities to secure a prompt and fair trial for the Government and the defendants in *United States* v. *Mitchell*, I am obliged to seek a subpoena for those materials we deem necessary for trial. Accordingly, on Tuesday, April 16, we will apply to Judge Sirica for a trial subpoena pursuant to Rule 17 (c) of the Federal Rules of Criminal Procedure.

Sincerely,
LEON JAWORSKI
Special Prosecutor

Statement of Information, House Judiciary Committee,
Jaworski to St. Clair, April 11, 1974, pp. 974–75.

Judge Sirica's Opinion in *United States* v. *Nixon*, May 20, 1974

This matter comes before the Court on motion of President Richard M. Nixon to quash a subpoena *duces tecum* issued to him by the Watergate Special Prosecutor with leave of this Court. . . .

In entering a special appearance, the President contends that the Court lacks jurisdiction to enforce the instant subpoena on two grounds: First, courts are without authority to rule on the scope or applicability of executive privilege when asserted by the President, and Second, a dispute between the President and Special Prosecutor regarding the production of evidence is an intra-branch controversy wholly within the jurisdiction of the executive branch to resolve. The first contention, as the President admits, is without legal force in this Circuit.

The second argument, whatever its merits in the setting of a disagreement between the President and a cabinet officer, for example, has no application to the present situation. The current Special Prosecutor is vested with the powers and authority conferred upon his predecessor pursuant to regulations which have the force of law. Among other prerogatives, the Special Prosecutor has "full authority" to determine "whether or not to contest the assertion of 'Executive Privilege' or any other testimonial privilege." The Special Prosecutor's independence has been affirmed and reaffirmed by the President and his representatives, and a unique guarantee of unfettered operation accorded him: "the jurisdiction of the Special Prosecutor will not be limited without the President's first consulting with such Members of Congress [the leaders of both Houses and the respective Committees on the Judiciary] and ascertaining that their consensus is in accord with his proposed action." The President not having so consulted, to the Court's knowledge, his attempt to abridge the Special Prosecutor's independence with the argument that he cannot seek evidence from the President by court process is a nullity and does not defeat the Court's jurisdiction.

The President advances three principal arguments on the merits supporting his motion to quash. Primary among these is his assertion that the subpoena, together with the Special Prosecutor's showing of relevancy and evidentiary value filed May 10, 1974, fails to comply with the requirements of Rule 17(c). It is conceded by all parties that Rule 17(c) cannot be employed as a vehicle for discovery, and that a showing of good cause is necessary. . . . Basically, good cause under Rule 17(c) requires a showing that (1) subpoenaed materials are evidentiary and relevant; (2) they are not otherwise procurable reasonably in advance of trial; (3) the party cannot properly prepare for trial without them, and failure to obtain them may delay the trial; and (4) the application is made in good faith, and does not constitute a "fishing expedition." See *United States* v. *Iozia, supra*, 13 F.R.D. at 338. It is the Court's position that the Special Prosecutor's May 10, 1974 memorandum correctly applies the Rule 17(c) standards, particularly in the more unusual situation of this kind where the subpoena, rather than being directed to the government by defendants, issues to what, as a practical matter, is a third party. It is the Court's conclusion as well, supported again by reference to the Special Prosecutor's memorandum and appendix, that the requirements of Rule 17(c) are here met.

With regard to the confidentiality privilege interposed by the President, the Court agrees that his claim is presumptively valid. The Special Prosecutor's submissions, however, in the Court's opinion, constitute a *prima facie* showing adequate to rebut the presumption in each instance, and a demonstration of need sufficiently compelling to warrant judicial examination in chambers incident to weighing claims of privilege where the privilege has not been relinquished. In citing relinquishment of privilege, the Court has reference to the portions of subpoenaed recordings which the President has caused to be reduced to transcript form and published. For such, the Court finds the privilege claimed nonexistent since the conversations are, to that extent at least, no longer confidential. . . .

U.S. v. Nixon, U.S.D.C., Dist. of Columbia, 74–110.

Address to the Nation, April 29, 1974

The President's Address to the Nation Announcing His Answer to the Subpoena From the House Judiciary Committee. April 29, 1974

Good evening:

I have asked for this time tonight in order to announce my answer to the House Judiciary Committee's subpoena for additional Watergate tapes, and to tell you something about the actions I shall be taking tomorrow—about what I hope they will mean to you and about the very difficult choices that were presented to me.

These actions will at last, once and for all, show that what I knew and what I did with regard to the Watergate break-in and coverup were just as I have described them to you from the very beginning. . . .

In these folders that you see over here on my left are more than 1,200 pages of transcripts of private conversations I participated in between September 15, 1972, and April 27 of 1973, with my principal aides and associates with regard to Watergate. They include all the relevant portions of all of the subpoenaed conversations that were recorded, that is, all portions that relate to the question of what I knew about Watergate or the coverup and what I did about it.

They also include transcripts of other conversations which were not subpoenaed, but which have a significant bearing on the question of Presidential actions with regard to Watergate. These will be delivered to the committee tomorrow.

In these transcripts, portions not relevant to my knowledge or actions with regard to Watergate are not included, but everything that is relevant is included—the rough as well as the smooth, the strategy sessions, the exploration of alternatives, the weighing of human and political costs.

As far as what the President personally knew and did with regard to Watergate and the coverup is concerned, these materials—together with those already made available—will tell it all.

For many days now, I have spent many hours of my own time personally reviewing these materials, and personally deciding questions of relevancy. I believe it is appropriate that the committee's review should also be made by its own senior elected officials, and not by staff employees. . . .

Ever since the existence of the White House taping system was first made known last summer, I have tried vigorously to guard the privacy of the tapes. I have been well aware that my effort to protect the confidentiality of Presidential conversations has heightened the sense of mystery about Watergate and, in fact, has caused increased suspicions of the President. Many people assume that the tapes must incriminate the President, or that otherwise, he would not insist on their privacy.

But the problem I confronted was this: Unless a President can protect the privacy of the advice he gets, he cannot get the advice he needs.

This principle is recognized in the constitutional doctrine of executive privilege, which has been defended and maintained by every President since Washington and which has been recognized by the courts whenever tested as inherent in the Presidency. I consider it to be my constitutional responsibility to defend this principle.

Three factors have now combined to persuade me that a major unprecedented exception to that principle is now necessary.

First, in the present circumstances, the House of Representatives must be able to reach an informed judgment about the President's role in Watergate.

Second, I am making a major exception to the principle of confidentiality because I believe such action is now necessary in order to restore the principle itself, by clearing the air of the central question that has brought such pressures upon it—and also to provide the evidence which will allow this matter to be brought to a prompt conclusion.

Third, in the context of the current impeachment climate, I believe all the American people, as well as their Representatives in Congress, are entitled to have not only the facts but also the evidence that demonstrates those facts.

I want there to be no question remaining about the fact that the President has nothing to hide in this matter.

The impeachment of a President is a remedy of last resort; it is the most solemn act of our entire constitutional process. Now, regardless of whether or not it succeeded, the action of the House in voting a formal accusation requiring trial by the Senate would put the Nation through a wrenching ordeal it has endured only once in its lifetime, a century ago, and never since America has become a world power with global responsibilities. . . .

I have been reluctant to release these tapes not just because they will embarrass me and those with whom I have talked—which they will—and not just because they will become the subject of speculation and even ridicule—which they will—and not just because certain parts of them will be seized upon by political and journalistic opponents—which they will.

I have been reluctant because in these and in all the other conversations in this office, people have spoken their minds freely, never dreaming that specific sentences or even parts of sentences would be picked out as the subjects of national attention and controversy.

I have been reluctant because the principle of confidentiality is absolutely essential to the conduct of the Presidency. In reading the raw transcripts of these conversations, I believe it will be more readily apparent why the principle is essential and must be maintained in the future. These conversations are unusual in their subject matter, but the same kind of uninhibited discussion—and it is that—the same brutal candor, is necessary in discussing how to bring warring factions to the peace table or how to move necessary legislation through the Congress. . . .

And then I was quite frankly concerned about the political implications. This represented potentially a devastating blow to the Administration and to its programs, one which I knew would be exploited for all it was worth by hostile elements in the Congress as well as in the media. I wanted to do what was right, but I wanted to do it in a way that would cause the least unnecessary damage in a highly charged political atmosphere to the Administration. . . .

Public Papers of the Presidents, Richard Nixon, 1974, 389–97.

Peter Rodino: A "grave matter"

The President
The White House
Washington, D.C.

Dear Mr. President:
The Committee on the Judiciary has authorized and directed me to reply to your letter of May 22 in which you decline to produce the tapes of Presidential conversations and Presidential diaries called for in the Committee's subpoenas served on you on May 15, 1974. You also decline to produce any other material dealing with Watergate that may be called for in any further subpoenas that may be issued by the Committee.

The Committee on the Judiciary regards your refusal to comply with its lawful subpoenas as a grave matter. Under the Constitution it is not within the power of the President to conduct an inquiry into his own impeachment, to determine which evidence, and what version or portion of that evidence, is relevant and necessary to such an inquiry. These are matters which, under the Constitution, the House has the sole power to determine.

In meeting their constitutional responsibility, Committee members will be free to consider whether your refusals warrant the drawing of adverse inferences concerning the substance of materials, and whether your refusals in and of themselves might constitute a ground for impeachment. . . .

Respectfully,
PETER W. RODINO, JR.
Chairman

House Judiciary Committee, Statement of Information,
Rodino to Nixon, May 30, 1974, pp. 1065–66.

Chicago Tribune, May 9, 1974

We saw the public man in his first administration, and we were impressed. Now in about 300,000 words we have seen the private man, and we are appalled.

What manner of man is the Richard Nixon who emerges from the transcripts of the White House tapes?

We see a man who, in the words of his old friend and defender, Sen. Hugh Scott, took a principal role in a "shabby, immoral and disgusting performance."

The key word here is immoral. It is a lack of concern for morality, a lack of concern for high principles, a lack of commitment to the high ideals of public office that make the transcripts a sickening exposure of the man and his advisers. He is preoccupied with appearance rather than substance. His aim is to find a way to sell the idea that disreputable schemes are actually good or are defensible for some trumped-up cause.

He is humorless to the point of being inhumane. He is devious. He is vacillating. He is profane. He is willing to be led. He displays dismaying gaps in knowledge. He is suspicious of his staff. His loyalty is minimal. His greatest concern is to create a record that will save him and his administration. The high dedication to grand principles that Americans have a right to expect from a President is missing from the transcript record.

Mr. Nixon's strategy backfired when he released the transcripts. It was also a strategic error for him to release the record of his income taxes. Both stripped the man to his essential character, and that character could not stand that kind of scrutiny. Both miscalculations demonstrated an essential Nixon defect—an insensitivity to the standards of ethics and morality that Americans expect of their leaders.

He thought disclosure of the records would help him. He has had a demonstration that his countrymen are not that tolerant.

And it should be noted here that the transcripts and the income tax statement were not the fabrications of his enemies. These were self-created instruments of destruction.

His decision Tuesday to disclose no more information leaves the record as it now stands. And as it stands that record leaves no doubt that he lacks the qualities that could edify and inspire his countrymen with confidence in these difficult times.

The statement of his counsel, James St. Clair, that the President is ready for a confrontation with Congress and his own special prosecutor is ominous.

The balance among the coordinate branches of our government—Executive, Judicial, and Legislative—is fragile. It has been established on rather comfortably loose terms by nearly 200 years of experience in practicing the special virtues of American government.

The limits of executive privilege, of congressional power, of judicial authority are not rigidly fixed. We would not relish the prospect of forcing the Supreme Court to make hard decisions in the distorting heat of partisan controversy. This is one confrontation this country does not need and we pray Mr. Nixon will not insist on it.

The President is right in urging a quick end to the Watergate affair. His country needs a swift and merciful termination of this agony.

Two roads are open. One is resignation. The other is impeachment. Both are legitimate and would satisfy the need to observe due process.

Resignation of the President would be quick and simple and a qualified successor stands ready to assume office.

Impeachment is the judicial process prescribed by the Constitution for removing a President. The House can, and probably will, vote a bill of impeachment quickly. A trial in the Senate would be, and indeed should be, long and deliberate. No suggestion of haste or mob justice could be tolerated. The White House could be expected to seize every opportunity for challenge and delay, and the final outcome might be two years in coming.

The objection to resignation that has been raised—and we have raised it ourselves—is that it would not resolve the issues. It would not answer many of the questions about the President's behavior and degree of complicity. It would leave at least a suspicion that the President had been persecuted instead of properly prosecuted out of office. To some he might remain a martyr. To many it would seem a miscarriage of justice, as an example of political exorcism. . . .

We do not share the White House belief that impeachment requires evidence of a specific crime. We believe a President may be removed simply for failing to do his job, or for so discrediting himself that he loses public respect and, with it, his ability to govern effectively.

It is true that this vagueness may tempt opponents to seek to remove a President for political or otherwise inadequate reasons, as they did with Andrew Johnson. But that risk must be accepted. The ultimate arbiter in this matter must be the public, and the public reaction today is clearly one of revulsion. Republican politicians are defecting in droves. The evidence against Mr. Nixon is in his own words, made public at his own direction. There can no longer be a charge that he was railroaded out of office by vengeful Democrats or a hostile press. The fundamental questions have been answered. Filling in the gaps in the transcripts can only make the case against the President stronger.

And so the objections to resignation have largely vanished.

Since the President has rejected this course, we urge the House to act quickly on a bill of impeachment. As the impeachment process progresses, as public opinion becomes clear, and as Mr. Nixon sees support dwindling in the Senate, he will have to reconsider his stand and recognize that resignation will spare the country the ordeal of a trial. . . .

It is saddening and hard to believe that for the first time in our history, it is better that the President leave office than fight to keep it. But things have reached such a state that Mr. Nixon's departure, one way or another, is the best course for the Presidency, the country, and the free world. To perpetuate a state of confrontation between the Executive and Congress—in order to define the limits of power which are probably better undefined—will be tragically costly in the eyes of history and the world.

The
Impeachment Inquiry

The Saturday Night Massacre in October 1973 had spurred the drive for impeachment. The House of Representatives, pursuant to its constitutional duties, began an inquiry in November. Formal House approval for an investigation came on February 6, 1974. Article I, Section 2 of the Constitution provides that the House has "the sole power of impeachment." But for nearly 185 years, political leaders and constitutional authorities had periodically debated the scope and meaning of the impeachment power. The House Judiciary Committee had its own staff, which sifted through evidence garnered by the Senate Select Committee, the United States Attorney's office, and the Special Prosecutor. For three days, beginning on July 18, the Committee heard from the President's Counsel, James St. Clair, who summarized the case for the President, and its own Chief Counsel, John Doar, who presented the argument for impeachment. The Judiciary Committee began televised hearings on the evening of July 24, following the Supreme Court's verdict in *U.S. v. Nixon*. Chairman Peter Rodino (D-NJ) and ranking minority member Edward Hutchinson (R-MI) opened the proceedings with partisan statements, but they underlined the solemnity and seriousness of the affair. Two days later, six Republicans joined twenty-one Democrats to vote three articles of impeachment, including charges of obstruction of justice, abuses of power, and contempt of the House for failing to respond to its subpoenas. The first charge passed by a vote of twenty-seven to eleven and the second by twenty-eight to ten, with six Republicans joining twenty-one Democrats. Two articles, relating to the President's alleged failure to notify Congress of his orders to bomb Cambodia and his tax liabilities, failed to pass. The bipartisan support resulted from the efforts of the "Fragile Coalition," a group of four Republicans and three southern Democrats who normally supported the President but now found the case for impeachment overwhelming.

Impeachment and the Constitution

I: Introduction

The Constitution deals with the subject of impeachment and conviction at six places. The scope of the power is set out in Article II, Section 4:

"The President, Vice President and all civil Officers of the United States, shall be removed from Office on Impeachment for, and Conviction of, Treason, Bribery, or other high Crimes and Misdemeanors."

Other provisions deal with procedures and consequences. Article I, Section 2 states:

"The House of Representatives . . . shall have the sole Power of Impeachment."

Similarly, Article I, Section 3, describes the Senate's role:

"The Senate shall have the sole Power to try all Impeachments. When sitting for that Purpose, they shall be on Oath or Affirmation. When the President of the United States is tried, the Chief Justice shall preside: And no Person shall be convicted without the Concurrence of two thirds of the Members present."

The same section limits the consequences of judgment in cases of impeachment:

"Judgment in Cases of Impeachment shall not extend further than to removal from Office, and disqualification to hold and enjoy any Office of honor, Trust or Profit under the United States: but the Party convicted shall nevertheless be liable and subject to Indictment, Trial, Judgment and Punishment, according to law."

Of lesser significance, although mentioning the subject, are: Article II, Section 2:

"The President . . . shall have Power to grant Reprieves and Pardons for Offenses against the United States, except in Cases of Impeachment."

Article III, Section 2:

"The Trial of all Crimes, except in Cases of Impeachment, shall be by Jury. . . ."

On February 6, 1974, the House of Representatives by a vote of 410 to 4 "authorized and directed" the Committee on the Judiciary "to investigate fully and completely whether sufficient grounds exist for the House of Representatives to exercise its constitutional power to impeach Richard M. Nixon, President of the United States of America."

To implement the authorization (H.Res. 803) the House also provided that "For the purpose of making such investigation, the committee is authorized to require . . . by subpoena or otherwise . . . the attendance and testimony of any person . . . and . . . the production of such things; and . . . by interrogatory, the furnishing of such information, as it deems necessary to such investigation."

This was but the second time in the history of the United States that the House of Representatives resolved to investigate the possibility of impeachment of a President. Some 107 years earlier the House had investigated whether President Andrew Johnson should be impeached. Understandably, little attention or thought has been given the subject of the presidential impeachment process during the intervening years. . . .

The House has set in motion an unusual constitutional process, conferred solely upon it by the Constitution, by directing the Judiciary Committee to "investigate fully and completely whether sufficient grounds exist for the House of Representatives to exercise its constitutional power to impeach." This action was not partisan. It was supported by the overwhelming majority of both political parties. Nor was it intended to obstruct or weaken the presidency. It was supported by Members firmly committed to the need for a strong presidency and a healthy executive branch of our government. . . .

IV: Conclusion

Impeachment is a constitutional remedy addressed to serious offenses against the system of government. The purpose of impeachment under the the Constitution is indicated by the limited scope of the remedy (removal from office and possible disqualification from future office) and by stated grounds for impeachment (treason, bribery and other high crimes and misdemeanors). It is not controlling whether treason and bribery are criminal. More important, they are constitutional wrongs that subvert the structure of government, or undermine the integrity of office and even the Constitution itself, and thus are "high" offenses in the sense that word was used in English impeachments.

The framers of our Constitution consciously adopted a particular phrase from the English practice to help define the constitutional grounds for removal. The content of the phrase "high Crimes and Misdemeanors" for the framers is to be related to what the framers knew, on the whole, about the English practice—the broad sweep of English constitutional history and the vital role impeachment had played in the limitation of royal prerogative and the control of abuses of ministerial and judicial power.

Impeachment was not a remote subject for the framers. Even as they labored in Philadelphia, the impeachment trial of Warren Hastings, Governor-General of India, was pending in London, a fact to which George Mason made explicit reference in the Convention. Whatever may be said on the merits of Hastings' conduct, the charges against him exemplified the central aspect of impeachment—the parliamentary effort to reach grave abuses of governmental power.

The framers understood quite clearly that the constitutional system they were creating must include some ultimate check on the conduct of the executive, particularly as they came to reject the suggested plural executive. While insistent that balance beween the executive and legislative branches be maintained so that the executive would not become the creature of the legislature, dismissable at its will, the framers also recognized that some means would be needed to deal with excesses by the executive. Impeachment was familiar to them. They understood its essential constitutional functions and perceived its adaptability to the American context.

While it may be argued that some articles of impeachment have charged conduct that constituted crime and thus that criminality is an essential ingredient, or that some have charged conduct that was not criminal and thus that criminality is not essential, the fact remains that in the English practice and in several of the American impeachments the criminality issue was not raised at all. The emphasis has been on the significant effects of the conduct—undermining the integrity of office, disregard of constitutional duties and oath of office, arrogation of power, abuse of the governmental process, adverse impact on the system of government. Clearly, these effects can be brought about in ways not anticipated by the criminal law. Criminal standards and criminal courts were established to control individual conduct. Impeachment was evolved by Parliament to cope with both the inadequacy of criminal standards and the impotence of courts to deal with the conduct of great public figures. It would be anomalous if the framers, having barred criminal sanctions from the impeachment remedy and limited it to removal and possible disqualification from office, intended to restrict the grounds for impeachment to conduct that was criminal.

The longing for precise criteria is understandable; advance, precise definition of objective limits would seemingly serve both to direct future conduct and to inhibit arbitrary reaction to past conduct. In private affairs the objective is the control of personal behavior, in part through the punishment of misbehavior. In general, advance definition of standards respecting private conduct works reasonably well. However, where the issue is presidential compliance with the constitutional requirements and limitations on the presidency, the crucial factor is not the intrinsic quality of behavior but the significance of its effect upon our constitutional system or the functioning of our government.

It is useful to note three major presidential duties of broad scope that are explicitly recited in the Constitution: "to take Care that the Laws be faithfully executed," to "faithfully execute the Office of President of the United States" and to "preserve, protect and defend the Constitution of the United States" to the best of his ability. The first is directly imposed by the Constitution; the second and third are included in the constitutionally prescribed oath that the President is required to take before he enters upon the execution of his office and are, therefore, also expressly imposed by the Constitution.

The duty to take care is affirmative. So is the duty faithfully to execute the office. A President must carry out the obligations of his office diligently and in good faith. The elective character and political role of a President make it difficult to define faithful exercise of his powers in the abstract. A President must make policy and exercise discretion. This discretion necessarily is broad, especially in emergency situations, but the constitutional duties of a President impose limitations on its exercise.

The "take care" duty emphasizes the responsibility of a President for the overall conduct of the executive branch, which the Constitution vests in him alone. He must take care that the executive is so organized and operated that this duty is performed.

The duty of a President to "preserve, protect, and defend the Constitution" to the best of his ability includes the duty not to abuse his powers or transgress their limits—not to violate the rights of citizens, such as those guaranteed by the Bill of Rights, and not to act in derogation of powers vested elsewhere by the Constitution.

Not all presidential misconduct is sufficient to constitute grounds for impeachment. There is a further requirement—substantiality. In deciding whether this further requirement has been met, the facts must be considered as a whole in the context of the office, not in terms of separate or isolated events. Because impeachment of a President is a grave step for the nation, it is to be predicated only upon conduct seriously incompatible with either the constitutional form and principles of our government or the proper performance of constitutional duties of the presidential office.

Impeachment Inquiry Staff, House Judiciary Committee, Constitutional Grounds for Presidential Impeachment, 93 Cong. 2 Sess. 1974, 1–3, 26–27.

Debate on Articles of Impeachment, July 24, 1974

Peter W. Rodino, Jr.

The CHAIRMAN. Before I begin, I hope you will allow me a personal reference. Throughout all of the painstaking proceedings of this committee, I as the chairman have been guided by a simple principle, the principle that the law must deal fairly with every man. For me, this is the oldest principle of democracy. It is this simple, but great principle which enables man to live justly and in decency in a free society.

It is now almost 15 centuries since the Emperor Justinian, from whose name the word "justice" is derived, established this principle for free citizens of Rome. Seven centuries have now passed since the English barons proclaimed the same principle by compelling King John, at the point of the sword, to accept a great doctrine of Magna Carta, the doctrine that the king, like each of his subjects, was under God and the law.

Almost two centuries ago the Founding Fathers of the United States reaffirmed and refined this principle so that here all men are under the law, and it is only the people who are sovereign. So speaks our Constitution, and it is under our Constitution, the supreme law of our land, that we proceed through the sole power of impeachment.

We have reached the moment when we are ready to debate resolutions whether or not the Committee on the Judiciary should recommend that the House of Representatives adopt articles calling for the impeachment of Richard M. Nixon.

Make no mistake about it. This is a turning point, whatever we decide. Our judgment is not concerned with an individual but with a system of constitutional government.

It has been the history and the good fortune of the United States, ever since the Founding Fathers, that each generation of citizens, and their officials have been, within tolerable limits, faithful custodians of the Constitution and of the rule of law.

For almost 200 years every generation of Americans has taken care to preserve our system, and the integrity of our institutions, against the particular pressures and emergencies to which every time is subject.

This committee must now decide a question of the highest constitutional importance. For more than 2 years, there have been serious allegations, by people of good faith and sound intelligence, that the President, Richard M. Nixon, has committed grave and systematic violations of the Constitution.

Last October, in the belief that such violations had in fact occurred, a number of impeachment resolutions were introduced by Members of the House and referred to our committee by the Speaker. On February 6, the House of Representatives, by a vote of 410 to 4, authorized and directed the Committee on the Judiciary to investigate whether sufficient grounds exist to impeach Richard M. Nixon, President of the United States. . . .

The Founding Fathers clearly did not mean that a President might be impeached for mistakes, even serious mistakes, which he might commit in the faithful execution of his office. By "high crimes and misdemeanors" they meant offenses more definitely incompatible with our Constitution.

The Founding Fathers, with their recent experience of monarchy and their determination that government should be accountable and lawful, wrote into the Constitution a special oath that the President, and only the President, must take at his inauguration. In that oath, the President swears that he will take care that the laws be faithfully executed.

The Judiciary Committee has for 7 months investigated whether or not the President has seriously abused his power, in violation of that oath and the public trust embodied in it.

We have investigated fully and completely what within our Constitution and traditions would be grounds for impeachment. For the past 10 weeks, we have listened to the presentation of evidence in documentary form, to tape recordings of 19 Presidential conversations, and to the testimony of nine witnesses called before the entire committee.

We have provided a fair opportunity for the President's counsel to present the President's views to the committee. We have taken care to preserve the integrity of the process in which we are engaged.

We have deliberated. We have been patient. We have been fair. Now, the American people, the House of Representatives, the Constitution, and the whole history of our Republic demand that we make up our minds. . . .

It must be decided whether the President was deceived by his subordinates into believing that his personal agents and key political associates had not been engaged in a systematic coverup of the illegal political intelligence operation, of the identities of those responsible, and of the existence and scope of other related activities; or whether, in fact, Richard M. Nixon, in violation of the sacred obligation of his constitutional oath, has used the power of his high office for over 2 years to cover up and conceal responsibility for the Watergate burglary and other activities of a similar nature.

In short, the committee has to decide whether in his statement of April 30 and other public statements the President was telling the truth to the American people, or whether that statement and other statements were part of a pattern of conduct designed not to take care that the laws were faithfully executed, but to impede their faithful execution for his political interest and on his behalf.

There are other critical questions that must be decided. We must decide whether the President abused his power in the execution of his office. . . .

Edward Hutchinson

During the next few days, we will be weighing the evidence and acting upon it. After a period of general debate, we will be discussing amendments and voting upon them. And finally, the end product of our deliberations will be manifest. Either we shall by majority vote have recommended one or more grounds for impeachment against the President, or all of those proposed for adoption will have been defeated in our deliberations.

The people will have an unusual glimpse into the discussions of those charged with the decisionmaking in a unique judicial process. But perhaps ours is more a political than a judicial function after all. The fact is that, of course, judges and juries deliberate behind closed doors, but by the committee's action in opening these discussions, it has, in effect, determined that our function is more political that judicial. I think the public should know that until now the only decisions made by this committee have been procedural ones. No substantive matter has yet been resolved.

Early in the inquiry the staff submitted a memorandum on what constitutes an impeachable offense within the meaning of the Constitution, but the committee took no action upon it, it being recognized that no definition could be drawn which would be agreed to probably by most members. Thus, as of this minute, the committee has not resolved just what an impeachable offense is.

As the staff assembled evidence, many of us felt that the committee should decide and give some direction to the staff as to the scope of the inquiry. We thought the committee should direct the staff to those areas of inquiry in which the committee itself determined that there might be merit so that time and effort would not be consumed in frivolous or other nonmeritorious allegations. But such a course of action would have required the committee to make decisions of substance, and no decisions were made.

The articles of impeachment which are to be exhibited tonight are, like any legislative bill, merely a vehicle upon which the committee may work its will. They will be open to additions, deletions, amendments, and substitutions. Each member of this committee individually weighing the evidence against his own concept of what warrants impeachment will come to his own conclusion on how he votes on the articles in their final form. Each of us is struck by the enormity of the decisions that we are called upon to make.

As I see it, and I state only my personal views, a vote for an article of impeachment means that a member is convinced that the article states an offense for which the President should be removed from office, and that there is evidence which supports the charge beyond a reasonable doubt.

Unlike criminal jurisprudence, there is discretion in the court to make the sentence fit the crime. The Constitution mandates that conviction on impeachment shall carry with it the removal from office, nothing less.

It seems to me that, then, that in determining in my own mind whether a specific charge states an impeachable offense, I would have to decide whether I thought the offense charged is of sufficient gravity to warrant removal of the President from office because of it. In other words, some offenses may be charged for which there is convincing evidence, and still such offenses may not, in the judgment of a member, be so serious as to justify impeachment and removal of a President of the United States from office. . . .

Committee on the Judiciary, H.R.,
93 Cong., 2 Sess. July 24, 1974, pp. 1–6.

Debate on Articles of Impeachment, July 24, 1974

Judiciary Committee's Articles of Impeachment

Article I (Approved 27–11)
In his conduct of the office of President of the United States, Richard M. Nixon, in violation of his constitutional oath faithfully to execute the office of President of the United States and, to the best of his ability, preserve, protect, and defend the Constitution of the United States, and in violation of his constitutional duty to take care that laws be faithfully executed, has prevented, obstructed, and impeded the administration of justice, in that:

On June 17, 1972, and prior thereto, agents of the Committee for the Re-election of the President:

Committed unlawful entry of the headquarters of the Democratic National Committee in Washington, District of Columbia, for the purpose of securing political intelligence. Subsequent thereto, Richard M. Nixon, using the powers of his high office, engaged personally and through his subordinates and agents in a course of conduct or plan designed to delay, impede, and obstruct the investigation of such unlawful entry; to cover up, conceal and protect those responsible; and to conceal the existence and scope of other unlawful covert activities.

The means used to implement this course of conduct or plan have included one or more of the following:

1. Making or causing to be made false or misleading statements to lawfully authorized investigative officers and employees of the United States.

2. Withholding relevant and material evidence or information from lawfully authorized investigative officers and employees of the United States.

3. Approving, condoning, acquiescing in, and counseling witnesses with respect to the giving of false or misleading statements to lawfully authorized investigative officers and employees of the United States and

false or misleading testimony in duly instituted judicial and Congressional proceedings.

4. Interfering or endeavoring to intefere with the conduct of investigations by the Department of Justice of the United States, the Federal Bureau of Investigation, the office of Watergate Special Prosecution Force, and Congressional committees.

5. Approving, condoning and acquiescing in the surreptitious payment of substantial sums of money for the purpose of obtaining the silence or influencing the testimony of witnesses, potential witnesses or individuals who participated in such illegal entry and other illegal activities.

6. Endeavoring to misuse the Central Intelligence Agency, an agency of the United States.

7. Disseminating information received from officers of the Department of Justice of the United States to subjects of investigations conducted by lawfully authorized investigative officers and employees of the United States, for the purpose of aiding and assisting such subjects in their attempts to avoid criminal liability.

8. Making false or misleading public statements for the purpose of deceiving the people of the United States into believing that a thorough and complete investigation had been conducted with respect to allegations of misconduct on the part of personnel of the executive branch of the United States and personnel of the Committee for the Re-election of the President, and that there was no involvement of such personnel in such misconduct: or

9. Endeavoring to cause prospective defendants, and individuals duly tried and convicted, to expect favored treatment and consideration in return for their silence or false testimony, or rewarding individuals for their silence or false testimony.

In all of this, Richard M. Nixon has acted in a manner contrary to his trust as President and subversive of constitutional government, to the great prejudice of the cause of law and justice and to the manifest injury of the people of the United States.

Wherefore Richard M. Nixon, by such conduct, warrants impeachment and trial, and removal from office.

Article II (Approved 28–10)

Using the powers of the office of President of the United States, Richard M. Nixon, in violation of his constitutional oath faithfully to execute the office of President of the United States, and to the best of his ability preserve, protect and defend the Constitution of the United States, and in disregard of his constitutional duty to take care that the laws be faithfully executed, has repeatedly engaged in conduct violating the constitutional rights of citizens, impairing the due and proper administration of justice in the conduct of lawful inquiries, of contravening the law of governing agencies of the executive branch and the purposes of these agencies.

This conduct has included one or more of the following:

1. He has, acting personally and through his subordinates and agents, endeavored to obtain from the Internal Revenue Service in violation of the constitutional rights of citizens, confidential information contained in income tax returns for purposes not authorized by law; and to cause, in violation of the constitutional rights of citizens, income tax audits or other income tax investigations to be initiated or conducted in a discriminatory manner.

2. He misused the Federal Bureau of Investigation, the Secret Service and other executive personnel in violation or disregard of the constitutional rights of citizens by directing or authorizing such agencies or personnel to conduct or continue electronic surveillance or other investigations for purposes unrelated to national security, the enforcement of laws or any other lawful function of his office.

He did direct, authorize or permit the use of information obtained thereby for purposes unrelated to national security, the enforcement of laws or any other lawful function of his office. And he did direct the concealment of certain records made by the Federal Bureau of Investigation of electronic surveillance.

3. He has, acting personally and through his subordinates and agents, in violation or disregard of the constitutional rights of citizens, authorized and permitted to be maintained a secret investigative unit within the office of the President, financed in part with money derived from campaign contributions which unlawfully utilized the resources of the Central Intelligence Agency, engaged in covert and unlawful activities, and attempted to prejudice the constitutional right of an accused to a fair trial.

4. He has failed to take care that the laws were faithfully executed by failing to act when he knew or he had reason to know that his close subordinates endeavored to impede and frustrate lawful inquiries by duly constituted executive, judicial and legislative entities concerning the unlawful entry into the headquarters of the Democratic National Committee and the cover-up thereof and concerning other unlawful activities including those relating to the confirmation of Richard Kleindienst as Attorney General of the United States, the electronic surveillance of private citizens, the break-in into the offices of Dr. Lewis Fielding and the campaign financing practices of the Committee to Re-Elect the President.

5. In disregard of the rule of law he knowingly misused the executive power by interfering with agencies of the executive branch including the Federal Bureau of Investigation, the Criminal Division and the office of Watergate special prosecution force of the Department of Justice, and the Central Intelligence Agency, in violation of his duty to take care that the laws be faithfully executed.

In all of this Richard M. Nixon has acted in a manner contrary to his trust as President and subversive of constitutional government to the great prejudice of the cause of law and justice and to the manifest injury of the people of the United States.

Wherefore, Richard M. Nixon by such conduct warrants impeachment and trial and removal from office.

Article III (Approved 21–17)

In his conduct of the office of President of the United States, Richard M. Nixon, contrary to his oath faithfully to execute the office of President of the United States and, to the best of his ability, preserve, protect and defend the Constitution of the United States, and in violation of his constitutional duty to take care that the laws be faithfully executed, has failed without lawful cause or excuse to produce papers and things as directed by duly authorized subpoenas issued by the Committee on the Judiciary of the House of Representatives on April 11, 1974, May 15, 1974, May 30, 1974, and June 24, 1974, and willfully disobeyed such subpoenas. The subpoenas, papers and things were deemed necessary by the Committee in order to resolve by direct evidence fundamental, factual questions relating to Presidential direction, knowledge or approval of actions demonstrated by other evidence to be substantial grounds for impeachment of the President. In refusing to produce these papers and things Richard M. Nixon, substituting his judgment as to what materials were necessary for the inquiry, interposed the powers of the presidency against the lawful subpoenas of the House of Representatives, thereby assuming to himself functions and judgments necessary to the exercise of the sole power of impeachment vested by the Constitution in the House of Representatives.

In all of this, Richard M. Nixon has acted in a manner contrary to his trust as President and subversive of constitutional government, to the great prejudice of the cause of law and justice, and to the manifest injury of the people of the United States.

Wherefore, Richard M. Nixon by such conduct, warrants impeachment and trial, and removal from office.

Article IV (Rejected 26–12)

In his conduct of the office of President of the United States, Richard M. Nixon, in violation of his constitutional oath faithfully to execute the office of President of the United States and to the best of his ability to preserve, protect and defend the Constitution of the United States and in disregard of his constitutional duties to take care that the laws be faithfully executed, on and subsequent to March 17, 1969, authorized, ordered and ratified the concealment from the Congress of the facts and submission to the Congress of false and misleading statements concerning the existence, scope and nature of American bombing operations in Cambodia in derogation of the power of the Congress to declare war, to make appropriations and to raise and support armies and by such conduct warrants impeachment and trial and removal from office.

Article V (Rejected 26–12)

In his conduct of the office of President of the United States, Richard M. Nixon, in violation of his constitutional oath faithfully to execute the office of the President of the United States, and to the best of his ability preserve, protect and defend the Constitution of the United States, and in violation of his constitutional duty to take care that the laws be faithfully executed, did receive emolument from the United States in excess of the compensation provided by law pursuant to Article II, Section I of the Constitution; and did willfully attempt to evade the payment of a portion of Federal income taxes due and owing by him for the years 1969, 1970, 1971, and 1972 in that (1) he during the period for which he had been elected President unlawfully received compensation in the form of Government expenditures at and on his privately owned property located in or near San Clemente, Calif., and Key Biscayne, Fla.; (2) he knowingly and fraudulently failed to report certain income and claimed deductions in the years 1969, 1970, 1971, and 1972 on his Federal income tax returns which were not authorized by law, including deductions for a gift of papers to the United States valued at approximately $576,000.

Roll Call Votes on Articles

	I	II	III	IV	V
Democrats					
Rodino (NJ)	Yes	Yes	Yes	No	Yes
Donohue (Mass)	Yes	Yes	Yes	No	No
Brooks (Tex)	Yes	Yes	Yes	Yes	Yes
Kastenmeier (Wis)	Yes	Yes	Yes	Yes	Yes
Edwards (Cal)	Yes	Yes	Yes	Yes	Yes
Hungate (Mo)	Yes	Yes	Yes	Yes	No
Conyers (Mich)	Yes	Yes	Yes	Yes	Yes
Eilberg (Pa)	Yes	Yes	Yes	No	Yes
Waldie (Cal)	Yes	Yes	Yes	Yes	No
Flowers (Ala)	Yes	Yes	No	No	No
Mann (SC)	Yes	Yes	No	No	No
Sarbanes (Md)	Yes	Yes	Yes	No	No
Seiberling (Ohio)	Yes	Yes	Yes	No	Yes
Danielson (Cal)	Yes	Yes	Yes	No	Yes
Drinan (Mass)	Yes	Yes	Yes	Yes	No
Rangel (NY)	Yes	Yes	Yes	Yes	Yes
Jordan (Tex)	Yes	Yes	Yes	Yes	Yes
Thornton (Ark)	Yes	Yes	Yes	No	No
Holtzman (NY)	Yes	Yes	Yes	Yes	Yes
Owens (Utah)	Yes	Yes	Yes	Yes	No
Mezvinsky (Iowa)	Yes	Yes	Yes	Yes	Yes
Republicans					
Hutchinson (Mich)	No	No	No	No	No
McClory (Ill)	No	Yes	Yes	No	No
Smith (NY)	No	No	No	No	No
Sandman (NJ)	No	No	No	No	No
Railsback (Ill)	Yes	Yes	No	No	No
Wiggins (Cal)	No	No	No	No	No
Dennis (Ind)	No	No	No	No	No

Fish (NY)	Yes	Yes	No	No	No
Mayne (Iowa)	No	No	No	No	No
Hogan (Md)	Yes	Yes	Yes	No	No
Butler (Va)	Yes	Yes	No	No	No
Cohen (Me)	Yes	Yes	No	No	No
Lott (Miss)	No	No	No	No	No
Froelich (Wis)	Yes	Yes	No	No	No
Moorhead (Cal)	No	No	No	No	No
Maraziti (NJ)	No	No	No	No	No
Latta (Ohio)	No	No	No	No	No

Committee on the Judiciary, H.R., 93 Cong., 2 Sess.
July 24, 1974, pp. 329–31, 445–47, 488–89, 515–17, 557–59.

U.S. v. Nixon

For nearly one year the President had tenaciously fought both the Special Prosecutor and Congress on the release of more tapes. But as often is the case in constitutional controversies, Americans move instinctively to the Supreme Court for a peaceful resolution of conflict. Nixon himself had bowed to the momentum for a court ruling, athough he occasionally hinted that he would be bound only by a "definitive" ruling. On July 24, 1974, the Supreme Court, in a unanimous verdict (Justice Rehnquist recusing himself) gave him just that. The Court, recognizing the doctrine of executive privilege, held it inapplicable in this controversy. Some five hours after the Supreme Court decision, Nixon announced his willingness to comply with the Court's decision. The decision had been delayed while Nixon and his staff frantically looked for "air" in the Court's opinion. In the meantime, Republican congressmen telegraphed Nixon, urging him to accept the ruling.

United States v. Nixon

Chief Justice Burger delivered the opinion of the Court

On March 1, 1974, a grand jury of the United States District Court for the District of Columbia returned an indictment charging seven named individuals with various offenses, including conspiracy to defraud the United States and to obstruct justice. Although he was not designated as such in the indictment, the grand jury named the President, among others, as an unindicted co-conspirator. On April 18, 1974, upon motion of the Special Prosecutor, . . . a subpoena *duces tecum* was issued pursuant to Rule 17 (c) to the President by the United States District Court and made returnable on May 2, 1974. This subpoena required the production, in advance of the September 9 trial date, of certain tapes, memoranda, papers, transcripts, or other writings relating to certain precisely identified meetings between the President and others. . . .

The District Court held that the judiciary, not the President, was the final arbiter of a claim of executive privilege. The court concluded that, under the circumstances of this case, the presumptive privilege was overcome by the Special Prosecutor's prima facie "demonstration of need sufficiently compelling to warrant judicial examination in chambers. . . ." . . .

Justiciability

In the District Court, the President's counsel argued that the court lacked jurisdiction to issue the subpoena because the matter was an intra-branch dispute between a subordinate and superior officer of the Executive Branch and hence not subject to judicial resolution. That argument has been renewed in this Court with emphasis on the contention that the dispute does not present a "case" or "controversy" which can be adjudicated in the federal courts. The President's counsel argues that the federal courts should not intrude into areas committed to the other branches of Government. He views the present dispute as essentially a "jurisdictional" dispute within the Executive Branch which he analogizes to a dispute between two congressional committees. Since the Executive Branch has exclusive authority and absolute discretion to decide whether to prosecute a case, . . . it is contended that a President's decision is final in determining what evidence is to be used in a given criminal case. Although his counsel concedes that the President has delegated certain specific powers to the Special Prosecutor, he has not "waived nor delegated to the Special Prosecutor the President's duty to claim privilege as to all materials . . . which fall within the President's inherent authority to refuse to disclose to any executive officer." . . .

Our starting point is the nature of the proceeding for which the evidence is sought—here a pending criminal prosecution. It is a judicial proceeding in a federal court alleging violation of federal laws and is brought in the name of the United States as sovereign. . . . Under the authority of Art. II, §2, Congress has vested in the Attorney General the power to conduct the criminal litigation of the United States Government. . . . It has also vested in him the power to appoint subordinate officers to assist him in the discharge of his duties. . . . Acting pursuant to those statutes, the Attorney General has delegated the authority to represent the United States in these particular matters to a Special Prosecutor with unique authority and tenure. The regulation gives the Special Prosecutor explicit power to contest the invocation of executive privilege in the process of seeking evidence deemed relevant to the performance of these specially delegated duties. . . .

The demands of and the resistance to the subpoena present an obvious controversy in the ordinary sense, but that alone is not sufficient to meet constitutional standards. In the contitutional sense, controversy means more than disagreement and conflict; rather it means the kind of controversy courts traditionally resolve. Here at issue is the production or nonproduction of specified evidence deemed by the Special Prosecutor to be relevant and admissible in a pending criminal case. It is sought by one official of the Executive Branch within the scope of his express authority; it is resisted by the Chief Executive on the ground of his duty to preserve the confidentiality of the communications of the President. Whatever the correct answer on the merits, these issues are "of a type which are traditionally justiciable.". . . The independent Special Prosecutor with his asserted need for the subpoenaed material in the underlying criminal prosecution is opposed by the President with his steadfast assertion of privilege against disclosure of the material. This setting assures there is "that concrete adverseness which sharpens the presentation of issues upon which the court so largely depends for illumination of difficult constitutional questions." *Baker* v. *Carr*, 369 U.S., at 204. Moreover, since the matter is one arising in the regular course of a federal criminal prosecution, it is within the traditional scope of Art. III power. *Id*. at 198.

In light of the uniqueness of the setting in which the conflict arises, the fact that both parties are officers of the Executive Branch cannot be viewed as a barrier to justiciability. It would be inconsistent with the applicable law and regulation, and the unique facts of this case to conclude other than that the Special Prosecutor has standing to bring this action and that a justiciable controversy is presented for decision. . . .

The Claim of Privilege

A

. . . [W]e turn to the claim that the subpoena should be quashed because it demands "confidential conversations between a President and his close advisors that it would be inconsistent with the public interest to produce." . . . The first contention is a broad claim that the separation of powers doctrine precludes judicial review of a President's claim of privilege. The second contention is that if he does not prevail on the claim of absolute privilege, the court should hold as a matter of constitutional law that the privilege prevails over the subpoena *duces tecum*.

In the performance of assigned constitutional duties each branch of the Government must initially interpret the Constitution, and the interpretation of its powers by any branch is due great respect from the others. The President's counsel, as we have noted, reads the Constitution as providing an absolute privilege of confidentiality for all Presidential communications. Many decisions of this Court, however, have unequivocally reaffirmed the holding of *Marbury* v. *Madison*, 1 Cranch 137 (1803), that "[i]t is emphatically the province and duty of the judicial department to say what the law is." *Id.*, at 177.

No holding of the Court has defined the scope of judicial power specifically relating to the enforcement of a subpoena for confidential Presidential communications for use in a criminal prosecution, but other exercises of power by the Executive Branch and the Legislative Branch have been found invalid as in conflict with the Constitution. *Powell* v. *McCormack*, 395 U.S. 486 (1969); *Youngstown Sheet & Tube Co.* v. *Sawyer*, 343 U.S. 579 (1952). . . .

B

In support of his claim of absolute privilege, the President's counsel urges two grounds, one of which is peculiar to our system of separation of powers. The first ground is the valid need for protection of communications between high Government officials and those who advise and assist them in the performance of their manifold duties; the importance of this confidentiality is too plain to require further discussion. Human experience teaches that those who expect public dissemination of their remarks may well temper candor with a concern for appearances and for their own interests to the detriment of the decisionmaking process. Whatever the nature of the privilege of confidentiality of Presidential communications in the exercise of Art. II powers, the privilege can be said to derive from the supremacy of each branch within its own assigned area of constitutional duties. Certain powers and privileges flow from the nature of enumerated powers; the protection of the confidentiality of Presidential communications has similar constitutional underpinnings.

The second ground asserted by the President's counsel in support of the claim of absolute privilege rests on the doctrine of separation of powers. Here it is argued that the independence of the Executive Branch within its own sphere . . . insulates a President from a judicial subpoena in an ongoing criminal prosecution, and thereby protects confidential Presidential communications.

However, neither the doctrine of separation of powers, nor the need for confidentiality of high-level communications, without more, can sustain an absolute, unqualified Presidential privilege of immunity from judicial process under all circumstances. The President's need for complete candor and objectivity from advisers calls for great deference from the courts. However, when the privilege depends solely on the broad, undifferentiated claim of public interest in the confidentiality of such conversations, a confrontation with other values arises. Absent a claim of need to protect military, diplomatic, or sensitive national security secrets, we find it difficult to accept the argument that even the very important interest in confidentiality of Presidential communications is significantly diminished by production of such material for *in camera* inspection with all the protection that a district court will be obliged to provide.

The impediment that an absolute, unqualified privilege would place in the way of the primary constitutional duty of the Judicial Branch to do justice in criminal prosecutions would plainly conflict with the function of the courts under Art. III. In designing the structure of our Government and dividing and allocating the sovereign power among three co-equal branches, the Framers of the Constitution sought to provide a comprehensive system, but the separate powers were not intended to operate with absolute independence. . . .

C

. . . The expectation of a President to the confidentiality of his conversations and correspondence, like the claim of confidentiality of judicial deliberations, for example, has all the values to which we accord deference for the privacy of all citizens and, added to those values, is the necessity for protection of the public interest in candid, objective, and even blunt or harsh opinions in Presidential decision-making. A President and those who assist him must be free to explore alternatives in the process of shaping policies and making decisions and to do so in a way many would be unwilling to express except privately. These are the considerations justifying a presumptive privilege for Presidential communications. The privilege is fundamental to the operation of Government and inextricably rooted in the separation of powers under the Constitution. In *Nixon* v. *Sirica*, 159 U.S. App. D.C. 58, 487 F. 2d 700 (1973), the Court of Appeals held that such Presidential communications are "presumptively privileged." . . .

But this presumptive privilege must be considered in light of our historic commitment to the rule of law. . . . We have elected to employ an adversary system of criminal justice in which the parties contest all issues before a court of law. The need to develop all relevant facts in the adversary system is both fundamental and comprehensive. The ends of criminal justice would be defeated if judgments were to be founded on a partial or speculative presentation of the facts. The very integrity of the judicial system and public confidence in the system depend on full disclosure of all the facts, within the framework of the rules of evidence. To ensure that justice is done, it is imperative to the function of courts that compulsory process be available for the production of evidence either by the prosecution or by the defense. . . .

In this case we must weigh the importance of the general privilege of confidentiality of Presidential communications in performance of the President's responsibilities against the inroads of such a privilege on the fair administration of criminal justice. The interest in preserving confidentiality is weighty indeed and entitled to great respect. However, we cannot conclude that advisers will be moved to temper the candor of their remarks by the infrequent occasions of disclosure because of the possibility that such conversations will be called for in the context of a criminal prosecution.

On the other hand, the allowance of the privilege to withhold evidence that is demonstrably relevant in a criminal trial would cut deeply into the guarantee of due process of law and gravely impair the basic function of the courts. A President's acknowledged need for confidentiality in the communications of his office is general in nature, whereas the constitutional need for production of relevant evidence in a criminal proceeding is specific and central to the fair adjudication of a particular criminal case in the administration of justice. Without access to specific facts a criminal prosecution may be totally frustrated. The President's broad interest in confidentiality of communications will not be vitiated by disclosure of a limited number of conversations preliminarily shown to have some bearing on the pending criminal cases.

We conclude that when the ground for asserting privilege as to subpoenaed materials sought for use in a criminal trial is based only on the generalized interest in confidentiality, it cannot prevail over the fundamental demands of due process of law in the fair administration of criminal justice. The generalized assertion of privilege must yield to the demonstrated, specific need for evidence in a pending criminal trial. . . .

United States v. *Nixon*, 418 U.S. 683 (1974).

Statement Announcing Intention To Comply With Supreme Court Decision Requiring Production of Presidential Tape Recordings, July 24, 1974

My challenge in the courts to the subpoena of the Special Prosecutor was based on the belief it was unconstitutionally issued and on my strong desire to protect the principle of Presidential confidentiality in a system of separation of powers.

While I am, of course, disappointed in the result, I respect and accept the Court's decision, and I have instructed Mr. St. Clair to take whatever measures are necessary to comply with that decision in all respects.

For the future, it will be essential that the special circumstances of this case not be permitted to cloud the rights of Presidents to maintain the basic confidentiality without which this office cannot function. I was gratified, therefore, to note that the Court reaffirmed both the validity and the importance of the principle of executive privilege—the principle I had sought to maintain. By complying fully with the Court's ruling in this case, I hope and trust that I will contribute to strengthening rather than weakening this principle for the future—so that this will prove to be not the precedent that destroyed the principle, but the action that preserved it.

Public Papers of the Presidents, Richard Nixon, 1974, 606.

Statement Announcing Availability of Additional Transcripts of Presidential Tape Recordings, August 5, 1974

I HAVE TODAY instructed my attorneys to make available to the House Judiciary Committee, and I am making public, the transcripts of three conversations with H. R. Haldeman on June 23, 1972. I have also turned over the tapes of these conversations to Judge Sirica, as part of the process of my compliance with the Supreme Court ruling.

On April 29, in announcing my decision to make public the original set of White House transcripts, I stated that "as far as what the President personally knew and did with regard to Watergate and the coverup is concerned, these materials—together with those already made available—will tell it all."

Shortly after that, in May, I made a preliminary review of some of the 64 taped conversations subpoenaed by the Special Prosecutor.

Among the conversations I listened to at that time were two of those of June 23. Although I recognized that these presented potential problems, I did not inform my staff or my Counsel of it, or those arguing my case, nor did I amend my submission to the Judiciary Committee in order to include and reflect it. At the time, I did not realize the extent of the implications which these conversations might now appear to have. As a result, those arguing my case, as well as those passing judgment on the case, did so with information that was incomplete and in some respects erroneous. This was a serious act of omission for which I take full responsibility and which I deeply regret.

Since the Supreme Court's decision 12 days ago, I have ordered my Counsel to analyze the 64 tapes, and have listened to a number of them myself. This process has made it clear that portions of the tapes of these June 23 conversations are at variance with certain of my previous statements. Therefore, I have ordered the transcripts made available immediately to the Judiciary Committee so that they can be reflected in the committee's report and included in the record to be considered by the House and the Senate.

In a formal written statement on May 22 of last year, I said that shortly after the Watergate break-in, I became concerned about the possibility that the FBI investigation might lead to the exposure either of unrelated covert activities of the CIA or of sensitive national security matters that the so-called "plumbers" unit at the White House had been working on, because of the CIA and plumbers connections of some of those involved. I said that I therefore gave instructions that the FBI should be alerted to coordinate with the CIA and to ensure that the investigation not expose these sensitive national security matters.

That statement was based on my recollection at the time—some 11 months later—plus documentary materials and relevant public testimony of those involved.

The June 23 tapes clearly show, however, that at the time I gave those instructions I also discussed the political aspects of the situation and that I was aware of the advantages this course of action would have with respect to limiting possible public exposure of involvement by persons connected with the reelection committee.

My review of the additional tapes has, so far, shown no other major inconsistencies with what I have previously submitted. While I have no way at this stage of being certain that there will not be others, I have no reason to believe that there will be. In any case, the tapes in their entirety are now in the process of being furnished to Judge Sirica. He has begun what may be a rather lengthy process of reviewing the tapes, passing on specific claims of executive privilege on portions of them, and forwarding to the Special Prosecutor those tapes or those portions that are relevant to the Watergate investigation.

It is highly unlikely that this review will be completed in time for the house debate. It appears at this stage, however, that a House vote of impeachment is, as a practical matter, virtually a foregone conclusion and that the issue will therefore go to trial in the Senate. In order to ensure that no other significant relevant materials are withheld, I shall voluntarily furnish to the Senate everything from these tapes that Judge Sirica rules should go to the Special Prosecutor.

I recognize that this additional material I am now furnishing may further damage my case, especially because attention will be drawn separately to it rather than to the evidence in its entirety. In considering its implications, therefore, I urge that two points be borne in mind.

The first of these points is to remember what actually happened as a result of instructions I gave on June 23. Acting Director Gray of the FBI did coordinate with Director Helms and Deputy Director Walters of the CIA. The CIA did undertake an extensive check to see whether any of its covert activities would be compromised by a full FBI investigation of Watergate. Deputy Director Walters then reported back to Mr. Gray that they would not be compromised. On July 6, when I called Mr. Gray, and when he expressed concern about improper attempts to limit his investigation, as the record shows, I told him to press ahead vigorously with his investigation—which he did.

The second point I would urge is that the evidence be looked at in its entirety and the events be looked at in perspective. Whatever mistakes I made in the handling of Watergate, the basic truth remains that when all the facts were brought to my attention, I insisted on a full investigation and prosecution of those guilty. I am firmly convinced that the record, in its entirety, does not justify the extreme step of impeachment and removal of a President. I trust that as the constitutional process goes forward, this perspective will prevail.

Public Papers of the Presidents, Richard Nixon, 1974, 621–23.

Resignation

The Supreme Court ruling forced Nixon to release the remaining subpoenaed tapes, including the famous "smoking gun" tape of June 23, 1972, recording the conversation in which Nixon and Haldeman conspired to use the CIA to thwart the FBI investigation. In a statement accompanying the release of the new tapes on August 6, Nixon sought to put the damaging testimony in the best light possible. But to no avail. A day later Republican congressional leaders visited the White House and urged the President to resign. Doubtless, he would have been impeached; but we cannot say for certain that he would have been convicted. In any event, Nixon himself chose not to run the risks of a trial and resigned on August 9, 1974. The night before, the thirty-seventh president addressed the nation for the thirty-seventh time from the White House, with a speech that referred hardly at all to the raging controversy that had engulfed the nation for more than two years and had brought about his downfall. Instead, Nixon insisted on reviewing his accomplishments. It was, in effect, the opening salvo in what became his twenty-year campaign to rewrite history in his favor. Wright Patman, chairman of the House Committee on Banking and Currency, immediately wrote to Peter Rodino, urging him to continue the investigation. Patman worried that in the future some would misconstrue events and the record. Rodino, however, promptly closed the inquiry. The next morning, Nixon bade farewell to his Administration's members. In his final statement as President,

Nixon once again laid bare his personal feelings and thoughts, as few other Presidents ever had done. Near the end, in a revealing comment, he noted that "those who hate you don't win unless you hate them, and then you destroy yourself." There was no more fitting epitaph for Watergate.

Resignation Statement, August 8, 1974

I have never been a quitter. To leave office before my term is completed is abhorrent to every instinct in my body. But as President, I must put the interest of America first. America needs a full-time President and a full-time Congress, particularly at this time with the problems we face at home and abroad.

To continue to fight through the months ahead for my vindication would almost totally absorb the time and attention of both the President and the Congress in a period when our entire focus should be on the great issues of peace abroad and prosperity without inflation at home.

Therefore, I shall resign the Presidency effective at noon tomorrow. Vice President Ford will be sworn in as President at that hour in this office.

As I recall the high hopes for America with which we began this second term, I feel a great sadness that I will not be here in the office working on your behalf to achieve those hopes in the next 2½ years. But in turning over direction of the Government to Vice President Ford, I know, as I told the Nation when I nominated him for that office ten months ago, that the leadership of America will be in good hands.

In passing this office to the Vice President, I also do so with the profound sense of the weight of responsibility that will fall on his shoulders tomorrow and, therefore, of the undersanding, the patience, the cooperation he will need from all Americans.

As he assumes that responsibility, he will deserve the help and the support of all of us. As we look to the future, the first essential is to begin healing the wounds of this Nation, to put the bitterness and the divisions of the recent past behind us and to rediscover those shared ideals that lie at the heart of our strength and unity as a great and as a free people.

By taking this action, I hope that I will have hastened the start of that process of healing which is so desperately needed in America.

I regret deeply any injuries that may have been done in the course of the events that led to this decision. I would say only that if some of my judgments were wrong, and some were wrong, they were made in what I believed at the time to be the best interest of the Nation.

To those who have stood with me during these past difficult months, to my family, my friends, to many others who joined in supporting my cause because they believed it was right, I will be eternally grateful for your support.

And to those who have not felt able to give me your support, let me say I leave with no bitterness toward those who have opposed me, because all of us, in the final analysis, have been concerned with the good of the country however our judgments might differ.

So, let us all now join together in affirming that common commitment and in helping our new President succeed for the benefit of all Americans.

I shall leave this office with regret at not completing my term, but with gratitude for the privilege of serving as your President for the past 5½ years. These years have been a momentous time in the history of our Nation and the world. They have been a time of achievement in which we can all be proud, achievements that represent the shared efforts of the Administration, the Congress and the people.

In all the decisions I have made in my public life, I have always tried to do what was best for the Nation. Throughout the long and difficult period of Watergate, I have felt it was my duty to persevere, to make every possible effort to complete the term of office to which you elected me.

In the past few days, however, it hs become evident to me that I no longer have a strong enough political base in the Congress to justify continuing that effort. As long as there was a base, I felt strongly that it was necessary to see the constitutional process through to its conclusion, that to do otherwise would be unfaithful to the spirit of that deliberately difficult process, and a dangerously destabilizing precedent for the future.

But with the disappearance of that base, I now believe that the constitutional purpose has been served, and there is no longer a need for the process to be prolonged.

I would have preferred to carry through to the finish whatever the personal agony it would have involved, and my family unanimously urged me to do so. But the interests of the Nation must always come before any personal considerations.

From the discussions I have had with Congressional and other leaders, I have concluded that because of the Watergate matter I might not have the support of the Congress that I would consider necessary to back the very difficult decisions and carry out the duties of this office in the way the interests of the Nation would require. . . .

Public Papers of the Presidents, Richard Nixon, 1974, 626–30.

Wright Patman to Peter Rodino, August 9, 1974

As I am sure you have already recognized, there is a need to make certain that all the records, correspondence, memoranda and other documents as well as tapes in any way relating to any aspect of the Watergate affair be preserved. With the rapid transition of Chief Executives and with the certain shift in key personnel, I am concerned that the steps necessary to assure preservation of these documents be undertaken immediately.

The Judiciary Committee, I hope, will expand its public record to include all pertinent transcripts and documents so that the American people will have a permanent record of the events which led to President Nixon's decision to resign. In the coming weeks and months, there will be some who will attempt to distort the record, misconstrue events and to cloud the real issues. This has been a wrenching experience for the nation and it would be sad indeed if we did not learn from this experience, and in my opinion, this is possible only if the record is complete in every respect.

Judge Sirica is receiving tapes under Superme Court order and I hope that the Judiiary Committee will take whatever steps are necessary to obtain those tapes and to publish the transcripts. However, there are additional tapes and documents covering this period and I think it is essential that all of this material be preserved so that it may be inspected and the pertinence to the Watergate inquiries be determined by the Judiciary Committee as well as the courts.

As I have mentioned previously, I feel that there are gaps in the public record as to the events during the fall of 1972—the period between John Dean's September 15, 1972 meeting with the President and H. R. Haldeman and his subsequent session in February of 1973.

The collection of tapes and material from this period may give the public and the Congress a fuller understanding of important aspects of the case.

House Banking Committee Files, courtesy of HBC staff.

Farewell Statement, August 9, 1974

Members of the Cabinet, Members of the White House staff, all of our friends here:

I think the record should show that this is one of those spontaneous things that we always arrange whenever the President comes in to speak, and it will be so reported in the press, and we don't mind because they have to call it as they see it.

But on our part, believe me, it is spontaneous.

You are here to say goodbye to us and we don't have a good word for it in English. The best here is au revoir. We will see you again.

I just met with the members of the White House staff, you know, those who serve here in the White House day in and day out, and I asked them to do what I ask all of you to do to the extent that you can and, of course, are requested to do so: To serve our next President as you have served me and previous Presidents—because many of you have been here for many years—with devotion and dedication. . . .

I am proud of this Cabinet. I am proud of all the members who have served in our Cabinet. I am proud of our sub-Cabinet. I am proud of our White House staff. As I pointed out last night, sure we have done some things wrong in this Administration, and the top man always takes the responsibility, and I have never ducked it. But I want to say one thing. We can be proud of it—5½ years—no man or no woman came into this Administration and left it with more of this world's goods than when he came in. No man or no woman ever profited at the public expense or the public till. That tells something about you.

Mistakes, yes. But for personal gain, never. You did what you believed in. Sometimes right, sometimes wrong. And I only wish that I were a wealthy man—at the present time I have got to find a way to pay my taxes (Laughter)—and if I were, I would like to recompense you for the sacrifices all of you have made to serve in Government. . . .

I remember my old man. I think that they would have called him sort of a little man, common man. He didn't consider himself that way. You know what he was? He was a streetcar motorman first, and then he was a farmer, and then he had a lemon ranch. It was the poorest lemon ranch in California. I can assure you. He sold it before they found oil on it. (Laughter)

And then he was a grocer. But he was a great man because he did his job and every job counts up to the hilt, regardless of what happens.

Nobody will ever write a book, probably, about my mother. Well, I guess all of you would say this about your mother—my mother was a saint. And I think of here, two boys dying of tuberculosis, nursing four others in order that she could take care of my older brother for three years in Arizona, and seeing each of them die, and when they died, it was like one of her own.

Yes, she will have no books written about her. But she was a saint. . . .

And as I leave, let me say that is an example I think all of us should remember. We think sometimes when things happen that don't go the right way; we think that when you don't pass the bar exam the first time—I happened to, but I was just lucky; I mean my writing was so poor the bar examiner said, "We have just got to let the guy through." (Laughter) We think that when someone dear to us dies, we think that when we lose an election, we think that when we suffer a defeat, that all is ended. We think, as T. R. said, that the light had left his life forever.

Not true. It is only a beginning always. The young must know it; the old must know it. It must always sustain us because the greatness comes not when things go always good for you, but the greatness comes when you are really tested, when you take some knocks, some disappointments, when sadness comes, because only if you have been in the deepest valley can you ever know how magnificent it is to be on the highest mountain.

And so I say to you on this occasion, as we leave, we leave proud of the people who have stood by us and worked for us and served this country.

We want you to be proud of what you have done. We want you to continue to serve in Government, if that is your wish. Always give it your best, never get discouraged, never be petty; always remember others may hate you, but those who hate you don't win unless you hate them, and then you destroy yourself.

Public Papers of the Presidents, Richard Nixon, 1974, 630–33.

The Pardon

On September 8, 1974, President Gerald R. Ford decided it would be best to put Watergate behind the nation and pardon Richard Nixon. Undoubtedly, many preferred not to see the former President in a criminal trial, but Ford failed to first secure a political consensus for a pardon. Leaders in both parties undoubtedly favored a pardon, but considered it premature to press for one so early. Many believe that the pardon contributed to Ford's defeat in the 1976 election. Certainly, he received heavy criticism for his failure to obtain a satisfactory statement of contrition from Nixon. Nevertheless, the prevailing legal principle has been that acceptance of a pardon is equivalent to the acceptance of guilt.

**Pardon Statement,
September 8, 1974**

Ladies and gentlemen, I have come to a decision which I felt I should tell you, and all of my fellow American citizens, as soon as I was certain in my own mind and in my own conscience that it was the right thing to do.

I have learned already in this office that the difficult decisions always come to this desk. I must admit that many of them do not look at all the same as the hypothetical questions that I have answered freely and perhaps too fast on previous occasions. My customary policy is to try and get all the facts and to consider the opinions of my countrymen and to take counsel with my most valued friends. But these seldom agree, and in the end the decision is mine.

To procrastinate, to agonize and to wait for a more favorable turn of events that may never come, or more compelling external pressures that may as well be wrong as right, is itself a decision of sorts and a weak course for a President to follow. . . .

The Constitution is the supreme law of our land it governs our actions as citizens. Only the laws of God, which govern our consciences are superior to it. As we are a nation under God, so I am sworn to uphold our laws with the help of God. And I have sought such guidance and searched my own conscience with special diligence to determine the right thing for me to do with respect to my predecessor in this place, Richard Nixon, and his loyal wife and family.

Theirs is an American tragedy in which we all have played a part. It could go on and on and on, or someone must write "The End" to it.

I have concluded that only I can do it. And if I can, I must.

There are no historic or legal precedents to which I can turn in this matter, none that precisely fit the circumstances of a private citizen who has resigned the presidency of the United States. But it is common knowledge that serious allegations and accusations hang like a sword over our former President's head, threatening his health, as he tries to reshape his life, a great part of which was spent in the service of this country and by the mandate of its people.

After years of bitter controversy and divisive national debate, I have been advised and I am compelled to conclude that many months and perhaps more years will have to pass before Richard Nixon could obtain a fair trial by jury in any jurisdiction of the United States under governing decisions of the Superme Court.

I deeply believe in equal justice for all Americans, whatever their station or former station. The law, whether human or divine, is no respecter of persons but the law is a respecter of reality. The facts as I see them are that a former President of the United States, instead of enjoying equal treatment with any other citizen accused of violating the law, would be cruelly and excessively penalized either in preserving the presumption of his innocence or in obtaining a speedy determination of his guilt in order to repay a legal debt to society.

During this long period of delay and potential litigation, ugly passions would again be aroused, and our people would again be polarized in their opinions, and the credibility of our free institutions of government would again be challenged at home and abroad. In the end, the courts might well hold that Richard Nixon had been denied due process and the verdict of history would even more be inconclusive with respect to those charges arising out of the period of his presidency of which I am presently aware.

But it is not the ultimate fate of Richard Nixon that most concerns me—though surely it deeply troubles every decent and every compassionate person. My concern is the immediate future of this great country. In this I dare not depend upon my personal sympathy as a longtime friend of the former President nor my professional judgment as a lawyer. And I do not.

As President, my primary concern must always be the greatest good of all the people of the United States, whose servant I am.

As a man, my first consideration is to be true to my own convictions and my own conscience.

My conscience tells me clearly and certainly that I cannot prolong the bad dreams that continue to reopen a chapter that is closed. My conscience tells me that only I, as President, have the constitutional power to firmly shut and seal this book. My conscience says it is my duty, not merely to proclaim domestic tranquility, but to use every means that I have to ensure it.

I do believe that the buck stops here, that I cannot rely upon public opinion polls to tell me what is right. I do believe that right makes might, and that if I am wrong 10 angels swearing I was right would make no difference. I do believe with all my heart and mind and spirit that I, not as President, but as a humble servant of God, will receive justice without mercy if I fail to show mercy.

Finally, I feel that Richard Nixon and his loved ones have suffered enough, and will continue to suffer no matter what I do, no matter what we as a great and good nation can do together to make his goal of peace come true.

Now, therefore, I, Gerald R. Ford, President of the United States, pursuant to the pardon power conferred upon me by Article II, Section 2, of the Constitution, have granted and by these presents do grant a full, free, and absolute pardon unto Richard Nixon for all offenses against the United States which he, Richard Nixon, has committed or may have committed or taken part in during the period from January 20, 1969, through August 9, 1974. . . .

Public Papers of the Presidents, Gerald R. Ford, 1974, 101–3.

Statement by Nixon, September 9, 1974

I have been informed that President Ford has granted me a full and absolute pardon for any charges which may be brought against me for actions taken during the time I was the President of the United States. In accepting this pardon, I hope that his compassionate act will contribute to lifting the burden of Watergate from our country.

Here in California, my perspective on Watergate is quite different than it was while I was embattled in the midst of the controversy while I was still subject to the unrelenting daily demand to the Presidency itself.

Looking back on what is still in my mind a complex and confusing maze of events, decisions, pressures, and personalities, one thing I can see clearly now is that I was wrong in not acting more decisively and more forthrightly in dealing with Watergate, particularly when it reached the stage of judicial proceedings and grew from a political scandal into national tragedy.

No words can describe the depths of my regret and pain at the anguish my mistakes over Watergate have caused the nation and the Presidency, a nation I so deeply love and an institution I so greatly respect.

I know that many fair-minded people believe that my motivations and actions in the Watergate affair were intentionally self-serving and illegal. I now understand how my own mistakes and misjudgments have contributed to that belief and seemed to support it. This burden is the heaviest one of all to bear.

That the way I tried to deal with Watergate was the wrong way, is a burden I shall bear for every day of the life that is left to me.

New York Times, September 9, 1974.

Appendix

Watergate Special Prosecution Force Criminal Actions Final Report, 1975

Watergate Cover-up

The following have been charged with offenses stemming from events following the break-in at Democratic National Committee Headquarters on June 17, 1972:

Charles W. Colson

Indicted on March 1, 1974, on one count of conspiracy to obstruct justice (18 USC Section 371) and one count of obstruction of justice (18 USC Section 1503). Pleaded not guilty March 9, 1974. Indictment dismissed by government June 3, 1974, after guilty plea in *U.S.* v. *Ehrlichman et al*.

John W. Dean III

Pleaded guilty on October 19, 1973, to an information charging one count of violation of 18 USC Section 371, conspiracy to obstruct justice. Sentenced August 2, 1974, to a prison term of one to four years. Began term September 3, 1974. Released January 8, 1975, pursuant to order reducing sentence to time served.

John D. Ehrlichman

Indicted on March 1, 1974, on one count of conspiracy to obstruct justice (18 USC Section 371), one count of obstruction of justice (18 USC Section 1503), one count of making false statements to agents of the FBI (18 USC Section 1001) and two counts of making a false statement to a Grand Jury (18 USC Section 1623). Pleaded not guilty March 9, 1974. Section 1001 count dismissed by judge. Found guilty on all other counts January 1, 1975. Sentenced February 21, 1975 to serve 2½ to 8 years in prison.

Harry R. Haldeman
Indicted on March 1, 1974, on one count of conspiracy to obstruct justice (18 USC Section 371), one count of obstruction of justice (18 USC Section 1503) and three counts of perjury (18 USC Section 1621). Pleaded not guilty March 9, 1974. Found guilty on all counts January 1, 1975. Sentenced February 21, 1975, to serve 2½ to 8 years in prison.

Fred C. LaRue
Pleaded guilty on June 28, 1973, to an information charging one count of violation of 18 USC Section 371, conspiracy to obstruct justice. Sentenced to serve one to three years in prison, all but six months suspended. Sentence reduced by court to six months total. Entered prison April 1, 1975. Released August 15, 1975.

Jeb S. Magruder
Pleaded guilty on August 16, 1973, to an information charging one count of violation of 18 USC Section 371, conspiracy to unlawfully intercept wire and oral communications, to obstruct justice and to defraud the United States. Sentenced on May 21, 1974, to a prison term of 10 months to four years. Began term June 4, 1974. Released January 8, 1975, pursuant to order reducing sentence to time served.

Robert Mardian
Indicted on March 1, 1974, on one count of conspiracy to obstruct justice (18 USC Section 371). Pleaded not guilty March 9, 1974. Found guilty January 1, 1975. Sentenced February 21, 1975 to serve 10 months to three years in prison. Conviction overturned on appeal.

John Mitchell
Indicted on March 1, 1974, on one count of conspiracy to obstruct justice (18 USC Section 371), one count of obstruction of justice (18 USC Section 1503), two counts of making a false statement to a Grand Jury (18 USC Section 1623), one count of perjury (18 USC Section 1621), and one count of making a false statement to an agent of the FBI (18 USC Section 1001). Section 1001 count was dismissed by judge. Pleaded not guilty March 9, 1974. Found guilty on all other counts January 1, 1975. Sentenced February 21, 1975 to serve 2½ to 8 years in prison.

Kenneth W. Parkinson
Indicted on March 1, 1974, on one count of conspiracy to obstruct justice (18 USC Section 371) and one count of obstruction of justice (18 USC Section 1503). Pleaded not guilty March 9, 1974. Acquitted January 1, 1975.

Herbert L. Porter
Pleaded guilty on January 28, 1974, to an information charging a

one-count violation of 18 USC Section 1001, making false statements to agents of the FBI. Information had been filed January 21, 1974. Sentenced on April 11, 1974, to a minimum of five months and maximum of 15 months in prison, all but 30 days suspended. Served April 22 to May 17, 1974.

Gordon Strachan
Indicted on March 1, 1974, on one count of conspiracy to obstruct justice (18 USC Section 371), one count of obstruction of justice (18 USC Section 1503), and one count of making a false statement to a Grand Jury (18 USC Section 1623). Pleaded not guilty March 9, 1974. Case severed September 30, 1974. Charges dismissed on motion of Special Prosecutor March 10, 1975.

Fielding Break-in
The following have been charged with offenses stemming from the September 3–4, 1971, break-in at the Los Angeles office of Dr. Lewis Fielding.

Bernard L. Barker
Indicted on March 7, 1974, on one count of conspiracy to violate civil rights (18 USC Section 241). Pleaded not guilty March 14, 1974. Found guilty July 12, 1974. Suspended sentence. Three years probation.

Charles W. Colson
Indicted on March 7, 1974, on one count of conspiracy to violate civil rights (18 USC Section 241). Indictment dismissed after Colson pleaded guilty on June 3, 1974, to an information charging one count of obstruction of justice (18 USC Section 1503). Sentenced June 21, 1974 to serve one to three years in prison and fined $5,000. Term started July 8, 1974. Released January 31, 1975, pursuant to order reducing sentence to time served.

Felipe De Diego
Indicted on March 7, 1974, on one count of conspiracy to violate civil rights (18 USC Section 241). Pleaded not guilty March 14, 1974. Indictment dismissed by judge on May 22, 1974. U.S. Court of Appeals overturned dismissal on April 16, 1975. Charges dismissed on motion of Special Prosecutor May 19, 1975.

John D. Ehrlichman
Indicted on March 7, 1974, on one count of conspiracy to violate civil rights (18 USC Section 241), one count of making a false statement to agents of the FBI (18 USC Section 1001), and three counts of making a false statement to a Grand Jury (18 USC Section 1623). Pleaded not guilty on March 9, 1974. On July 12, 1974, Ehrlichman was found guilty on all charges, except one of the counts of making a false statement to a Grand Jury. On July 22, Judge Gerhard Gesell entered an acquittal on

the Section 1001 charge. On July 31, 1974, he was sentenced to concurrent prison terms of 20 months to five years.

Egil Krogh, Jr.

Indicted on October 11, 1973, on two counts of violation of 18 USC Section 1623, making a false statement to a Grand Jury. Pleaded not guilty October 18, 1973. Indictment dismissed January 24, 1974, after Krogh pleaded guilty on November 30, 1973, to an information charging one count of violation of 18 USC Section 241, conspiracy to violate civil rights. Sentenced on January 24, 1974, to a prison term of two to six years, all but six months suspended. Began sentence Feburary 4, 1974. Released June 21, 1974.

G. Gordon Liddy

Indicted March 7, 1974, on one count of conspiracy to violate civil rights (18 USC Section 241). Pleaded not guilty March 14, 1974. Found guilty July 12, 1974. Sentenced July 31, 1974, to a prison term of one to three years, sentence to run concurrently with sentence in U.S. v. Liddy et al. Released on bail October 15, 1974, pending appeal, after serving twenty-one months. Bail revoked January 13, 1975.

Eugenio Martinez

Indicted on March 7, 1974, on one count of conspiracy to violate civil rights (18 USC Section 241). Pleaded not guilty March 14, 1974. Found guilty July 12, 1974. Received a suspended sentence and three years probation on July 31, 1974.

Original Watergate Defendants

Bernard L. Barker

Indicted September 15, 1972, on seven counts of conspiracy, burglary, wiretapping and unlawful possession of intercepting devices (one count of 18 USC Section 371, two counts of 22 DC Code Section 1801[b], two counts of 18 USC Section 2511, two counts of 23 DC Code 543[a]). Pleaded guilty January 15, 1973. Sentenced November 9, 1973, to a prison term of 18 months to six years. Motion to withdraw guilty plea denied. Freed January 4, 1974, pending outcome of appeal. Appeal denied February 25, 1975. Sentence reduced by Judge John J. Sirica to time served.

Virgilio Gonzalez

Indicted September 15, 1972, on seven counts of conspiracy, burglary, wiretapping and unlawful possession of intercepting devices (one count of 18 USC Section 371, two counts of 22 DC Code Section 1801[b1], two counts of 18 USC Section 2511, two counts of 23 DC Code 543[a]). Pleaded guilty January 15, 1973. Sentenced November 9, 1973, to a prison term of one to four years. Motion to withdraw guilty plea denied. Released on parole March 7, 1974. Appeal denied February 25, 1975.

E. Howard Hunt

Indicted September 15, 1972, on six counts of conspiracy, burglary, and wiretapping (one count of 18 USC Section 371, two counts of 22 DC Code Section 1801[b], three counts of 18 USC Section 2511). Pleaded guilty January 11, 1973. Sentenced November 9, 1973, to a prison term of 30 months to eight years and fined $10,000. Motion to withdraw guilty plea denied. Released on personal recognizance January 2, 1974, pending outcome of appeal. Appeal denied February 25, 1975. Re-entered prison on April 25, 1975.

G. Gordon Liddy

Indicted September 15, 1972, on six counts of conspiracy, burglary, and wiretapping (one count of 18 USC Section 371, two counts of 22 DC Code Section 1801[b], three counts of 18 USC Section 2511). Convicted January 30, 1973, on all counts. Sentenced March 23, 1973, to a prison term of six years and eight months to 20 years and fined $40,000. Released on bail October 15, 1974. Appeal denied. Re-entered prison February 16, 1975.

Eugenio R. Martinez

Indicted September 15, 1972, on seven counts of conspiracy, burglary, wiretapping and unlawful possession of intercepting devices (one count of 18 USC, Section 371, two counts of 22 DC Code Section 1801[b], two counts of 23 DC Code 543[a], two counts of 18 USC Section 2511). Pleaded guilty January 15, 1973. Sentenced November 9, 1973, to a prison term of one to four years. Motion to withdraw guilty plea denied. Released on parole March 7, 1974. Appeal denied February 25, 1975.

James W. McCord, Jr.

Indicted on September 15, 1972, on eight counts of conspiracy, burglary, wiretapping and unlawful possession of intercepting devices (one count of 18 USC Section 371, two counts of 22 DC Code Section 1801[b], three counts of 18 USC Section 2511, two counts of 23 DC Code Section 543[a]). Convicted January 30, 1973. Sentenced November 9, 1973, to a prison term of one to five years. Conviction upheld by U.S. Court of Appeals. Entered prison on March 21, 1975. Released May 29, 1975, pursuant to order reducing sentence to time served.

Frank A. Sturgis

Indicted September 15, 1972, on seven counts of conspiracy, burglary, wiretapping and unlawful possession of intercepting devices (one count of 18 USC Section 371, two counts of 22 DC Code Section 1801[b], two counts of 18 USC Section 2511, two counts of 23 DC Code Section 543[a]). Pleaded guilty January 15, 1973. Sentenced November 9, 1973, to a prison term of one to four years. Motion to withdraw guilty plea denied. Released by court order on January 18, 1974, pending outcome of appeal. Parole Board announced on March 25, 1974, that parole would commence on termination of appeal bond. Appeal denied February 25, 1975.

Campaign Activities and Related Matters

The following individuals entered pleas of guilty to misdemeanor non-willful violations of 18 USC Section 610, the federal statute prohibiting corporate campaign contributions:

Raymond Abendroth . October 23, 1974	$2,000 fine
Time Oil Corp.		
James Allen . . . . . . May 1, 1974	$1,000 fine
Northrop Corp.		
Richard L. Allison . . . May 17, 1974	$1,000 fine
Lehigh Valley Co-operative Farmers		
Orin E. Atkins . . . . . November 13, 1973 . .	$1,000 fine
Ashland Petroleum Gabon, Inc.		
Russell DeYoung . . . October 17, 1973	$1,000 fine
Goodyear Tire and Rubber Co.		
Ray Dubrowin . . . . . March 7, 1974	$1,000 fine
Diamond International Corp.		
Harry Heltzer . . . . . October 17, 1973	$ 500 fine
Minnesota Mining and Manufacturing Co.		
Charles N. Huseman . December 3, 1974 . . .	$1,000 fine
HMS Electric Corp.		
William W. Keeler . . . December 4, 1973 . . .	$1,000 fine
Phillips Petroleum Co.		
Harding L. Lawrence . November 13, 1973 . .	$1,000 fine
Braniff Airways		
William Lyles, Sr. . . . September 17, 1974 . .	$2,000 fine
LBC & W, Inc.		
H. Everett Olson . . . . December 19, 1973 . .	$1,000 fine
Carnation Co.		
Claude C. Wild, Jr. . . November 13, 1973 . .	$1,000 fine
Gulf Oil Corp.		
Harry Ratrie . . . . . . January 28, 1975	Suspended
Ratrie, Robbins and Schweitzer, Inc.	sentence
Augustus Robbins, III . January 28, 1975	Suspended
Ratrie, Robbins and Scheiwtzer, Inc.	sentence

The following individuals entered pleas of guilty to misdemeanor non-willful violations of 18 USC Sections 2 and 610, aiding and abetting an illegal campaign contributions:

Francis X. Carroll . . . May 28, 1974	Suspended
	sentence
Norman Sherman . . . August 12, 1974	$500 fine
John Valentine . . . . August 12, 1974	$500 fine

The following corporations entered pleas of guilty to violations of 18 USC Section 610, illegal campaign contributions:

American Airlines . . . October 17, 1973	$5,000 fine
Ashland Oil, Inc. . . . . December 30, 1974 . .	$25,000 fine
Ashland Petroleum		
Gabon, Inc. . . . . . . November 13, 1973 . .	$5,000 fine

Braniff Airways	November 12, 1973 . .	$5,000 fine
Carnation Company . .	December 19, 1973 . .	$5,000 fine
Diamond		
International Corp. .	March 7, 1974	$5,000 fine
Goodyear Tire and Rubber		
Company	October 17, 1973	$5,000 fine
Greyhound Corp. . . .	October 8, 1974	$5,000 fine
Gulf Oil Corp.	November 13, 1973 . .	$5,000 fine
Lehigh Valley Co-operative		
Farmers	May 6, 1974	$5,000 fine
Minnesota Mining and		
Manufacturing Co. .	October 17, 1973	$3,000 fine
National		
By-Products, Inc. . .	June 24, 1974	$1,000 fine
Phillips Petroleum Co.	December 4, 1973 . . .	$5,000 fine
Time Oil Corp.	October 23, 1974	$5,000 fine
Ratrie, Robbins and		
Schweitzer, Inc. . . .	January 28, 1975	$2,500 fine

The following corporations entered pleas of guilty to violations of 18 USC Section 611, illegal campaign contributions by government contractor:

LBC & W, Inc.	September 17, 1974 . .	$5,000 fine
Northrop Corporation	May 1, 1974	$5,000 fine

The following individual and corporation entered pleas of not guilty to an information filed October 19, 1973, charging four counts of misdemeanor non-willful violation of 18 USC Section 610, illegal campaign contribution. Both were acquitted on July 12, 1974, by a U.S. District Court judge in Minneapolis, Minnesota:

Dwayne O. Andreas
 Chairman of the Board, First Interoceanic Corp.
First Interoceanic Corp.

The following related campaign contribution matters were under the jurisdiction of the Watergate Special Prosecution Force:

American Ship Building Company
 Pleaded guilty August 23, 1974, to one count of conspiracy (18 USC Section 371) and one count of violation of 18 USC Section 610, illegal campaign contribution. Fined $20,000.

Associated Milk Producers, Inc.
 Pleaded guilty on August 1, 1974, to one count of conspiracy (18 USC Section 371) and five counts of violation of 18 USC Section 610, illegal campaign contribution. Fined $35,000.

Tim M. Babcock
 Pleaded guilty on December 10, 1974, to an information charging a

one-count violation of 2 USC Section 440, making a contribution in the name of another person. Sentenced to one year in prison and fined $1,000, with all but four months of the prison sentence suspended. Sentence under appeal.

Jack L. Chestnut
Indicted December 23, 1974, on one count of willful violation of 18 USC Section 610, aiding and abetting an illegal campaign contribution. Pleaded not guilty January 6, 1975. Found guilty May 8, 1975, after jury trial by Office of U.S. Attorney for Southern District of New York. Sentenced June 26, 1975, to serve four months in prison and fined $5,000. Conviction under appeal.

John B. Connally
Indicted on July 29, 1974, on two counts of accepting an illegal payment (18 USC Section 201 [g]), one count of conspiracy to commit perjury and obstruct justice (18 USC Section 371) and two counts of making a false statement to a Grand Jury (18 USC Section 1623). Pleaded not guilty August 9, 1974. Judge severs last three counts for separate trial. Found not guilty on first two counts April 17, 1975. Remaining counts dismissed April 18, 1975, on motion of Special Prosecutor.

Harry S. Dent, Sr.
Pleaded guilty on December 11, 1974, to an information charging one count violation of the Federal Corrupt Practices Act (2 USC Sections 242 and 252). Sentenced to one month unsupervised probation.

DKI for '74
Pleaded guilty on December 13, 1974, to an information charging a violation of 2 USC Sections 434 [a] and [b], and 441, failure to report receipt of contributions and failure to report names, addresses, occupations and principal places of business of the persons making such contributions. Suspended sentence.

Jack A. Gleason
Pleaded guilty on November 15, 1974, to an information charging a one-count violation of the Federal Corrupt Practices Act, (2 USC Section 252). Suspended sentence.

Jake Jacobsen
Indicted on February 21, 1974, on one count of violation of 18 USC Section 1623, making a false statement to a Grand Jury. Indictment dismissed by Chief Judge George L. Hart May 3, 1974. Indicted July 29, 1974, on one count of making an illegal payment to a public official (18 USC Section 201[f]). Pleaded guilty August 7, 1974. Sentencing deferred.

Thomas V. Jones
Pleaded guilty on May 1, 1974, to an information charging a one-

count violation of 18 USC Sections 2 and 611, willfully aiding and abetting a firm to commit violation of statute prohibiting campaign contributions by government contractors. Fined $5,000.

Herbert W. Kalmbach
Pleaded guilty on February 25, 1974, to a one-count violation of the Federal Corrupt Practices Act, (2 USC Sections 242[a] and 252[b]), and one count of promising federal employment as a reward for political activity and support of a candidate (18 USC Section 600). Sentenced to serve six to eighteen months in prison and fined $10,000 on the first charge. On the second charge, Kalmbach was sentenced to serve six months in prison, sentence to run concurrent with other sentence. Began term July 1, 1974. Released January 8, 1975. Sentence modified to time served.

John H. Melcher, Jr.
Pleaded guilty April 11, 1974, to an information charging a one-count violation of 18 USC Sections 3 and 610, being an accessory after the fact to an illegal corporate campaign contribution. Fined $2,500.

Harold S. Nelson, former general mgr., Associated Milk Producers, Inc.
Pleaded guilty on July 31, 1974, to a one-count information charging conspiracy to violate 18 USC Section 201 [f], (illegal payment to government official), and 18 USC Section 610, (illegal campaign contribution) 18 USC Section 371. Sentenced November 1, 1974, to serve four months in prison and fined $10,000. Term began November 8, 1974. Released February 21, 1975.

David L. Parr, former special counsel, Associated Milk Producers, Inc.
Pleaded guilty on July 23, 1974, to a one-count information charging conspiracy to violate 18 USC Section 610, illegal campaign contribution. Sentenced November 1, 1974, to serve four months in prison and fined $10,000. Term began November 8, 1974. Released February 21, 1975.

Stuart H. Russell
Indicted December 19, 1974, on one count of conspiracy to violate 18 USC Section 610, illegal campaign contribution (18 USC Section 371), two counts of aiding and abetting a willful violation of 18 USC Section 610, illegal campaign contribution (18 USC Sections 2 and 610). Pleaded not guilty. Found guilty in San Antonio, Texas, July 11, 1975. Sentenced in August 1975, to a prison term of two years.

Maurice Stans
Pleaded guilty March 12, 1975, to three counts of violation of the reporting sections of the Federal Election Campaign Act of 1971, 2 USC Sections 434[a] and [b], 441; and two counts of violation of 18 USC Section 610, accepting an illegal campaign contribution. Fined $5,000 on May 14, 1975.

George M. Steinbrenner III, Chairman of the Board, American Ship Building Co.

Indicted April 5, 1974, on one count of conspiracy (18 USC Section 371); five counts of willful violation of 18 USC Section 610, illegal campaign contribution; two counts of aiding and abetting an individual to make a false statement to agents of the FBI (18 USC Sections 2 and 1001), four counts of obstruction of justice (18 USC Section 1503); and two counts of obstruction of a criminal investigation (18 USC Section 1510). Pleaded not guilty April 19, 1974. Convicted, later pardoned.

On August 23, 1974, Steinbrenner pleaded guilty to the count of the indictment charging a violation of 18 USC Section 371, conspiracy to violate 18 USC Section 610, and an information charging one count of violation of 18 USC Sections 3 and 610, being an accessory after the fact to an illegal campaign contribution. He was fined $15,000 on August 30, 1974. The remaining counts of the indictment were dismissed.

Wendell Wyatt

Pleaded guilty on June 11, 1975, to a one-count information charging violation of the reporting provisions of the Federal Election Campaign Act (18 USC Section 2[b] and 2 USC Sections 434[a] and [b] and 441). Fined $750 on July 18, 1975.

Bibliographical Note

The literature on Richard Nixon, his career, and his presidency is a burgeoning enterprise. Watergate, of course, is so important that even Nixon's favorably-inclined biographers feel compelled to address the issue. When they argue that it is but a minor note in his career, they nevertheless spend a great deal of time arguing that point. The major biographical works, written after Nixon's resignation, are by Stephen Ambrose, Roger Morris, and Jonathan Aitken. Joan Hoff's *Nixon Reconsidered* emphasizes the domestic achievements of Nixon's presidency, holding that these overshadow Watergate.

Students should consult the journalistic accounts of Watergate at the time, among them reporting by Carl Bernstein and Bob Woodward, J. Anthony Lukas, as well as the numerous memoirs by various participants, including Haldeman, Ehrlichman, Magruder, Kleindienst, Sirica, Dean, Dash, and Ervin. But none of these is as important as Richard Nixon in his own words, whether it be his memoir, *RN: The Memoirs of Richard Nixon*, or the published edition of the first tapes (*The White House Transcripts*).

For Watergate specifically, many of the essays in Leon Friedman and William F. Levantrosser (eds.), *Watergate and Afterward: The Legacy of Richard Nixon*, are very useful. Stanley I. Kutler in *The Wars of Watergate* integrates Watergate with the career of Richard Nixon and the context of the Vietnam Era.

Acknowledgments

Adam Land provided invaluable aid throughout this project. He helped to compile the documents and he has been a wonderful sounding board for ideas. Shari Osborn gathered documents for me at an early stage. David Burner has prodded me to do this book for several years, and he, too, has helped in numerous ways. Finally, my family continues to be my greatest inspiration.

Madison, Wisconsin
September 1996